ORDEAL BY FIRE

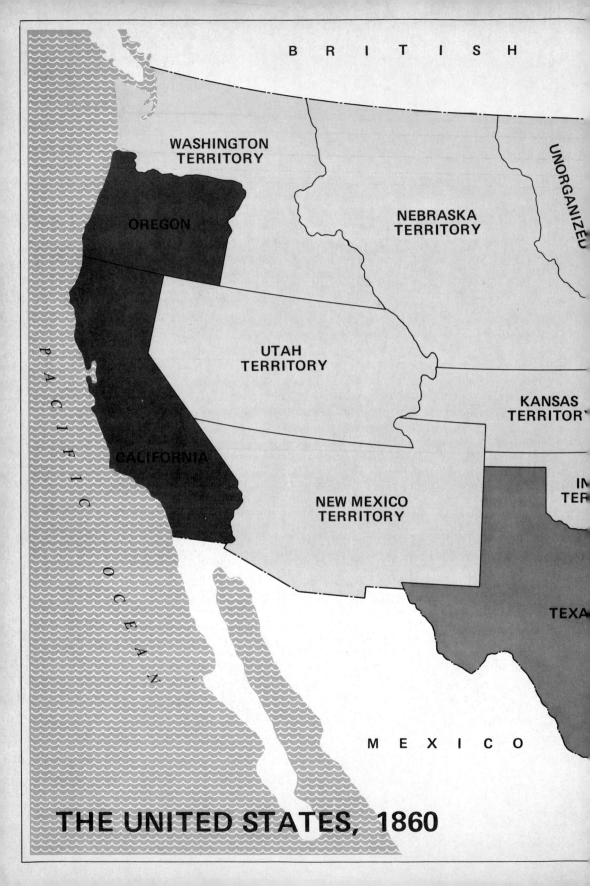

THE UNITED STATES, 1860

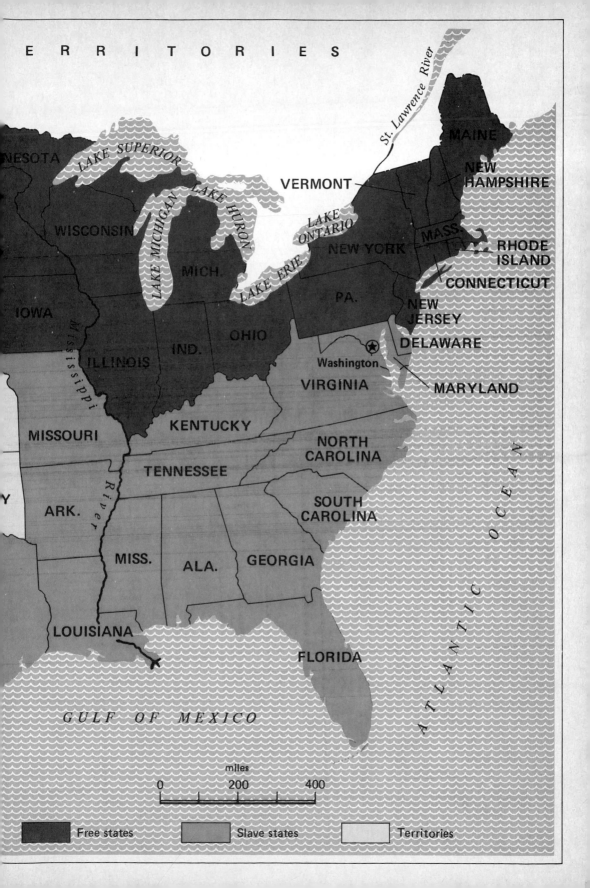

E R R I T O R I E S

St. Lawrence River

MAINE

VERMONT

NEW HAMPSHIRE

LAKE SUPERIOR

NESOTA

WISCONSIN

LAKE MICHIGAN

LAKE HURON

LAKE ONTARIO

NEW YORK

MASS.

RHODE ISLAND

MICH.

LAKE ERIE

CONNECTICUT

IOWA

ILLINOIS

IND.

OHIO

PA.

NEW JERSEY

DELAWARE

Washington

VIRGINIA

MARYLAND

Mississippi

MISSOURI

KENTUCKY

NORTH CAROLINA

TENNESSEE

River

ARK.

SOUTH CAROLINA

MISS.

ALA.

GEORGIA

Y

LOUISIANA

FLORIDA

ATLANTIC OCEAN

GULF OF MEXICO

miles

0   200   400

Free states   Slave states   Territories

ORDEAL BY FIRE

Volume I
The Coming of War

SECOND EDITION

James M. McPherson

Princeton University

McGraw-Hill, Inc.

New York St. Louis San Francisco Auckland Bogotá
Caracas Lisbon London Madrid Mexico Milan Montreal New Delhi
Paris San Juan Singapore Sydney Tokyo Toronto

Ordeal by Fire:
Volume I, The Coming of War

1 2 3 4 5 6 7 8 9 0   HAL HAL   9 0 9 8 7 6 5 4 3 2

ISBN 0-07-045837-5

This book was set in Garamond Book by The Clarinda Company.
The editors were Niels Aaboe and Laura D. Warner;
the production supervisor was Louise Karam.
The cover was designed by Joan Greenfield.
Arcata Graphics/Halliday was printer and binder.

Library of Congress Cataloging-in-Publication Data

McPherson, James M.
    Ordeal by fire / James M. McPherson.—2nd ed.
        p.   cm.
    Includes bibliographical references and index.
    Contents: v. 1. The coming of war—v. 2. The Civil War.
    ISBN 0-07-045837-5 (v. 1) (pbk.)—ISBN 0-07-045838-3 (v. 2) (pbk.)
    1. United States—History—Civil War, 1861–1865—Causes.
    2. United States—History—Civil War, 1861–1865.   3. United States—History—1865–1898.   I. Title.
E468.M23   1993
973.7—dc20   92-23635

★

About the Author

JAMES M. McPHERSON is George Henry Davis '86 Professor of American History at Princeton University, where he has taught since 1962. He was born in Valley City, North Dakota, in 1936. He received his B.A. from Gustavus Adolphus College in 1958 and his Ph.D. from The Johns Hopkins University in 1963. He has been a Guggenheim Fellow, a National Endowment for the Humanities Fellow, a Fellow at the Center for Advanced Studies in Behavioral Sciences at Stanford, and a Seaver Institute Fellow at the Henry E. Huntington Library in San Marino, California. In 1982, he was Commonwealth Fund Lecturer at University College, London.

A specialist in Civil War–Reconstruction history and in the history of race relations, McPherson is the author of *The Struggle for Equality: Abolitionists and the Negro in the Civil War and Reconstruction* (1964), *The Negro's Civil War* (1965), *Marching Toward Freedom: The Negro in the Civil War* (1968), *The Abolitionist Legacy: From Reconstruction to the NAACP* (1975), *Battle Cry of Freedom: The Civil War Era* (1988), and *Abraham Lincoln and the Second American Revolution* (1991).

For Jenny

Contents

PHOTOGRAPHS

MAPS

TABLES

FIGURES

★
A Note on
This Paperback Edition

This volume is part of a separate printing or *Ordeal by Fire*, Second Edition, not a new or revised edition. Many teachers who have used the full edition of *Ordeal by Fire* have suggested separate publication of two of its parts—"The Coming of War" and "The Civil War"—as individual volumes for adaptation to various types and structures of courses. This edition, then, is intended as a convenience for those instructors and students who wish to use one part or another of *Ordeal by Fire* rather than the full edition. The pagination of the full edition is retained here, but the table of contents, bibliography, and index cover only the material in this volume.

★
Preface to the Second Edition

The decade that has passed since publication of the first edition of this book has seen an astonishing increase in the already high level of interest in the American Civil War. The number of Civil War Round Tables has doubled to a total of two hundred; hundreds of thousands of people watched reenactments of Civil War battles during the 125th-anniversary observances of those battles from 1986 to 1990; more visitors than ever have walked Civil War battlefields; a nationwide conservation movement has mobilized to preserve these battlefields from further commercial and residential encroachment; Civil War books reached the national best-seller lists and stayed there for months; millions watched the film *Glory,* which dealt with the black 54th Massachusetts Infantry, as well as the eleven-hour documentary *The Civil War* on public television. And new books about almost every conceivable facet of the Civil War era continue to pour from the presses.

I have tried to incorporate this scholarship into the second edition of *Ordeal by Fire.* While it has been a matter of quiet satisfaction that the main outlines of the story require little or no revision in the light of these new studies, I welcome the opportunity to refine or expand my treatment of several subjects that have been the focus of particularly intensive scholarship in recent years: the changing status of women during this era; the impact of economic growth on the antebellum working class; and the ambivalent position of nonslaveholding whites in a slave society.

In this edition I have also expanded the captions for many of the photographs and have added new illustrations. Citation endnotes have been moved to the bottom of the page to enable students more readily to identify my sources. I have updated the bibliography and added a new section on biographies.

I am grateful to many reviewers of the first edition as well as to colleagues, students, and other readers who have called to my attention minor errors, shaky interpretations, and ambiguous or misleading phraseology. Their suggestions have enabled me to correct, sharpen, and clarify the information and interpretations in this edition. I wish also to express my gratitude to the College Division of McGraw-Hill for maintaining the high standards of Knopf's College Division, and especially to my editor, Niels Aaboe, whose contribution has been invaluable.

James M. McPherson

★
Preface to the First Edition

The Civil War was America's greatest trauma. More than a million of the three million men who fought it were killed or wounded; the republic that had been born in 1776 was also wounded and nearly killed by the conflict. In the end that republic healed stronger than ever because the radical surgery of war had removed the cancer of slavery. But the scars from this surgery have never disappeared. The issues that brought on the Civil War are with us yet: relations between whites and blacks, nation and states, North and South. Because of that, and because of its intense drama, its heroes and knaves, its record of grand events and awful violence, the story of the Civil War era remains the most crucial and compelling in American history.

This book explores the questions of how and why the United States broke apart and went to war in 1861. It delineates the social and economic structure of the antebellum republic, with special attention to the roots of conflict between North and South. It describes the rise in sectional tensions over the issue of slavery's expansion, from the annexation of Texas in 1845 to the election in 1860 of Abraham Lincoln as president—the event that triggered secession and war. It analyzes the main cause of war as a clash over the future of American society: would slavery continue to exist in this republic of freedom, or would the institution of bondage, as Lincoln hoped, be placed "in the course of ultimate extinction"? The political process could not resolve this life-and-death question; by 1861 both sides were willing to fight for what they viewed as the survival of their way of life.

This volume is intended for use in college courses in American history. It can be assigned in conjunction with the author's succeeding volume on America's *Ordeal by Fire,* Volume II: *The Civil War.* Or it can be assigned separately in courses on the antebellum era, on the Civil War, on Southern history, in the survey course, or in other courses.

James M. McPherson

★
Acknowledgments

A good many people and institutions have helped me produce this book. Students, colleagues, and lecture audiences over the years have knowingly or unknowingly helped to shape my knowledge and understanding of this era. The resources and staffs of the Princeton University Library and the Henry E. Huntington Library were indispensable. I am especially indebted to Martin Ridge, the late Ray Billington, James Thorpe, Virginia Renner, and Noelle Jackson for making my year of research and writing at the Huntington Library so pleasant and productive. Thanks must also go to the National Endowment for the Humanities and to Princeton University, which provided the funds and a leave for my year at the Huntington.

Several colleagues and friends read drafts of these chapters and made fruitful suggestions for improvement. For their careful and honest reading, I am indebted to William J. Cooper, Jr., Richard N. Current, Michael F. Holt, Peyton McCrary, and Emory M. Thomas. I also owe thanks to members of the editorial staff at Alfred A. Knopf, especially to David C. Follmer, who as history editor for the college department first suggested the project from which this book grew and who faithfully supported it from the beginning, to his successor Christopher J. Rogers, who has shepherded this paperback edition to completion, and to James Kwalwasser, who gave this project more editorial time, effort, care, and enthusiasm than the most demanding author could expect. I am grateful to Louis Masur for his checking of quotations and references, and to my wife Patricia for her time and patience in helping me with the tedious task of reading proofs. Writing this book has been an intellectually rewarding experience, and all of these people have helped in various ways to enrich this experience.

The Setting of Conflict

During the first half of the nineteenth century, the United States grew at a rate unparalleled in modern history. This growth occurred in three dimensions: territory, population, and economy. The Louisiana Purchase in 1803 doubled the nation's territory. The acquisitions of Florida (1810 and 1819), Texas (1845), and Oregon (1846) and the cessions from Mexico (1848 and 1854) nearly doubled it again. Population growth exceeded this fourfold increase of territory: the six million Americans of 1803 became twenty-six million by 1853. The economy grew even faster: during these fifty years the gross national product increased sevenfold. No other country could match any single one of these components of growth; the combined impact of all three made the United States a phenomenon of the Western world.

This growth, however, was achieved at high cost to certain groups in North America. White men ruthlessly and illegally seized Indian lands and killed the native Americans or drove them west of the Mississippi. The land hunger of Americans provoked armed conflicts with Spaniards and Mexicans whose territory they seized by violence and war. American economic expansion was based in part on slave-grown tobacco and cotton. Born of a revolution that proclaimed all men free and equal, the United States became the largest slaveholding country in the world.

The social and political strains produced by rapid growth provoked repeated crises that threatened to destroy the republic. From the beginning, these strains were associated mainly with slavery. The geographical division of the country into free and slave states ensured that the crises would take the form of sectional conflict. Each section evolved institutions and values based on its labor system. These values in turn generated ideologies that justified each section's institutions and condemned those of the other.

For three-quarters of a century the two sections coexisted under one flag because the centripetal forces of nationalism—the shared memories of a common struggle for nationhood—proved stronger than the centrifugal forces of sectionalism. But as early as 1787, conflict over slavery at the constitutional convention almost broke up the Union before it was fairly launched. To forestall Southern threats to reject the Constitution, Northern states finally accepted three compromises to protect slavery: a provision adding three-fifths of the slaves to the free population as a basis of representation in the lower house and in the electoral college (Article I, Section 2); a clause forbidding for twenty years the passage of a federal law to prohibit the importation of slaves (Article I, Section 9); and a clause requiring the return of slaves who escaped into free states (Article IV, Section 2).

In subsequent decades a powerful impetus for territorial expansion came from the South, which hoped to gain new slave states to counterbalance the more rapid population growth of the free states. The Louisiana Purchase, the annexation of Texas, and the conquest of the Southwest from Mexico were accomplished by Southern presidents and Southern-dominated congressional majorities over significant Northern opposition. Southern-born settlers tried unsuccessfully to legalize slavery in Indiana and Illinois, in defiance of the provision in the Northwest Ordinance banning the institution in the territories from which these states were formed.

Northern antislavery men produced their own counterthrusts to Southern maneuvers. In 1819, Northern congressmen tried to exclude slavery from the proposed new state of Missouri, part of the Louisiana Purchase. The ensuing sectional conflict in Congress provoked angry rhetoric and fears of disunion. The lawmakers resolved the impasse in 1820 by a compromise that admitted Missouri as a slave state but prohibited slavery in the remaining portion of the Louisiana Purchase that lay north of 36°30'.

The Missouri Compromise settled the question of slavery in the territories for a generation, until the Mexican War caused it to flare up anew. Before 1850, Congress admitted free and slave states alternately to the Union, enabling the South to maintain parity in the Senate (at fifteen slave states and fifteen free states by 1848) even though the region's slower population growth reduced the South to a permanent minority in the House and in the electoral college. The selection of Supreme Court justices by geographical circuits gave the slave states, with their larger territory, a majority on the Supreme Court. And the South's domination of the Democratic party allowed the section to wield political power out of proportion to its population. For two-thirds of the years from 1789 to 1861, the Presidents of the United States, the Speakers of the House and presidents pro tem of the Senate, and the chairmen of key congressional committees were Southerners.

But this Southern domination of national politics could not last forever. By 1860, the free states had a population of nineteen million, and the slave states just over twelve million. Four million of the latter were slaves. The election of a President by a Northern antislavery party in 1860 was the handwriting on the wall. To escape the perceived threat to their way of life, most of the slave states seceded and brought on a civil war.

The Coming of War

ONE

American Modernization, 1800-1860

*E*verything new is quickly introduced here, and all the latest inventions. There is no clinging to old ways, the moment an American hears the word "invention" he pricks up his ears.

—Friedrick List, a Prussian visitor to the United States, 1829

★ Changes in the Economy

A middle-aged American in the 1850s could look back on remarkable economic changes during his lifetime. The first half of the nineteenth century brought the industrial revolution to the United States, where it greatly transformed the material conditions of life.

In 1800, when steam power, machines, and factories had already turned Britain into the world's leading industrial power, the United States was still an agricultural society whose few manufactured goods were made by hand in homes and in small artisan shops or were imported from Britain. Only 6 percent of the population lived in towns or cities larger than 2,500 people, a percentage that had remained roughly constant for more than a century. Sailing vessels carried most of the trade between cities. Overland travel had improved little since the days of the Roman Empire; indeed, the Roman highway was probably superior to the American—with few exceptions, the American road was little more than a dirt path almost impassable in wet weather. Inland water transport was mainly confined to downriver flatboats that were broken up and sold for firewood when they reached their destinations. Farming techniques had undergone little alteration since the arrival of the first colonists. Output per farm worker was no higher—and in some areas lower—than a century earlier. Farms more than a few miles from population centers or navigable rivers existed largely on a subsistence basis, for the absence of adequate transportation made it difficult to get crops to market.

All of this began to change after the War of 1812. Before then, the American colonies and states had experienced what economists call "extensive" economic growth: a growth rate little if any greater than the increase in population. After 1815, the economy sustained "intensive" growth: a rate of increase in wealth and output exceeding population growth. This intensive, or *per capita,* economic growth averaged about 1.5 percent annually from 1815 to 1860—enough to double per capita output during those forty-five years.

The economic changes during the first half of the nineteenth century were qualitative as well as quantitative. One can conceive of intensive economic growth without any important changes in economic structures or techniques. An agricultural economy, for example, may increase its per capita output by moving onto more fertile land or by utilizing traditional methods more efficiently. This happened in the Southern states between 1800 and 1860. The Northern economy, however, underwent a process of *development*—that is, qualitative as well as quantitative growth—during this period. The following analysis of economic development, therefore, will apply mainly to the North.[1]

Changes in Transportation

The first and probably most important qualitative changes came in transportation. The decades from 1800 to 1830 constituted the turnpike era in early American history. Construction crews built thousands of miles of new or improved all-weather, macadamized roads (compacted stones and crushed rock), mostly in the Northern states. The turnpike era overlapped the canal era, which began with the astounding success of the Erie Canal, completed from Albany to Buffalo in 1825. By 1850, the United States had 3,700 miles of canals, also mostly in the free states. The canal era in turn overlapped the beginning of the railroad age. The opening of the first railroad westward from Baltimore in 1830 was followed by a boom in railroad construction, especially during the 1850s. As early as 1840, the United States had 3,328 miles of rail—more than Britain, the pioneer in this mode of transport. By 1860, the United States had nearly 31,000 miles of rail—as much as the rest of the world combined.

These decades also witnessed the great age of the river steamboat. Robert Fulton introduced the first successful steamboat on the Hudson River in 1807. After the War of 1812, this novel form of transport developed rapidly and became the principal means of transport in the area served by the Ohio and Mississippi rivers. The dozen or so steamboats on American rivers in 1815 multiplied to about 3,000 by 1860. Canals were widened and deepened in the 1840s to accommodate steamboats. These paddle-wheeled vessels also plied the Great Lakes. The ocean steamer had appeared before the Civil War, but the United States continued to rely mainly on sailing ships for its salt-water merchant marine.

---

[1]In this book, geographical terms will be defined as follows: "South" refers to the slave states and "North" to the free states, except during the Civil War when the four "border states" that did not secede—Delaware, Maryland, Kentucky, and Missouri—are included in the "North." These "border states" plus Virginia, North Carolina, and Tennessee will sometimes be referred to as the "upper South"; all other slave states are designated the "lower South" and sometimes the "cotton South." "Section" and "sectional" refer, according to context, to the slave states or the free states and to comparisons or relations between them. "Region" will designate smaller groupings of states within each section: "New England" and the "Mid-Atlantic states" (New York, Pennsylvania, and New Jersey) will sometimes be grouped together as the "Northeast"; the "Old Northwest," or after the acquisition of the Oregon Territory in 1846, the "Midwest," will be the label for states west of the Appalachian Mountains and north of the Ohio River; the "Southeast" will refer to slave states east of the Appalachians; the "Old Southwest" will be used for the slave states west of the Appalachians and should not be confused with the new "Southwest"—the territory acquired from Mexico in 1848.

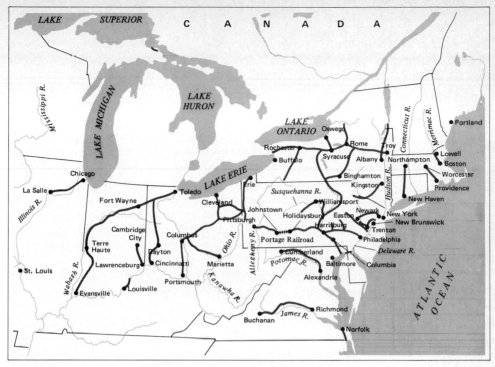

PRINCIPAL CANALS IN 1860

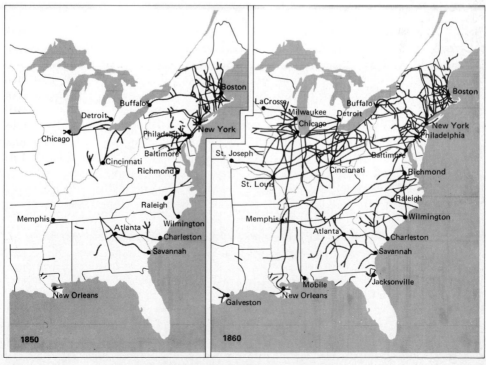

RAILROADS IN 1850 AND 1860

The expansion of canals and railroads plus the development of Great Lakes shipping had an impact on regional alignments. Before 1840, most interregional trade flowed in a north-south direction. Coastal shipping along the Atlantic seaboard and river transport along the Ohio-Mississippi network dominated trading patterns. But the major canals and railroads ran generally in an east-west direction to link the Northeast with the Old Northwest. By the 1840s, the tonnage transported over the Great Lakes–Erie Canal route exceeded tonnage on the Mississippi; by the 1850s, tonnage on the east-west water and rail routes was more than twice the north-south river volume. This reorientation of trade patterns strengthened interregional ties among the free states—a development that would help weld them together against the South in the secession crisis of 1861.

Nineteenth-century Americans called their transport facilities "internal improvements." Modern economists term them "social overhead capital." This is a form of capital investment that, because construction takes a long time, does not yield quick returns. Indeed, even the ultimate direct profits to investors may be low or nonexistent, though the benefits to society in the form of improved transportation are high. Private capital is often unwilling or unable to undertake such projects. Thus the state governments built most of the canals, and the state and federal governments built most of the improved roads outside of New England. Turnpikes constructed by private capital rarely returned a profit, and the states eventually took over many of them. The federal as well as state governments dredged harbors and river channels, built levees, and in other ways helped to improve and maintain inland waterways. Although private capital built most of the railroads, many cities, states, and the federal government provided vital assistance with loans, land grants, and guarantees of bond issues.

Whether we call them internal improvements or social overhead capital, these investments provided the basis for intensive economic growth. By reducing the time and costs of transportation, they made possible the creation of an interregional market economy. Freight shipped from Cincinnati to New York in 1817 took more than fifty days to reach its destination; by 1852 it required only six days. The same trip for passengers was reduced from three weeks to two days. The accompanying graph of inland freight rates illustrates the dramatic reduction in transport costs. Western farmers could now ship their products to the East, where consumers could afford to buy them. The difference between the wholesale price of western pork in Cincinnati and New York declined from $9.53 to $1.18 a barrel between 1818 and 1858. The price difference between Cincinnati and New York for a barrel of western flour declined from $2.48 to $0.28 during the same years. The cumulative effect of many such cost reductions lowered the wholesale price index for the United States by about 40 percent, and the cost-of-living index by about 15 percent, during these four decades.

Increased Food Production

By creating a national market, improved transportation enabled farmers and manufacturers to achieve specialization and economies of scale (lower unit costs because of larger volume). During the four antebellum decades, the total output of food crops increased fourfold and the percentage of that production sold in the market instead of

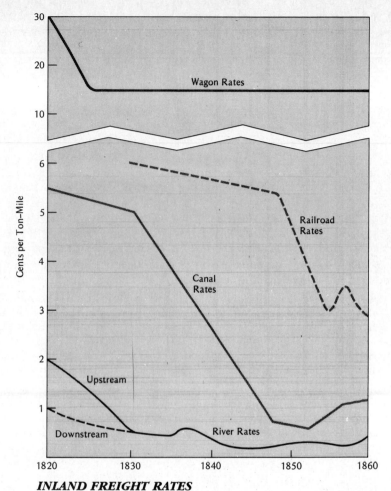

INLAND FREIGHT RATES

(Adapted from Douglass C. North, Growth and Welfare in the American Past, 2d ed., Englewood Cliffs, N.J., 1974, p. 108.)

consumed on the farm nearly doubled. This made it possible for farmers to feed the rapidly growing cities even though the proportion of the labor force in agriculture declined from 76 to 57 percent between 1820 and 1860. The urban population grew three times as fast as the rural population during these four decades, raising the urban proportion of the total from 7 percent in 1820 to 20 percent in 1860. This was the fastest rate of urbanization in American history.

The increase in food production could not have occurred without the numerous technological innovations in agriculture that took place during this period. Before 1800, there had been few improvements in farm implements over the centuries. "In culture, harvesting, and threshing of grains," wrote one historian, "the [American] colonists were not much advanced beyond Biblical times." But in the first half of the nineteenth century, a host of inventors developed a variety of horse-drawn implements and machines that, in the words of another historian, "revolutionized the technology of agriculture."[2]

The first improvements came with the development of moldboard iron plows in the 1810s and steel plows in the 1830s. Beginning in the 1820s, inventors also patented a variety of seed drills, harrows, and cultivators. But these implements, which increased the acreage a farmer could sow, actually made worse the chief bottleneck of agriculture—the harvest. Farmers could now grow more grain than they could reap and thresh. The invention of horse-drawn reapers by Cyrus Mc-Cormick of Virginia and Obed Hussey of Maine in the 1830s was therefore one of the most important developments in nineteenth-century agriculture. Two men and a horse could now harvest as much grain in a day as eight men using cradles or twenty men using sickles. This leap in productivity, however, would have meant little if similar improvements in threshing had not occurred at the same time. John and Hiram Pitts of Maine patented a successful horse-powered threshing and fanning machine in 1834. By the 1850s, farmers in the Northern states were overcoming their traditional conservatism and buying thousands of the new machines being mass-produced by factories in the Midwest. This substitution of machines and horses for human labor began the transition of American agriculture from the labor-intensive livelihood it had been until then to the capital-intensive business it is today.

The American System of Manufactures

Similar changes took place in manufacturing. Household production of hand-crafted goods for subsistence and for local markets reached a peak about 1815 and then gave way to shop- and factory-produced goods for regional and national markets. In the United States, as in Britain, textiles were the leading sector of the industrial revolution. The factory system (defined as wage-earning employees with different skills working together in a large building to manufacture a product with the aid of power-driven machinery) came first to this industry in the 1810s with the introduction of the power loom at Waltham, Massachusetts. New England textile mills increased their annual output of cloth from 4 million yards in 1817 to 308 million yards in 1837.

The factory system spread from textiles to other industries after 1830, as inventors and enterpreneurs developed new machines and new methods of organizing production. Britain, of course, pioneered many of these developments. Other western European countries also led the United States in basic science and in early industrial technology. But American businessmen and engineers, much like those of Japan today, had a knack for adapting foreign technology to their own needs and improving it through dozens of incremental changes. Thus, while the basic inventions of textile machinery were British, most of the improvements during the 1820s and 1830s were American. Perhaps the most important American contribution to the clothing industry was the sewing machine, invented by Elias Howe of Massachusetts in the 1840s.

American technology was more change-oriented than its European counterpart. Americans built cheap and light textile machinery, often of wood. This horrified British engineers, who built their machines of metal to last for decades. But there was

[2]Ulysses Prentiss Hedrick, *A History of Agriculture in the State of New York* (Albany, 1933), p. 67; Clarence H. Danhof, *Change in Agriculture: The Northern United States, 1820–1870* (Cambridge, Mass., 1969), p. 181.

method in the apparent American madness. Technology was advancing so rapidly that when an American machine wore out after a few years, it could be cheaply replaced by a better one, while the heavier and more expensive British machines could not be so readily scrapped. "Everything new is quickly introduced here," wrote a foreign visitor to the United States in 1829. "There is no clinging to old ways, the moment an American hears the word 'invention' he pricks up his ears."[3]

By the 1840s, the United States had partly reversed the earlier flow of technology from Europe to America. British industrialists discovered that they could learn much from their upstart rivals across the Atlantic. Perhaps the most important Yankee contribution to the industrial revolution was what the British called "the American system of manufactures"—the mass production of machine-made, interchangeable parts. Introduced first in the manufacture of firearms in the early nineteenth century, the concept of interchangeable parts was a revolutionary one. Previously, skilled craftsmen had fashioned each part of a musket, and each musket had been a unique creation whose parts were not exactly the same as the similar parts of other muskets. The manufacture of muskets (or any other item) was therefore a slow process requiring many skilled workers. The final product was expensive, and if any of its parts broke or wore out they could be replaced only by a craftsman, who would make a new and expensive replacement. If each part, on the other hand, was machine-produced in large quantities, all the parts in one musket would be interchangeable with the similar parts of another one. Both the manufacturing and the replacement costs would be reduced. The first crude machine tools did not always produce parts that were perfectly interchangeable, but as the century advanced and machine-tool technology improved, the American system of mass production expanded to include scores of products: clocks and watches, nails, screws, nuts and bolts, locks, furniture, plows, sewing machines, boots and shoes—even large items such as the parts for steam engines, locomotives, and McCormick reapers.

Such American machine-made products were the marvel of the international Crystal Palace exhibition in London in 1851. Impressed by American methods of firearms manufacture, the British imported Yankee engineers and machinists to help build their new Enfield Armoury for the production of army rifles. Britain also sent industrial commissions to visit American factories in the 1850s and invited Samuel Colt, the Connecticut inventor of the six-shooting revolver, to testify before Parliament in 1854. In his testimony, Colt summed up the American system of manufactures in a single sentence: "There is nothing that cannot be produced by machinery."[4] This attitude enabled the United States to become the world leader in machine-tool technology by the third quarter of the nineteenth century. Americans played a particularly important role in the development of turret lathes and milling machines, the forerunners of modern machine tools.

★ Causes of American Modernization

From its beginnings, therefore, American industry—like much of American agriculture—was capital-intensive rather than labor-intensive. There were four basic reasons

[3]Stuart Bruchey, *The Roots of American Economic Growth, 1607–1861* (New York, 1965), p. 166.
[4]Eugene S. Ferguson, "Technology as Knowledge," in Edwin T. Layton (ed.), *Technology and Change in America* (New York, 1973), p. 23.

for this: a shortage of labor, especially skilled labor; a generous endowment of resources; a high level of mass education and literacy; and an openness to change, a willingness to innovate and experiment.

The low population density of the United States, the lure of cheap land on the frontier, and the rapid growth of the economy kept the supply of labor below the demand. American wage levels were consequently higher than European. The shortage and high cost of labor impelled technological innovation, to substitute machines for human workers.

If labor was scarce and expensive in comparison with Europe, the opposite was true of key resources, especially water and wood. Water powered the textile mills of New England, and wood fueled the steam engines that powered steamboats, locomotives, and some factories. American forests also supplied a plentiful and cheap source of building material for machinery, ships, railroad ties and cars, and a host of other items whose cost was greater in wood-deficient Europe. Just as the abundance of capital, in the form of cheap land, stimulated capital-intensive agriculture, so the abundance of raw materials and power stimulated capital-intensive industry.

Education and values also played crucial roles in American economic development. Not counting the slave population, the United States in 1850 had the highest literacy rate (89 percent) and the highest percentage of children in school of any country in the world save Sweden and Denmark. The free states, when considered alone, surpassed the Scandinavian countries, while New England stood in a class by itself. Foreign observers pointed out the importance of education in producing the "adaptative versatility" of Yankee workers. A visiting British industrial commission reported in 1854 that having been "educated up to a far higher standard than those of a much superior social grade in the Old World, the American working boy develops rapidly into the skilled artizan, and having once mastered one part of his business, he is never content until he has mastered all." With examples "constantly before him of ingenious men who have solved economic and mechanical problems to their own profit and elevation . . . there is not a working boy of average ability in the New England States, at least, who has not an idea of some mechanical invention or improvement in manufactures."[5] Many American technological innovations were indeed contributed by the workers themselves: Elias Howe, for example, was a journeyman machinist in Boston when he invented the sewing machine.

Americans were less bound than Europeans by tradition and by inherited institutions that inhibited change. The heritage of revolution and republicanism gave them a sense of being a new and unique people. They oriented themselves toward the future rather than the past; they valued change more than tradition; they proclaimed their belief in "progress," "advancement," "improvement"; they exhibited a "go-ahead spirit," a belief that "the sky is the limit." "We are THE PEOPLE OF THE FUTURE," exulted American nationalists in the 1840s. "Custom hath lost its sway, and Time and Change are the Champions against the field."[6] This optimism, this willingness to experiment, underlay the Yankee genius for innovation.

Many Americans considered machinery an agent of moral improvement and democratic equality. The railroads, said one enthusiast, were God's instrument "to quicken the activity of men; to send energy and vitality where before were silence and barrenness; to multiply cities and villages, studded with churches, dotted with

---

[5]Nathan Rosenberg (ed.), *The American System of Manufactures* (Edinburgh, 1969), pp. 203–204.
[6]Arthur A. Ekirch, *The Idea of Progress in America, 1815–1860* (New York, 1944), p. 52.

schools." A writer in *Scientific American* asserted in 1851 that "every new and useful machine, invented and improved, confers a general benefit upon all classes,—the poor as well as the rich." The Whig political leader William H. Seward believed that "popular government follows in the track of the steam-engine and the telegraph." The increased output and rising standard of living produced by technological progress, declared an early economist, were "marked by a tendency to equality of physical and intellectual condition."[7]

The antebellum United States was undergoing a process that some social scientists term "modernization": heavy investment in social overhead capital, which transforms a localized subsistence economy into a nationally integrated market economy; rapid increases in output per capita, resulting from technological innovation and the shift from labor-intensive toward capital-intensive production; the accelerated growth of the industrial sector compared with other sectors of the economy; rapid urbanization, made possible by an increase in agricultural productivity that enables farmers to feed the growing cities; an expansion of education, literacy, and mass communications; a value system that emphasizes change rather than tradition; an evolution from the traditional, rural, village-oriented system of personal and kinship ties, in which status is "ascriptive" (inherited), toward a fluid, cosmopolitan, impersonal, and pluralistic society, in which status is achieved by merit. In most of these reports, the United States—with the partial and significant exception of the South— was the most rapidly modernizing country in the world in the middle decades of the nineteenth century.

★ The Modernizing Ethos

American modernization had its roots in a value system associated with the Protestant work ethic. Nearly a century ago, the German sociologist Max Weber called attention to the connection between *The Protestant Ethic and the Spirit of Capitalism*—to cite the title of his most famous book. Weber wondered why the most advanced capitalist societies were Protestant—and in particular, Calvinist. He pointed to Calvinist theology as an explanation: the doctrine of salvation by election; the belief that worldly success was a sign of God's favor; the concept of the "calling," according to which all people are called by God to vocations that, no matter how great or humble, are equal in his sight and whose diligent performance is a sacred duty; and the injunction against waste, according to which wealth must be used for the glory of God through stewardship to mankind rather than squandered in conspicuous consumption and easy living. This combination of beliefs created a value system that Weber described as "worldly asceticism": hard work, thrift, sobriety, reliability, self-discipline, self-reliance, and the deferral of immediate gratification for long-range goals. These were precisely the values best suited to modernizing capitalism.[8]

In a more secular age, these values have become known as the work ethic. But during the nineteenth century, they were still very much anchored in religion. And because in Britain and America they were exhibited most forcefully by the Puritans (as

---

[7]Ibid., pp. 102, 119; Eric Foner, *Free Soil, Free Labor, Free Men: The Ideology of the Republican Party Before the Civil War* (New York, 1970), p. 39.

[8]Although influential, the Weber thesis is not universally accepted. Critics maintain that religious factors alone cannot explain economic developments and point out that several non-Protestant societies— for example, Japan—have also experienced remarkable economic growth and modernization.

well as by those seventeenth- and eighteenth-century offshoots of Puritanism, the Quakers and Unitarians), they are sometimes known as the Puritan ethic. Puritan theology, sermons, and maxims contained many biblical quotations and aphorisms emphasizing work as the glorification of God and idleness as the instrument of Satan: "Walk worthy of the vocation wherewith ye are called" (Eph. 4:1); "If any would not work, neither shall he eat" (2 Thess. 3:10); "Wealth gotten by vanity shall be diminished; but he that gathereth by labor shall increase" (Prov. 13:11); "The hand of the diligent shall bear rule: but the slothful shall be under tribute" (Prov. 13:24); "Satan finds mischief for idle hands to do" (Isaac Watts).

These maxims were also disseminated by schoolbooks and by the extraordinary outpouring of "how to succeed" books. The main message of the latter was that success is attainable through hard work, good works, sobriety, and thrift. Many of the authors were clergymen, who told their readers that, in the words of a New England minister, "religion will teach you that industry is a SOLEMN DUTY you owe to God, whose command is, 'BE DILIGENT IN BUSINESS!' " American schoolbooks, especially the widely used Speller by Noah Webster and the Readers by Presbyterian clergyman William Holmes McGuffey, inculcated the same message: "Persevering industry will enable one to accomplish almost anything."[9]

The Puritan work ethic was strongest among New Englanders in general and among Congregationalists, Unitarians, Presbyterians, and Quakers in particular. It was no coincidence that New England was at the cutting edge of American modernization or that a disproportionate number of entrepreneurs and inventors were New England Yankees of Calvinist background. Tables 1.1 and 1.2 illustrate this predominance.[10]

Other studies have confirmed the data in these tables. An analysis of property ownership based on the 1860 census revealed that, no matter where they lived, men of New England birth enjoyed greater average wealth than men born in any other part of the country. Surveys of prominent businessmen and of millionaires during the nineteenth century found that New Englanders were represented in both groups at twice their proportion of the population. Two studies of scientists found Yankees overrepresented by two and a half times their population percentage.[11] In 1847, an Argentine visitor to the United States reported that men of New England birth carried "to the rest of the Union the . . . moral and intellectual aptitude [and] . . . manual aptitude which makes an American a walking workshop. . . . The great colonial and railroad enterprises, the banks, and the corporations are founded and developed by them."[12]

[9]Irvin G. Wyllie, *The Self-Made Man in America: The Myth of Rags to Riches* (New Brunswick, N.J., 1954), pp. 63, 42-43.

[10]The data on business executives are from Frances W. Gregory and Irene Neu, "The American Industrial Elite in the 1870's: Their Social Origins," in William Miller (ed.), *Men in Business* (Cambridge, 1952), pp. 193-204. Data on inventors were calculated from the list in Roger Burlingame, *March of the Iron Men: A Social History of Union Through Invention* (New York, 1938), pp. 468-476. Data on religious affiliation of the American population were calculated from Edwin S. Gaustad, *Historical Atlas of Religion in America* (New York, 1962), pp. 52, 140.

[11]Lee Soltow, *Men and Wealth in the United States 1850-1870* (New Haven, 1975), pp. 148-149, 152; C. Wright Mills, "The American Business Elite: A Collective Portrait," in Economic History Association, *Tasks of Economic History* (New York, 1945), pp. 20-44; Pitirim Sorokin, "American Millionaires and Multi-Millionaires," *Journal of Social Forces,* 3 (1925), 634 (this article includes data on scientists also); *American Men of Science* (New York, 1910).

[12]Domingo Faustino Sarmiento, *Sarmiento's Travels in the United States in 1847,* trans. Michael A. Rockland (Princeton, 1970), p. 198.

Table 1.1   ORIGINS OF NINETEENTH-CENTURY AMERICAN BUSINESS EXECUTIVES AND INVENTORS

| Region | AMERICAN BUSINESS EXECUTIVES (MEDIAN BIRTH DATE 1825) | | Birthplace and/or Residence of Inventors of Main Technological Innovations, 1790-1860 | Residence of All Americans in 1825 |
	Birthplace (N = 247)	Father's Birthplace (N = 175)		
New England	51%	65%	42%	16%
Rest of North	34	22	51	38
South	3	2	7	46
Abroad or unspecified	12	11		

Table 1.2   RELIGIOUS AFFILIATIONS OF NINETEENTH-CENTURY BUSINESS EXECUTIVES

Denomination	Business Executives (N = 144)		American Population c. 1840 (Estimated)	
Congregational	22%		5%	
Presbyterian	14	54%	10	17%
Unitarian	10		1	
Quaker	8		1	
Episcopal	25		2	
Other Protestant	21		51	

★ Modernization and Reform

The modernizing ethos of Yankee Protestantism also gave rise to some of the principal reform movements in antebellum America: temperance, education, women's rights, and antislavery.[13] These movements grew out of the Second Great Awakening, a prolonged series of Protestant revivals in the first third of the nineteenth century. Inspired by a zealous sense of mission, many evangelicals—especially those of Yankee heritage—strove not only for the conversion of individual sinners but also for the purification of society from such sins as drunkenness, prostitution, ignorance, and above all slavery. The evangelicals hoped to reform society by first reforming individuals—by inculcating in them the Protestant ethic values of industry, piety, sobriety, thrift, and self-improvement through self-discipline.

The Temperance Movement

The temperance movement displayed all of these reform traits. In the early nineteenth century, Americans consumed an extraordinary amount of alcohol—more than three

[13]The antislavery movement is discussed in Chapter 3.

times as much per person as today. No social occasion was complete without heavy drinking. Liquor was cheap, untaxed in most areas, and constituted a considerable portion of people's caloric intake. Many persons greeted each day with a gill (four ounces) of whiskey or rum; John Adams regularly drank a pint of hard cider (about 20 proof) before breakfast. European visitors voiced astonishment at the "universal practice of sipping a little at a time [every] half an hour to a couple of hours, during the whole day."[14]

The temperance movement arose as a reaction against this excessive consumption. Beginning as a local religious and moral reform, it expanded into a national crusade by the 1830s. At the height of its influence in 1836, the American Temperance Union (ATU), a federation of local and regional societies, claimed a membership of a million and a half. But the ATU fragmented thereafter as its members divided over the question of temperance versus prohibition. At first, the movement had favored moderation in drinking; but by the 1830s its radical wing was pushing the organization toward the goal of prohibiting all alcoholic beverages. The requirement that members pledge total abstinence caused a dramatic drop in ATU membership by 1840.

Up to this point, temperance had been a middle-class Protestant movement. It had tried by moral suasion to infuse values of sobriety and self-restraint into the whole society. In this respect, the temperance movement fostered the process of modernization. Work patterns in preindustrial societies were task-oriented rather than time-oriented. Artisans worked in bursts of effort to complete a particular job, then took several days off, perhaps to spend their time and money in tippling. This irregularity did not fit the clockwork pace of factories, in which the operation of machines required punctuality, reliability, and sobriety. Work became time-oriented instead of task-oriented, a transition aided by the mass production of clocks and watches, itself an achievement of the American system of manufacturing. It was not merely an accident of history that the temperance movement in both Britain and America coincided with the industrial revolution. As part of the effort to inculcate discipline and steadiness among workers, many employers supported the temperance movement, and some forbade their employees to drink on *or* off the job.

Many workers, especially Irish and German immigrants, resented and resisted such efforts to impose temperance. But by 1840 some skilled Protestant workingmen had internalized temperance values and had begun to form "Washington Temperance Societies."[15] Proudly declaring themselves reformed drunkards, they expanded the membership of these societies to a purported 600,000 by 1847. The Washingtonian movement rejuvenated the temperance crusade, which turned from moral suasion to legal coercion in the 1840s. Fifteen states legislated against the sale of liquor during the decade after Maine passed the first such law in 1846.

These laws, however, were poorly enforced, and most were eventually repealed or struck down by the courts. The phenomenal success of the temperance movement was due chiefly to moral suasion and self-denial. Between 1830 and 1850, the per capita consumption of alcohol declined fourfold. During the same years, the per capita consumption of coffee and tea nearly doubled. The impact of these changes on

[14]J. C. Furnas, *The Americans: A Social History* (New York, 1969), p. 505.
[15]Named for George Washington, in order to symbolize their professed patriotic and republican virtues.

the values associated with the work ethic—such as sobriety, punctuality, and reliability—scarcely needs to be spelled out.

Education

Another major focus of antebellum reform was public education. Economists consider education a means of "human capital formation" crucial to economic growth and modernization. Investment in education temporarily removes young people from the labor force but increases their aptitudes, skills, and productivity in the long run. "Intelligent laborers," wrote a businessman in 1853, "can add much more to the capital employed in a business than those who are ignorant."[16] As noted earlier, British industrialists explained the adaptive versatility of American workers and the technological proficiency of American industry by reference to the high level of education and literacy in the United States.

Like other aspects of modernization, education owed much of its impetus to Protestantism. The Puritan emphasis on the ability to read the Bible and to understand theology made New England the most literate society in the world during the seventeenth century. The same religious motivation underlay education in Presbyterian Scotland and Lutheran Sweden, which caught up with New England during the eighteenth century. In nineteenth-century America, higher education was sustained primarily by Protestant denominations, and Protestant influences imbued even the public schools.

As early as 1830, New England and New York had public school systems that reached at least three-quarters of the population. Although in other areas a combination of local free schools, church schools, private schools, apprenticeship programs, and home tutoring provided education for most of the white population, little in the way of a public school *system* existed outside New England and New York. And even there the system was haphazard; formal teacher training scarcely existed; educational standards varied widely; classes were ungraded and rarely went beyond the grammar-school level.

Under the tutelage of New England progressives, especially Horace Mann, educational reforms spread through much of the North beginning in the 1830s. As secretary of the Massachusetts State Board of Education, Mann led a drive to rationalize the patchwork pattern of public schools, to professionalize the teachers, and to carry the message of reform into other states. Mann founded the first "normal" school for teacher training in 1839. During the next two decades several Northern states established such institutions. Massachusetts also pioneered in other innovations: a standardized graded curriculum, the first compulsory attendance law (1852), and extension of public education to the secondary level. By 1860, most Northern states sustained public school systems at least through the eighth grade, and about three-quarters of the Northern children between five and sixteen years of age were enrolled in school. Although some Southern states began modest educational reforms in the 1850s, the South lacked an effective public school system before the Civil War.

An essential task of education, wrote the Massachusetts superintendent of schools in 1857, was "by moral and religious instruction daily given" to "inculcate habits of regularity, punctuality, constancy, and industry." Although religious overtones remained strong, as this quotation indicates, many educational reformers

16Ekirch, *Idea of Progress*, p. 197.

began to view the function of schooling in more secular terms. Horace Mann in particular had a modern vision of the schools as agents of economic growth and social mobility. Education "[is] the grand agent for the development or augmentation of national resources," he wrote in 1848, "more powerful in the production and gainful employment of the total wealth of a country than all the other things mentioned in the books of the political economists." Schooling would also uplift the poor by equipping them with the values and skills necessary to function in a modern capitalist economy. Education "does better than to disarm the poor of their hostility toward the rich; it prevents their being poor."[17] If this belief proved to be too optimistic, it nevertheless bespoke the faith that most Americans have placed in education as a lever of upward mobility.

Not all education took place in schools, of course. In addition to such institutions as the family and the church, many channels existed for the dissemination of information and ideas. One of the most important was the public lecture. Reformers discovered lecturing to be the most effective way to spread their message. In 1826 Josiah Holbrook, a Massachusetts educator, founded the American Lyceum of Science and the Arts. The lyceum was the first national agency for adult education. It brought lecturers on almost every conceivable subject to cities and hamlets throughout the country.

Overshadowing all other means of communication in the nineteenth century was the press. The United States was the world's preeminent newspaper-reading country. Technological advances in printing caused explosive growth in newspaper circulation after 1830. The installation of the first steam press in 1835 increased the capacity of a single press from 200 to 5,500 copies per hour. New machines for making and cutting paper also lowered prices and thereby boosted circulation. In the 1820s, a single issue of a newspaper cost five or six cents; less than two decades later, several New York dailies sold for a penny. The growth of the railroads enabled urban dailies to print weekly editions for rural areas. By 1860, the weekly edition of Horace Greeley's *New York Tribune* reached the unprecedented circulation of 200,000 copies. The commercial development of the telegraph after 1844 made possible the instantaneous transmission of news over long distances and led to the formation of the Associated Press in 1848. The number of newspapers doubled between 1825 and 1840 and doubled again by 1860, reaching a total of 3,300. Circulation grew twice as fast as population. By 1860, the United States had twice as many newspapers as Britain—indeed, it had nearly one-third of the newspapers in the entire world.

Women

Economic modernization had an ambivalent impact on women. When most Americans lived on farms or in farm villages, before 1815, the family had been the principal unit of production as well as of consumption. Mothers and daughters had tended gardens and farm animals, spun and woven cloth, sewed garments, dipped candles, and helped to make many other items that the family consumed. But as the economy diversified and industrialized after 1815, production of cloth, shoes, candles, and even food moved increasingly outside the home. Some girls and unmarried young women

[17]Michael B. Katz, *The Irony of Early School Reform: Educational Innovation in Mid-Nineteenth Century Massachusetts* (Cambridge, Mass., 1968), p. 43; Horace Mann, "Annual Report of 1848," in *The Life and Works of Horace Mann*, 5 vols. (Boston, 1891), IV, 245-251.

THE CHANGING STATUS OF WOMEN.
By the second quarter of the nineteenth century a growing number of young, unmarried women were joining the wage labor force, especially in New England textile mills such as the one above. At the same time, middle-class women like Elizabeth Cady Stanton, photographed here with two of her children in the 1840s, obtained an excellent education at women's secondary schools (called "seminaries") but were denied political rights and excluded from many occupations. Having broken through some traditional barriers, women led by Stanton launched the modern women's rights movement at a convention in Seneca Falls, New York, in 1848, calling for removal of remaining obstacles to their equal rights and opportunities.

went to work in the new textile mills; others stayed at home and helped their mothers bind shoes or sew shirts for low piecework wages in the "putting out" system organized by the shoemaking and ready-made clothing industry during the 1820s. But very few married women worked for wages outside the home, and only the poorest did so within the household. As production shifted from household to shop, factory, office, and commercial agriculture, men went *out* of the home to work while women stayed at home to raise children and manage the household. Thus there arose a concept of "separate spheres" for men and women. Man's sphere was the bustling world of work, commerce, politics; woman's sphere was the domestic circle of household and children.

In some respects this marked a decline in woman's status. But in other ways it laid the groundwork for modern feminism. If woman's sphere was confined mainly to the home, at least she now ruled that sphere. The old patriarchal domination of wife and children eroded as the father went out of the house each day to his sphere, leaving mother in charge of nurturing, socializing, and educating the children. As the family became less of a productive unit, it became a locus of love and nurture of children. Childhood emerged as a separate stage of life. As middle-class parents lavished more affection on children, they began having fewer of them by practicing a rudimentary form of birth control (mainly sexual abstinence). The birth rate declined by 23 percent between 1810 and 1860. This meant that a woman in the 1850s was less continuously burdened by pregnancy, childbirth, and nursing of children than her mother and grandmother had been. This freed women, especially those of the middle and upper classes, for more activities outside the home.

Thus in a seeming paradox, the notion that woman's sphere was in the home became a sort of springboard for extension of that sphere outside the home. Many of the activists in the temperance movement, antislavery societies, church-related and missionary organizations, and other reform movements of this era were women. But perhaps the most important change during these decades was the rising prominence of women in the enlarged public education system. As families began having fewer children, they sent them to school longer and more frequently. As the function of schools expanded beyond the Three R's to include socializing of children in the values of the society, women began to play a larger role in the process. In a sense, this represented an expansion of woman's "sphere" of nurturing and training children. By the 1850s nearly three-fourths of the public school teachers in New England were women, and the institution of the "schoolma'am" was spreading through the rest of the North and into the South.

And, of course, if women were to be teachers, they must themselves become better educated. In every society before the middle of the nineteenth century, men were more literate than women. The United States in 1860 was the first country in which as many girls as boys went to school and in which literacy rates for the two sexes were about equal. Higher education was still mostly a male domain, but a few women's "seminaries" got started during this period, and Oberlin College in the 1830s became the first coeducational college. Women also forged to the front in two important media of communication during this era: magazines and popular literature. More than one hundred "ladies' magazines" flourished in the antebellum generation, to which women were principal contributors. The best-selling novelists and short-story writers, whose work was serialized in newspapers and magazines, were mainly women—including Harriet Beecher Stowe, author of one of the most popular and powerful novels of all time, *Uncle Tom's Cabin*.

In many ways, American women by midcentury had emerged into more prominent social and public roles than women had previously played in any Western society. All the more galling, then, were laws that turned their property over to husbands when they married, made divorce from cruel, exploitative, or philandering husbands almost impossible, and denied women the right to vote or hold public office. It was to attack these injustices that Elizabeth Cady Stanton, Lucretia Mott, and other feminists held a convention at a church in the upstate New York village of Seneca Falls in 1848 to launch the modern women's rights movement. Although the movement's crowning achievement—enfranchisement of women on an equal basis with men—was not secured until the twentieth century, the movement did win more liberal divorce laws, married women's property acts in most states, broader educational and professional opportunities for women, and other gains during the quarter century after 1848.

★ Modernization and Social Tensions

Not all groups in American society participated equally in the modernizing process or accepted the values that promoted it. The most important dissenters were found in the South (see Chapter 2). In the North, three groups resisted aspects of modernization and the Yankee Protestant hegemony that accompanied it: Catholics, especially the Irish; residents of the southern Midwest, most of them descendants of settlers from the slave states; and some wage laborers.

Catholic versus Protestant Values

The Catholic Irish in both Ireland and America during the nineteenth century possessed cultural values that were in many ways antithetical to modernization. The experience of poverty and oppression had bred in the Irish a profound pessimism that amounted almost to fatalism. Since others possessed all the wealth and power, the practice of self-discipline, self-denial, and investment in the future seemed pointless. Many Irish did not share the conviction that reform or "progress" could lead to improvement for either individuals or society.

Roman Catholic doctrine reinforced this conservatism. A prominent Catholic layman wrote in 1859: "The age attaches . . . too much importance to what is called the progress of society or the progress of civilization, which, to the man whose eye is fixed on God and eternity, can appear of not great value." The church opposed the ferment of reform that flourished in the yeast of Yankee Protestantism. Such reform movements, said Catholic leaders, are "against all the principles and maxims of the past, and all the moral, religious, social, and political institutions of the present." The "spirit of radical Protestantism" had "infected our whole society and turned a large portion of our citizens into madmen." Under the influence of this fanaticism, said a New York Catholic newspaper in 1856, "the country has for a number of years been steadily tending toward revolution."[18] The pope from 1846 to 1878 was Pius IX, whose opposition to modernism and liberalism set the tone for the entire church. In

---

[18]Ekirch, *Idea of Progress,* p. 173; Benjamin J. Blied, *Catholics and the Civil War* (Milwaukee, 1945), p. 30; Oscar Handlin, *Boston's Immigrants: A Study in Acculturation,* rev. ed. (Cambridge, Mass., 1959), pp. 132, 139; *Freeman's Journal,* June 7, 1856.

his *Syllabus of Errors* (1864) Pius declared: "It is an error to believe that the Roman Pontiff can and ought to reconcile himself to, and agree with, progress, liberalism, and contemporary civilization."

These ethnic and religious values contributed to the gulf between the conservative, antireformist Catholic population and the modernizing, reform-minded Yankee Protestants. Class distinctions widened the gulf, for native-born Protestants predominated in the upper and middle classes while Irish Catholics clustered in the lower. Each group viewed the other with suspicion, which increased after the onset of heavy Irish and German immigration in the 1840s (see Chapter 5). Yankee reform movements such as those promoting temperance and public education tried to impose middle-class Protestant values and behavior patterns on the Catholic population. But drinking remained popular among the Irish and Germans even as it declined among Protestants of native or English birth. The proportion of immigrant children attending school in 1850 was only one-third that of native-born children of native-born parents. Catholic parents resented the reading of the King James Bible and the recital of Protestant prayers in the public schools. During the 1840s a movement began to establish Catholic parochial schools.

The Midwest: Butternuts versus Yankees

The "Butternuts" of the southern Midwest constituted another antimodernization subculture. American westward migration tended to follow the lines of latitude. Thus the southern part of the Midwest was settled mostly by emigrants from the upper South and Pennsylvania, and the northern part mostly by emigrants from New England and upstate New York (which in turn had been settled by New Englanders). The two streams of migration met in central Ohio, Illinois, and Indiana, where they mixed about as readily as oil and water. The Butternuts (so-called because many of them wore homespun clothing dyed with an extract from butternuts or walnuts) were mostly Methodists and Baptists of Southern origin who developed a largely rural economy based on corn, hogs, and whiskey. Their economic as well as cultural orientation was Southern, for the region's transportation network was tied into the southward-flowing tributaries of the Ohio and Mississippi rivers.

The somewhat later-arriving Yankees in the northern half of the Midwest developed a diversified commercial-agricultural economy. This region grew faster and became more prosperous than the Midwest's southern tier during the last two antebellum decades. Its trade orientation along the newly built canal and railroad networks linked it to the industrializing Northeast. The "Yankee" Midwesterners gained control of the major economic institutions in their states: banks, railroads, commercial enterprises, industries, and so on. They also organized temperance, antislavery, and other reform movements. In nearly every index of modernization— per capita wealth and economic growth, schools and literacy, railroads and commerce, rate of urbanization, technological innovation, and support for measures favoring social and economic change—the Yankee areas were ahead of Butternut areas by 1850. Butternuts disliked what they viewed as Yankee economic dominance and "Puritan" cultural imperialism. The politics of these states were marked by bitter conflicts over banking laws, corporation charters, temperance legislation, antislavery agitation, and anti-Negro measures, with the Butternuts consistently hostile to banks, corporations, temperance, and blacks.

Workers

Some members of the wage-earning class looked sourly upon the economic changes associated with modernization. This was not because the economic transition between 1815 and 1860 impoverished the working class. On the contrary, real wages (a combined index of changes in actual wages and in the cost of living) increased at least 50 percent during those years. Nevertheless, workers did not share equally with other segments of the society in the economic benefits of modernization, for the average per capita income of all Americans increased nearly 100 percent during the same period. The poor were getting richer, but not as fast as the rich and middle class were, leading to a widening gap between rich and poor and a growing sense of class consciousness among wage-earners. And the emergence of child labor in the textile industry, sweatshop conditions for women in the garment industry of big cities, and other low-wage occupations for recent immigrants, women, and children created a substantial group of workers who earned less than a living wage and could make ends meet only if several members of the family worked.

Even when earnings were adequate, the whole concept of "wages" seemed alien to the American notion of independence and equality among white men. In the Jeffersonian world of landowning farmers and independent artisans, the great majority of white males owned the means of production—and/or the tools of their trade. But in the post-1815 era of capitalist modernization, more and more men owned nothing but their labor power, which they sold to employers in return for wages. Those who worked for wages were dependent for a living on the owner of the business who paid them; they were not equal in status or independence to the "boss" or "capitalist" (words that entered the American language during the first half of the nineteenth century). Skilled craftsmen like shoemakers, tailors, cabinetmakers, gunsmiths, handloom weavers, and others resented the downgrading or displacement of their skills by the new techniques of production or new machines. Spokesmen for these workers, and others, protested the granting by state legislatures of bank and corporation charters, or subsidies to transportation companies, as a form of "special privilege" that enriched the few at the expense of the many. Labor unions and workingmen's political parties proliferated during the 1830s. Their protests against privilege and in favor of preserving the old status of independence for skilled workers fueled political activism during the presidencies of Andrew Jackson and Martin Van Buren (1829–1841). But the economic depression from 1837 to 1843 killed off many labor unions. Thereafter most workers seemed to accept, with varying degrees of reluctance or enthusiasm, the economic changes that transformed and expanded the working class, because rising wages brought a higher standard of living and technological innovation created new high-status occupations like telegrapher, railroad engineer, steamboat pilot, machinist, and the like that enabled many workers to achieve upward occupational mobility. Nevertheless, an undercurrent of hostility to modernization persisted among elements of the working class.

★ Political Parties and Modernization

By the 1830s, a two-party system had emerged as an apparently permanent feature of American politics. Issues associated with modernizing developments in the first half of the nineteenth century helped to define the ideological position of the two parties

Table 1.3 ROLL-CALL VOTES IN SEVEN STATE LEGISLATURES, 1832–1849

Legislation Favoring	Whigs	Democrats
Banks (N = 92)	83%	31%
Incorporation of business enterprises (N = 49)	77	39
Internal improvements (N = 49)	63	45
Incorporation of nonprofit voluntary associations (N = 10)	71	37
Social reforms (temperance, prison and asylum reform, abolition of capital punishment) (N = 22)	66	41
Public schools (N = 15)	68	47
Antislavery and problack measures (N.H., Pa., and Ohio) (N = 19)	82	10
Total (unweighted average) (N = 256)	74%	38%

and the constituencies to which they appealed. Democrats inherited the Jeffersonian commitment to states' rights, limited government, traditional economic arrangements, and religious pluralism; Whigs inherited the Federalist belief in nationalism, a strong government, economic innovation, and cultural homogeneity under the auspices of established Protestant denominations. Catholics and Butternuts provided the most solid support for the Democratic party in the North, while Protestants of New England and British birth formed the strongest Whig constituency. In areas with few Catholics or Butternuts, different but analogous patterns emerged. In states as dissimilar as Alabama and New Hampshire, the Whigs were most prevalent in urban areas and in prosperous farming regions linked by good transportation to the market economy. Merchants and skilled workers in New Hampshire and merchants and large planters in Alabama tended to be Whigs; farmers on poorer soils—those less involved with the market economy—leaned toward the Democrats. Similar patterns existed in other states—though often with significant exceptions.

These patterns suggest a generalization that can be stated, at the risk of oversimplification, as follows: Whigs were the party of modernization, Democrats the party of tradition. Whigs wanted to use the federal and state governments to promote economic growth through aid to internal improvements and the chartering of banks; Democrats tended to oppose such institutions of economic growth as banks and corporations, especially after 1840, because they feared that state-legislated economic privilege would threaten equal rights. Most advocates of temperance and public schools and black rights and prison reform were Whigs; most opponents were Democrats. Most Whigs subscribed to an enterpreneurial ethic that favored industrialization and urban growth; many Democrats retained the Jeffersonian agrarian heritage of hostility or at least unease toward these things. Most Whigs welcomed the future; many Democrats feared it. In the words of historian Marvin Meyers, "the Whig party spoke to the explicit hopes of Americans" while the Democrats "addressed their diffuse fears and resentments."[19] Table 1.3, showing the roll-call votes in seven state legislatures (New Hampshire, New Jersey, Pennsylvania, Ohio, Virginia, Ala-

[19]Marvin Meyers, *The Jacksonian Persuasion* (Stanford, 1957), p. 13.

bama, and Missouri) from 1832 to 1849, provides a graphic illustration of these party differences.[20]

In national politics, the most dramatic Whig-Democratic conflicts occurred over the issues of rechartering the Second Bank of the United States in the 1830s and the Mexican War in the 1840s. The Whigs favored the bank and opposed the war, but lost both contests. The latter issue points up another difference between the parties. Both believed in American expansion. But the Whigs favored expansion *over time* by means of economic growth and modernization. Democrats supported expansion *over space* by the acquisition of new territory in which to replicate the traditional institutions of older states. Democrats believed in the removal of Indians from their lands east of the Mississippi; Whigs provided what little defense existed for Indian rights in antebellum America—feeble and ineffective though it was. To the Whigs, "progress" meant internal development; to the Democrats it meant external growth. In a pamphlet entitled *Why I Am a Whig,* Horace Greeley explained: "Opposed to the instinct of boundless acquisition stands that of Internal Improvement. A nation cannot simultaneously devote its energies to the absorption of others' territories and the improvement of its own."[21]

The Democratic ideology of Jeffersonian agrarianism, small government, states' rights, and territorial expansion best suited the interests of the South and slavery. Chattel slavery in the United States became known as "the peculiar institution," not least because it seemed like an anomaly in a modernizing society. In the end, the party contests over banks, tariffs, internal improvements, and the like faded into the background of the greater conflict over slavery.

[20]This table is derived from the tables in Herbert Ershkowitz and William G. Shade, "Consensus or Conflict? Political Behavior in State Legislatures During the Jacksonian Era," *Journal of American History,* 58 (December 1971), 591–621, and in J. Mills Thornton, *Politics and Power in a Slave Society: Alabama, 1800–1860* (Baton Rouge, 1978), pp. 463–471.

[21](New York, 1851), p. 6.

TWO

The Antebellum South

W*e are an agricultural people. . . . We have no cities—we don't want them. . . . We want no manufactures; we desire no trading, no mechanical or manufacturing classes. As long as we have our rice, our sugar, our tobacco, and our cotton, we can command wealth to purchase all we want.*
                    —Louis T. Wigfall, Confederate senator from Texas, 1861

★ *The Southern Economy*

The South was the great exception to many of the foregoing generalizations about American modernization. The slave states remained overwhelmingly rural and agricultural. Their economy grew, but it did not develop a substantial commercial and industrial sector. Southern agriculture was as labor-intensive in 1860 as it had been in 1800. Upward social mobility was impossible for the half of the Southern labor force who lived in slavery. In contrast to the vigorous educational system and near-universal literacy of the North, the South's commitment to education was weak, and nearly half of its population was illiterate. The proliferation of voluntary associations, reform movements, and self-improvement societies that flourished in the free states largely by-passed the South. The slave states valued tradition and stability more than change and progress.

Some North-South Comparisons

Tables 2.1 through 2.5 illustrate some key statistical differences between North and South. In the tables, the category "slave states" includes the four border states that remained in the Union in 1861; had it included only the eleven states that eventually seceded, the North-South contrasts would have been even greater.

Other kinds of data confirm the picture presented by these tables. In 1860 Massachusetts produced more manufactured goods than all the future Confederate states combined, while New York and Pennsylvania *each* produced more than twice the goods manufactured by all the future Confederate states combined. The states that grew all the cotton possessed only 6 percent of the nation's cotton manufacturing

Table 2.1 PERCENTAGE OF URBANIZED POPULATION (LIVING IN TOWNS OF 2,500 OR MORE)

	Free States	Slave States
1820	10%	5%
1840	14	6
1860	26	10

Table 2.2 PERCENTAGE OF LABOR FORCE IN AGRICULTURE

	Free States	Slave States
1800	68%	82%
1860	40	81

Table 2.3 VALUE OF FARMLAND AND IMPLEMENTS, 1860

	Value of Farmland per Acre	Value of Farm Machinery and Implements per Acre	Value of Farm Machinery and Implements per Worker
Free states	$25.67	$0.89	$66
Slave states	10.40	0.42	38

Table 2.4 CAPITAL INVESTED IN MANUFACTURING

	FREE STATES		SLAVE STATES	
	Percentage of U.S. Total	Per Capita	Percentage of U.S. Total	Per Capita
1840	80%	$21.92	20%	$ 7.25
1860	84	43.73	16	13.25

Table 2.5 LITERACY AND EDUCATION, 1860

	PERCENTAGE OF POPULATION LITERATE			Percentage of Free Population Aged 5-19 Enrolled in School	Average Number of School Days per Year
	Total Population	Free Population	Slaves		
Free states	94%	94%	—	72%	135
Slave states	58	83	10% (est.)	35	80

capacity. New York state had nearly as much banking capital in 1860 as all fifteen slave states combined, while Massachusetts had as much banking capital as the cotton states of the lower South. The per capita circulation of newspapers and magazines among Southern whites was less than half that among the Northern population. With one-third of the country's white population, Southerners contributed only 7 percent of the important inventions from 1790 to 1860. The inventor of the cotton gin, which revolutionized the Southern economy, was the Massachusetts native Eli Whitney, who had gone to Georgia in 1792 as a tutor. A large proportion of antebellum Southern college presidents and professors, academy principals, tutors, and newspaper editors came from the North.

The South as a "Colonial" Economy

From the first Virginia experiments with tobacco culture in the 1610s, the growing of staple crops for the world market dominated Southern economic life. Four-fifths of all colonial exports to England before 1776 came from the Southern colonies—tobacco from Virginia and Maryland, rice and indigo and naval stores from the Carolinas and Georgia. Indigo virtually disappeared and tobacco underwent a relative decline after the Revolution. But Whitney's invention of the cotton gin made the commercial growing of short-staple cotton feasible,[1] while the rise of the textile industry in England and in New England created a vast new demand for cotton. Southern plantations and farms doubled their cotton output each decade from 1800 to 1860. Cotton exports provided more than half of all American exports from 1815 to 1860. Defenders of slavery and of the South argued with much truth that King Cotton ruled the American economy.

Much of the capital and entrepreneurship to finance and market Southern crops came from outside the South. The key figure in this process was the "factor," or commission merchant. The origins of factoring went back to the colonial period, when tobacco-importing firms in London sent their agents to Virginia to buy and ship the crop. The factor advanced credit to the planter, with future crops as collateral, and functioned as the planter's purchasing agent to obtain consumer goods from London or elsewhere. This system adapted itself easily to the marketing of cotton in the nineteenth century, except that factors became increasingly the representatives of Northern rather than British firms. Although they lived in the South, most of the factors—two-thirds by a contemporary estimate—were Yankees or Englishmen.

The factor took charge of the planter's crop when it reached Memphis or New Orleans or Mobile or Charleston or Savannah—or any of several other cities. He provided storage facilities and contracted for transportation and sale to the ultimate purchaser. He arranged for insurance and credit and supplies for the planter. For each of these services he charged a commission. The total amount of the commissions— including interest if the planter went into debt, as many of them did—might be as much as 20 percent of the value of the crop. Factoring represented a drain of wealth

---

[1]Before 1793, little "short-staple" cotton was grown, as the amount of hand labor required to remove the seeds from the short and tenacious cotton fibers made this crop commercially unprofitable. The cotton gin was a simple device in which a spiked cylinder rotating through a grid of bars separated the fiber from the seeds. The higher-quality (but more expensive) long-staple cotton, in which the seed could be easily separated from the fibers, had been grown commercially before 1793, but its growing area was limited to the coastal and sea-island areas of Georgia and South Carolina. The adaptability of short-staple cotton to widespread areas of the South set off a veritable cotton boom after Whitney's invention in 1793.

PRINCIPAL STAPLE CROP REGIONS OF THE SOUTH, 1860

from the South estimated at between $100 million and $150 million annually in the late antebellum period.

Thus while plantation agriculture was a profitable enterprise, many of the profits on marketing the crop—not to speak of the profits on its manufacture into finished goods—went to outsiders. Indeed, as an exporter of raw materials and an importer of manufactured goods, the South sustained something of a colonial economic relationship to the North and with Britain. Complained a resident of Mobile in 1847, "our whole commerce except a small fraction is in the hands of Northern men. $7/_8$ of our Bank Stock is owned by Northern men. . . . Our wholesale and retail business— everything in short worth mentioning is in the hands of [Yankees]. . . . Financially we are more enslaved than our negroes."[2] "At present, the North fattens and grows rich upon the South," declared an Alabama newspaper in 1851.

> We purchase all our luxuries and necessities from the North. . . . Northerners abuse and denounce slavery and slaveholders, yet our slaves are clothed with Northern manufactured goods, have Northern hats and shoes, work with Northern hoes, ploughs, and other implements. . . . The slaveholder dresses in Northern goods, rides in a Northern saddle . . . sports his Northern carriage . . . reads Northern books. . . . In Northern vessels his products are carried to market, his cotton is ginned with Northern gins, his sugar is crushed and preserved by Northern machinery; his rivers

[2]J. Mills Thornton, *Politics and Power in a Slave Society: Alabama, 1800–1860* (Baton Rouge, 1978), p. 255.

are navigated by Northern steamboats. . . . His son is educated at a Northern college, his daughter receives the finishing polish at a Northern seminary; his doctor graduates at a Northern medical college, his schools are furnished with Northern teachers, and he is furnished with Northern inventions.[3]

In 1852, Southerners who wanted to do something about this state of affairs revived the Southern Commercial Convention (originally founded in 1837), which met annually through the rest of the 1850s. Its purpose was to promote the construction with Southern capital of railroads, steamship lines, port facilities, banks, factories, and other enterprises to achieve economic independence from the North. The leaders of this movement exhorted fellow Southerners to buy only Southern-made goods, to boycott Northern textbooks and teachers, to patronize only Southern authors and vacation resorts. South Carolina's William Gregg urged the creation of a Southern textile industry, and led the way by building a model textile mill at Graniteville in the 1840s. The fierce Southern partisan Edmund Ruffin wore only clothes of Southern manufacture. Senator James Mason of Virginia proudly appeared in the U.S. Senate wearing a homespun suit.

But all of this availed little. The achievements of the Southern Commercial Convention turned out to be more political than economic. The Convention became increasingly a forum for secessionists. While Southern per capita investment in manufacturing nearly doubled between 1840 and 1860, as illustrated by Table 2.4 on page 27, this increase lagged behind the Northern growth rate, and the South's share of the nation's manufacturing capacity actually declined. James B. D. DeBow of New Orleans, publisher of the commercial magazine *DeBow's Review* and a leading advocate of Southern economic independence, found it necessary to have his *Review* printed in New York because of inadequate facilities in New Orleans. Three-quarters of DeBow's advertising income came from Northern businesses, and an important collection of *Review* articles on the industrial potential of the South sold six times as many copies in the North as in the South. Even William Gregg was obliged to hire a Northern superintendent and Yankee foremen for his Graniteville textile mill.

A crucial aspect of the Southern economy helps to explain its failure to modernize: slaves were both capital and labor. On a typical plantation, the investment in slaves was greater than the investment in land and implements combined. Slave agriculture could not follow the path blazed by Northern agriculture and become more capital-intensive because, paradoxically, an increase of capital became an increase of labor. Instead of investing substantial sums in machinery, planters invested in more slaves. As a contemporary observer put it: "To sell cotton in order to buy negroes—to make more cotton to buy more negroes, 'ad infinitum,' is the aim and direct tendency of all the operations of the thorough going cotton planter."[4]

Antebellum Southern agriculture underwent little technological change after the invention of the cotton gin in 1793. As indicated by Table 2.3 (page 27), the absorption of capital by labor meant that the per-unit value of land and machinery in the South was less than half the Northern average. The per capita output of Southern agriculture did increase between 1800 and 1860—perhaps as much as did that of Northern agriculture—but the cause was not primarily technological change. Rather,

[3]Quoted in Robert R. Russel, *Economic Aspects of Southern Sectionalism, 1840-1861* (Urbana, Ill., 1924), p. 48.

[4]Harold D. Woodman, *King Cotton and His Retainers: Financing and Marketing the Cotton Crop of the South, 1800-1925* (Lexington, Ky., 1968), p. 135.

it was the improved organization of the plantation labor force and the westward movement of the plantation frontier to virgin soil, as indicated by the maps on pages 29 and 32.

Thus the Southern economy *grew,* but it did not *develop.* As indicated by Table 2.2, the proportion of the Southern labor force in agriculture was virtually the same in 1860 as it had been in 1800. The South failed to develop a substantial urban middle class and skilled-labor population or to generate a diversified economy producing a wide variety of goods and services. Because slaves along with other kinds of personal and real property were counted as wealth, the per capita wealth of Southern whites in 1860 ($3,978) was nearly double the Northern average ($2,040). With only 30 percent of the nation's free population, the South furnished 60 percent of the nation's wealthiest men. On the other hand, the estimated Southern per capita income of $103 was 27 percent lower than the Northern average of $141.[5]

Economic historians have demonstrated that slavery was profitable. But profitable for whom? Certainly for cotton and sugar planters (probably less so for tobacco, rice, and hemp planters), whose average return on investment probably equaled that of Northern industrialists and exceeded that of Northern farmers. It was also profitable for the many slave owners in the upper South who sold their surplus slaves to the thriving cotton plantations of the Southwest. But it was not "profitable" for the slaves. Two economic historians have calculated that slaves on cotton plantations received in the form of food, clothing, and shelter only 22 percent of the earnings produced by these plantations. With emancipation, the proportion of output retained by labor rose to 56 percent.[6] It was also not profitable for the small-holding Southern farmers, who were crowded off the best land by large planters and could scarcely afford to buy slaves in the rising market.

Another way to look at the economics of slavery is to ask whether the institution promoted or inhibited Southern development. Many contemporaries believed that in this respect slavery's impact was negative. Observers of Southern life—ranging from the French visitor Alexis de Tocqueville to the British economist John Elliott Cairnes to the Yankee traveler Frederick Law Olmsted—maintained that slavery caused Southern backwardness. As Tocqueville steamed down the Ohio River in 1831, with Kentucky on his left and Ohio on his right, he mused on the contrast between slave and free society.

> On the left bank of the river the population is sparse; from time to time one sees a troop of slaves loitering through half-deserted fields. . . . One might say that society had gone to sleep. But on the right bank a confused hum proclaims from afar that men are busily at work; fine crops cover the fields . . . there is evidence of comfort; man appears rich and contented; he works.

Equally harsh were Olmsted's conclusions after three extended trips through the South in the 1850s, each of which resulted in a book. The slave states, wrote Olmsted, lacked "the characteristic features of a free-labor community, including an abundance and variety of skilled labor, a home market for a variety of crops, dense settlements

---

[5]Lee Soltow, *Men and Wealth in the United States 1850-1870* (New Haven, 1975), pp. 65, 101; Roger L. Ransom, *Conflict and Compromise: The Political Economy of Slavery, Emancipation, and the American Civil War* (Cambridge, 1989), p. 76.

[6]Roger L. Ransom and Richard Sutch, *One Kind of Freedom: The Economic Consequences of Emancipation* (Cambridge, 1977), pp. 3-4.

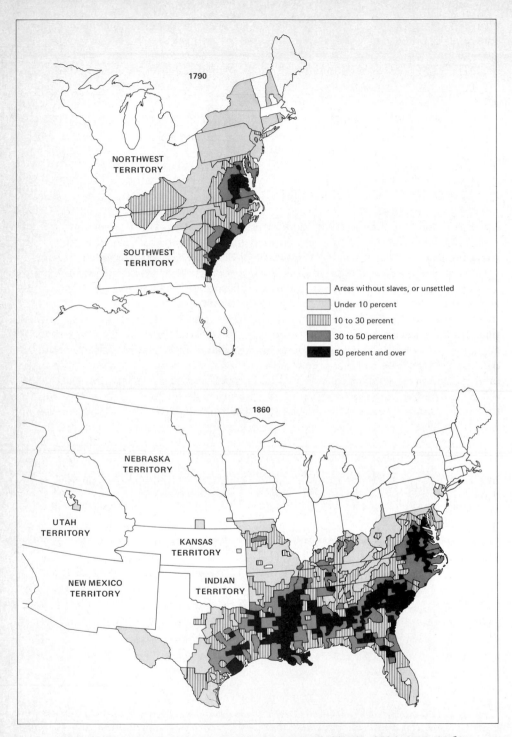

Areas without slaves, or unsettled
Under 10 percent
10 to 30 percent
30 to 50 percent
50 percent and over

PERCENTAGE OF SLAVES IN TOTAL POPULATION, 1790 AND 1860

[and] a large body of small proprietors." If a man returned to a Northern state after twenty years' absence, he would be struck by:

> . . . what we call the "improvements" which have been made: better buildings, churches, schoolhouses, mills, railroads . . . roads, canals, bridges . . . the better dress and evidently higher education of the people. But where will the returning traveller see the accumulated cotton profits of twenty years in Mississippi? Ask the cotton-planter for them, and he will point in reply, not to dwellings, libraries, churches, schoolhouses, mills, railroads, or anything of the kind; he will point to his negroes— to almost nothing else.[7]

A fundamental reason for the South's failure to modernize and become economically independent was a lack of diversity in its economy—that is, too great a dependence on a single staple crop, cotton. The soaring demand for cotton in the 1850s intensified this problem. As the nation's economy recovered from the 1837-1843 depression, cotton prices rose from their 1844 low of five cents a pound to an average of eleven cents a pound throughout the 1850s. Planters scrambled to put every available acre into cotton, and they set new production records almost every year. This also bid up the price of slaves, which nearly doubled during the 1850s and thereby absorbed most of the available capital in the South. A discouraged promoter of textile mills in Georgia asked rhetorically: "Why should all our cotton make so long a journey to the North, to be manufactured there, and come back to us at so high a price? It is because all spare cash is sunk here in purchasing negroes."[8] Although the cotton South enjoyed unprecedented prosperity in the 1850s, its economy became even more narrowly specialized in staple-crop agriculture.

Yet another reason for the South's failure to develop economically was rooted in the values of Southern society.

Southern Values versus Economic Change

In the South the voices of those calling for industrial development were sometimes drowned out by the voices of those who branded the entrepreneurial ethic a form of vulgar Yankee materialism. The South's ideal image of itself portrayed country gentlemen as practicing the arts of gracious living, hospitality, leisure, the ride and the hunt, chivalry toward women, honor toward equals, and kindness toward inferiors. The Yankees, on the other hand, appeared as a nation of shopkeepers—always chasing the almighty dollar, shrewd but without honor, hardworking but lacking the graces of a leisured class. "The Northerner loves to make money," said a Mississippian, "the Southerner to spend it." The author George Cary Eggleston recalled after the Civil War how he had come from Indiana to Virginia to inherit the family plantation. "I quitted the rapidly developing, cosmopolitan, kaleidoscopic West [for] the restful leisureliness of life in Virginia [with] its repose, the absence of stress or

[7]Alexis de Tocqueville, *Democracy in America*, ed. J. P. Mayer, trans. George L. Lawrence (Garden City, N.Y., 1969), pp. 345-346; Frederick Law Olmsted, *The Cotton Kingdom: A Selection*, ed. David Freeman Hawke (Indianapolis, 1971), pp. 184-185; Frederick Law Olmsted, *The Slave States Before the Civil War*, ed. Harvey Wish (New York, 1959), p. 253.

[8]Ulrich B. Phillips, *American Negro Slavery* (New York, 1918), p. 396.

strain or anxious anticipation, the appreciation of tomorrow as the equal of today in the doing of things."[9]

Many leading Southerners in the 1850s echoed Thomas Jefferson's praise of farmers as the "peculiar deposit for substantial and genuine virtue" and his warning against the industrial classes in the cities as sores on the body politic. "We have no cities," said a Texas politician at the outset of the Civil War. "We don't want them. . . . We want no manufactures; we desire no trading, no mechanical or manufacturing classes. As long as we have our rice, our sugar, our tobacco, and our cotton, we can command wealth to purchase all we want." In 1857, Governor Henry Wise of Virginia gloried in the gentleman slaveholder class, "civilized in the solitude, gracious in the amenities of life, and refined and conservative in social habits . . . who have leisure for the cultivation of morals, manners, philosophy, and politics." A South Carolina planter rejected the concept of progress as defined in Northern terms of commerce, industry, internal improvements, cities, and reform. The goals of these "noisy, brawling, roistering *progressistas,*" he warned, could be achieved in the South "only by the destruction of the planter class."[10] The popularity of such views posed a powerful obstacle to economic change in the South.

★ Slavery in the American South

Slavery formed the foundation of the South's distinctive social order. Although some historians have argued that plantation agriculture rather than slavery per se was the basic institution of the Southern economy, the distinction scarcely seems important. Slavery and the plantation were inextricably linked from the seventeenth century onward. In the 1850s, only 10 percent of the slave labor force worked in mining, transportation, construction, lumbering, and industry; another 15 percent were domestic servants or performed other nonagricultural labor. The overwhelming majority of slaves, about 75 percent, worked in agriculture—55 percent raising cotton, 10 percent tobacco, and the remaining 10 percent sugar, rice, or hemp. Slave labor raised more than half of the tobacco, three-quarters of the cotton, and nearly all of the rice, sugar, and hemp, as well as a major portion of the South's food crops.

Although only one-third of the South's white families owned slaves, this was a remarkably widespread distribution of ownership for such expensive property. By contrast, only 2 percent of American families in 1950 owned corporation stocks comparable in value to one slave a century earlier. Nearly half of all owners in the 1850s held fewer than five slaves, but more than half of all slaves belonged to the 12 percent of owners who possessed twenty or more—the number that unofficially distinguished a plantation from a farm.

Herrenvolk Democracy

What stake did nonslaveholding whites have in the slave system? A number of different views have existed concerning this group. To some observers they have

[9]Eugene D. Genovese, *The Political Economy of Slavery* (New York, 1965), p. 30; George Cary Eggleston, *Recollections of a Varied Life* (New York, 1910), pp. 46–49.

[10]William Howard Russell, *My Dairy North and South* (Boston, 1861), p. 179; David Bertelson, *The Lazy South* (New York, 1967), p. 190; "The Prospects and Policy of the South, as They Appear to the Eyes of a Planter," *Southern Quarterly Review,* 26 (October 1854), 432, 448.

appeared as an undifferentiated mass of ragged, dirty, illiterate "poor whites" eking out a miserable living on the margins of the plantation economy. At the opposite pole, some Southern historians have portrayed these "plain folk" as a proud, intelligent, prosperous, and politically important rural middle class who raised food crops and small amounts of tobacco or cotton or hogs for the market. Many contemporaries, Northern and Southern alike, viewed the nonslaveholding whites as a potential antislavery force who, because they had no stake in the plantation system, might feel that slavery degraded all labor to the level of bond labor.

None of these viewpoints is entirely correct, though all possess elements of truth. To disentangle truth from stereotype, one must distinguish among three distinct groups of rural nonslaveholding whites. One group consisted of the residents of the "hill country"—the Appalachian highlands and valleys stretching from western Maryland and eastern Kentucky to northern Alabama, and the Ozark Plateau of southern Missouri and northern Arkansas. These regions contained few slaves. Their inhabitants were mainly small-holding farmers who raised food crops and livestock. In politics, the hill-country residents often opposed the piedmont and lowland areas of their states over matters of legislative apportionment, state aid to internal improvements, and taxation of land and slaves. No friends of the plantation regime, the hill-country folk came closest to fitting the image of an antislavery fifth column within the South. During the Civil War many of them remained loyal to the Union.

A second group of nonslaveholders lived in the "piney woods" or "wiregrass" regions—areas of sandy or marshy soil in eastern North Carolina, southern Georgia and Alabama, eastern Mississippi, and numerous pockets elsewhere. These people came closest to fitting the traditional image of poor whites. They raised a few acres of corn and grazed scraggy herds of livestock in the woods. Although they sold some of their hogs to richer areas of the South, these whites, like those in the upcountry, participated minimally in the staple-crop economy.

The largest group of nonslaveholding whites, however, played an important role in that economy. They lived in the piedmont districts or in the less fertile areas of the tidewater, where they raised each year a bale or two of cotton or a hogshead of tobacco, as well as food crops. They were linked to the plantation regime by numerous ties of self-interest and sentiment. They ginned their cotton and perhaps sold some of their pork at the nearest plantation. Many of them aspired to become slaveholders, and the more successful or lucky achieved this goal. Moreover, given the traditional patterns of kinship in the South, a nonslaveholder was quite likely to be a cousin or a nephew of the planter down the road. The big planter was in the habit of treating his poorer neighbors once or twice a year to a barbecue—especially if he happened to be running for the legislature.

While subtle ties of kinship and mutual interest blunted potential class conflict between slaveholders and some nonslaveholders, the most important tie was the bond of race. Not all Southern whites owned slaves, but they all owned white skins. And slavery was not only a system of labor exploitation, it was also a method of racial control. However much some nonslaveholders may have disliked slavery, few of them could see any alternative means of preserving white supremacy. An Alabama farmer told Frederick Law Olmsted that he believed slavery to be wrong—but he did not believe emancipation to be right. "Now suppose they was free, you see they'd all think themselves just as good as we. . . . How would you like to hev a nigger feelin' just as good as a white man? How'd you like to hev a nigger steppin' up to your darter?" Another dirt farmer said to Olmsted that he wished "there warn't no niggers here. They are a great cuss to this country. . . . But it wouldn't never do to free 'em and leave 'em here. I don't know anybody, hardly, in favor of that. Make 'em free and leave 'em here and they'd steal everything we made. Nobody couldn't live here then."[11]

Olmsted perceptively concluded that "from childhood, the one thing in their condition which has made life valuable to the mass of whites has been that the niggers are yet their inferiors." The South's leading proslavery political spokesman, John C. Calhoun of South Carolina, also grasped this truth. "With us," said Calhoun in 1848, "the two great divisions of society are not the rich and the poor, but white and black; and all the former, the poor as well as the rich, belong to the upper class, and are respected and treated as equals . . . and hence have a position and pride of character of which neither poverty nor misfortune can deprive them."[12]

The sociologist Pierre L. van den Berghe has described this rationalization for slavery and white supremacy as "Herrenvolk democracy"—the equal superiority of all who belong to the Herrenvolk (master race) over all who do not.[13] The Herrenvolk concept had a powerful appeal in both the South and the North. "Your fathers and my fathers built this government on two ideas," said the Alabama champion of Southern rights William L. Yancey. "The first is that the white race is the citizen, and the master race, and the white man is the equal of every other white man. The second idea is that the Negro is the inferior race." The Declaration of Independence, in this interpretation, affirmed that all *white* men were created equal. The man who wrote that Declaration was a slaveholder. President Andrew Jackson, whose name is linked with the egalitarian ethos of Jacksonian Democracy, was a slaveholder. The Jacksonian Democrats aggressively championed white supremacy; their Herrenvolk ideology helped attract Irish, Butternuts, and unskilled laborers in the North to the Democratic party, for it proclaimed that no matter how poor they might be, these people were still better than blacks. Like the Southern nonslaveholders, they feared emancipation because it would render their whiteness meaningless. "Break down slavery," said Governor Wise of Virginia, "and you would with the same blow destroy the democratic principle of equality among men."[14] Here was the central paradox of American history: slavery became for many whites the foundation of liberty and equality.

The Conditions of Slavery

For the slaves there was no paradox: slavery was slavery, and freedom was its opposite. Chattel bondage gave the master great power over his slaves to buy or sell, to punish without sanction of the courts, to separate families, to exploit sexually, even to kill with little fear of being held legally responsible. As a form of property, the slaves had few human rights in the eyes of the law. They could not legally marry, nor

[11]Olmsted, *Cotton Kingdom*, pp. 106, 192.

[12]Olmsted, *Slave States Before the Civil War*, p. 251; *The Works of John C. Calhoun*, ed. Richard K. Crallé, 6 vols. (New York, 1854–57), IV, 505–506.

[13]Pierre van den Berghe, *Race and Racism: A Comparative Perspective* (New York, 1967). George M. Fredrickson, *The Black Image in the White Mind* (New York, 1971), chap. 2, applies this concept to antebellum race relations in a penetrating analysis.

[14]Yancey and Wise quoted in Fredrickson, *Black Image*, pp. 61, 62.

SLAVES IN THE AMERICAN SOUTH. *The photograph above portrays a typical slave cabin—this one in Georgia—with dirt floors and no glass in the windows. The photograph below shows slaves gathered before "the Great House" and outbuildings on a large plantation near Baton Rouge.*

own property, nor be taught to read or write in most states. Owners might let them have a family, earn money, or (in rare cases) even buy their freedom; but until they were free, money, spouse, and children could be taken away at any moment. Several states permitted manumission only on condition that the manumitted slave leave the state. Of the 250,000 free blacks in the slave states in 1860, only 35,000 lived in the eight lower-South cotton states, where they suffered galling restrictions that made life for many of them little better than slavery.

In practice, the master's power over his slaves was often tempered by economic self-interest and sometimes by paternalism. Masters and overseers could not rule by the whip alone. Dead, maimed, brutalized, or runaway slaves could grow little if any cotton. Persuasion, inducement, rewards for good work, and concessions were necessary in this as in other relationships between employer and employees. The gentleman planter's code of *noblesse oblige* required beneficence toward inferiors. The slaves spoke the same language and worshipped the same Christian God as their owners. Relations of trust and affection as well as alienation and hatred could exist between slave and master.

Slavery was, in short, a human institution as well as a legal and economic one. This helped to neutralize its dehumanizing tendencies and to give the slaves latitude to create cultural institutions that sustained them through generations of bondage. Natural leaders in the slave quarters often became eloquent preachers in the "invisible institution" of the black church, whose congregations worshipped apart from whites (sometimes secretly) in spite of laws to the contrary. The slaves created the most original and moving music in antebellum America—the spirituals—which expressed their longing for freedom as well as their resignation to sorrow, and evolved after the Civil War into the blues and eventually into jazz. While slavery made stable family life difficult, a majority of slaves nevertheless formed strong ties of kinship and family. Thus although slavery's impact on black people could be repressive, the countervailing force of a positive black culture provided an impressive example of survival in the face of adversity.

Slavery in the United States operated with less physical harshness than in most other parts of the Western Hemisphere. For most slaves on West Indian sugar plantations or Brazilian coffee plantations, life was indeed nasty, brutish, and short. Climatic conditions and disease took a higher toll of black lives there than in North America. Food, clothing, medical care, and the material necessities of life were less abundant, and the pace of work on tropical sugar plantations was more brutally demanding than work in the cotton or tobacco fields further north.

Slavery in the Caribbean and in South America flourished while the African slave trade was still open. In the United States, by contrast, the slave system reached its height only after the African slave trade had ended in 1808. This had important implications for the physical treatment of slaves. In Latin America, many planters had considered it cheaper to import slaves from Africa and almost literally work them to death than to create an environment in which the slaves could raise families and maintain their population through natural reproduction. In the United States, the cutoff of imports made planters dependent on natural reproduction for the maintenance and increase of their slave "stock." It was in the slave owner's interest to encourage good health and a high birth rate among his slaves. One former slave said that his master "fed us reg'lar on good, 'stantial food, just like you'd tend to you hoss, if you had a real good one." Another former slave recalled a Louisiana planter who liked to point out healthy slave children to visitors. " 'Dat one be worth a t'ousand dollars,' or 'Dat one be a whopper.' You see, 'twas just like raisin' young mules."[15]

The U.S. slave population increased by an average of 27 percent per decade after 1810, almost the same natural growth rate as for the white population. This rate of increase was unique in the history of bondage. No other slave population in the Western Hemisphere even maintained, much less increased, its population through natural reproduction. In Barbados, for example, the decennial natural *decrease* from 1712 to 1762 was 43 percent. At the time of emancipation, the black population of the United States was ten times the number of Africans who had been imported, but the black population of the West Indies was only half the number of Africans who had been imported. Of the eleven million Africans brought across the Atlantic by the slave trade, the United States received only 5 percent; yet at the time of emancipation it had more than 30 percent of the hemisphere's black population.

Important social implications underlie these bare demographic facts. For example, Spanish and Portuguese laws in Latin America allowed slaves to marry and provided some protection to their families, whereas slave marriages had no legal basis in the United States. But because West Indian and Latin American countries relied on the slave trade to maintain their supply of slaves, and because twice as many male as female Africans were imported, marriage and a family were impossible for large numbers of male slaves in these countries. By contrast, the sex ratio among slaves in the United States was virtually equal from 1820 onward. This enabled most slaves to form families, and helps to explain why the natural reproduction rate was so much higher in North America than elsewhere. It also helps to explain why large-scale slave revolts were rarer in the United States than in the Caribbean or in Latin America: men with family responsibilities were less likely to start an insurrection than men with no such responsibilities.

Lacking legal protection, however, slave families in the United States were fragile. One of the most tragic aspects of slavery was the breakup of families. Even a master who refused to sell family members apart from each other could not always prevent such sales to settle debts after his death. Several studies of slavery have found that from one-fifth to one-third of slave marriages were broken by owners—generally by selling one or both of the partners separately.[16] The percentage of children sold apart from their parents or siblings cannot even be estimated.

Slavery and the Work Ethic

In a modernizing society, status depends on achievement as well as on ascription. But slaves experienced the most extreme form of ascribed status. Most of them could achieve upward mobility only within the narrowest of ranges: from field hand to driver or house servant, for example. Even those few slaves who earned their freedom

---

[15]Paul D. Escott, *Slavery Remembered: A Record of the Twentieth-Century Slave Narratives* (Chapel Hill, N.C., 1979), p. 25.

[16]John W. Blassingame, *The Slave Community* (New York, 1972), pp. 89-92; Herbert Gutman and Richard Sutch, "The Slave Family: Protected Agent of Capitalist Masters or Victim of the Slave Trade?" in Paul A. David et al., *Reckoning with Slavery* (New York, 1976), pp. 127-129; Herbert Gutman, *The Black Family in Slavery and Freedom* (New York, 1976), pp. 146-147; Escott, *Slavery Remembered,* pp. 46-48.

found their mobility circumscribed by racism and by the legal restrictions on free blacks.

Slavery also undermined the work ethic among Southern whites. When most kinds of manual labor are associated with bondage, work becomes servile rather than honorable. The Virginia statesman George Mason acknowledged that "slavery discourages arts and manufactures. The poor despise labor when performed by slaves." The South Carolina industrialist William Gregg lamented that his state was "destitute of every feature which characterizes an industrious people."[17] Primarily because of the paucity of employment opportunities and the lack of esteem for white labor, only one-eighth of the immigrants to the United States settled in the South. Twice as many native-born whites migrated from slave to free states as vice versa.

Perhaps the most outspoken critic of the work habits of both whites and blacks in the South was Frederick Law Olmsted, whose writings on the South portrayed slipshod farming practices, wretched roads and public services, trains and steamboats that ran late or not at all, and a general air of shiftlessness. The root of the problem, as Olmsted and others saw it, was the inefficiency of slave workers. Forced labor was reluctant labor. Slaves "seem to go through the motions of labor without putting strength into them," wrote Olmsted, who believed that the average free worker in the North accomplished twice as much as the average slave. Most slaves, he argued, had little motivation to improve their output through harder work or greater efficiency. They lacked the time discipline of modern work habits. "Their time isn't any value to themselves," said one Southern white in a remark that Olmsted considered profound.[18]

Planters' records as well as black folklore also provide evidence that slaves engaged in slowdowns and careless practices, as a form of resistance to compulsory labor: they feigned illness, ceased to work when the overseer looked the other way, pretended to misunderstand orders, broke tools, abused work animals, ran away to the woods or swamps. Slavery helped cause the technological lag in Southern agriculture. Southern hoes were heavy and clumsy because slaves were said to break the lighter ones customarily used on Northern farms. Slaves continued to use hoes for tillage and cultivation long after Northern farmers had begun to use horse-drawn plows and cultivators. The plows that *were* used in Southern agriculture tended to be the old shallow-furrow mule-drawn shovel plows, rather than the new deep-furrow horse-drawn moldboard plows common in the North by the 1830s. Mules were the common Southern draft animals because, while less strong than horses, they could better withstand the reputed carelessness and abuse of slaves. In 1860, the slave states contained 90 percent of the mules but only 40 percent of the horses in the United States.[19]

[17]Mason and Gregg quoted in Bertelson, *Lazy South,* pp. 159, 195.

[18]Olmsted, *Cotton Kingdom,* pp. 28, 153–154.

[19]Two economic historians, Robert Fogel and Stanley Engerman, have challenged the thesis of slave inefficiency. Indeed, they maintain that because of careful management, high morale among slave workers, and economies of scale on large plantations, Southern agriculture was more efficient than Northern. Few other historians, however, have accepted this argument. See Robert W. Fogel and Stanley L. Engerman, *Time on the Cross: The Economics of American Negro Slavery* (Boston, 1974), and two volumes criticizing these arguments: Paul A. David et al., *Reckoning with Slavery* (New York, 1976), and Herbert G. Gutman, *Slavery and the Numbers Game* (Urbana, Ill., 1975). In a subsequent study, Robert Fogel reiterated the thesis about the superior efficiency of slave-labor agriculture, but now attributed it mainly to "the enormous, almost unconstrained degree of force available to masters." Fogel, *Without Consent or Contract: The Rise and Fall of American Slavery* (New York, 1989), p. 34.

The denial of education to slaves produced the most jarring disjunction between slavery and modernization. At least 90 percent of the slave population was illiterate. Although the slaves developed a vigorous oral tradition, their inability to read and write barred them from the principal means of communicating knowledge, ideas, and culture in a modernizing society. The low level of literacy was one of the chief features distinguishing the slave from the free population and the South from the North (see Table 2.5, page 27). In the eyes of abolitionists, it was one of the main reasons for the "backwardness" of the South and the immorality of slavery.

THREE

The Ideological Conflict over Slavery

*M*any *in the South once believed that slavery was a moral and political evil. That folly and delusion are gone. We see it now in its true light, and regard it as the most safe and stable basis for free institutions in the world.*

—John C. Calhoun, 1838

★ The Antislavery Movement

Few white men questioned the morality of black slavery before the eighteenth century. Bondage was the most ancient and universal form of labor in the history of civilization. Philosophy and religion in the premodern era justified slavery as one of many forms of subordination to authority necessary for social order. But by the second half of the eighteenth century, four currents of Anglo-American and French thought converged to form the basis for the emergence of an international antislavery movement.

The first was the growth of post-Reformation radical Protestant denominations, especially the Quakers. Traditional Christianity had justified slavery as God's will, a necessary part of the divine order. But the explosive forces loosed by the Reformation generated numerous sectarian challenges to the status quo. The Quakers became one of the most successful sects in England and America. By 1760 they had begun to purge themselves of slaveholding. In 1775 they founded the first American antislavery organization, the Pennsylvania Society for Promoting the Abolition of Slavery. Meanwhile the Great Awakening of the 1740s (the first of several major revival movements in the history of American Protestantism) had produced an evangelical faith in conversion and spiritual regeneration. This in turn caused many Congregationalists and Methodists as well as Quakers to transform the traditional Christian view of sin as a form of slavery into a conviction that slaveholding was a sin.

The second current of thought that helped to undermine the intellectual rationalizations for bondage was the Enlightenment, which questioned slavery's place in a social order designed to produce the greatest good for the greatest number. The third was the maturation of a laissez-faire economic theory that rejected feudal and mercantilistic restrictions on free enterprise and free labor. Adam Smith's *Wealth of Nations* (1776) was the most influential statement of this theory. The labor of slaves, wrote Smith, "though it appears to cost only their maintenance, is in the end the dearest of any. A person who can acquire no property, can have no other interest but to eat as much, and to labour as little as possible."[1]

The fourth development that worked against slavery was the series of revolutions that rocked the transatlantic world in the half-century after 1775. The Age of Revolution produced the abolition of slavery in all of the new states of the Union north of Maryland, in the French West Indies,[2] and in most of the Central and South American countries that won their independence from Spain. In 1808, Britain and the United States prohibited their citizens from engaging in the international slave trade; in subsequent years, Britain used diplomacy and naval power to enforce this prohibition on a growing list of additional nations. In 1833, Britain abolished slavery in its own West Indian colonies, and in 1848, during a second wave of European revolutions, France and Denmark followed suit.

These were impressive achievements. Nearly two million slaves attained freedom. The slave trade was curtailed if not fully halted. On the other hand, slavery survived in the southern United States, Brazil, and Cuba, where the increasing production respectively of cotton, coffee, and sugar after 1800 entrenched the institution more firmly than ever. The expansion of slavery in these countries produced a slave population in the Western Hemisphere larger in 1850 than it had been a half-century earlier. Americans and the nationals of other countries participated in a flourishing illicit slave trade to Brazil and Cuba. The illegal slavers even continued to bring Africans to the United States after 1808.[3]

Abolition versus Colonization

After the achievements of the Revolutionary generation, the antislavery movement in the United States lost some of its impetus. The libertarian sentiments of Southern Jeffersonians were neutralized by the class benefits they derived, as planters, from slavery. Whites also feared the racial consequences of "letting loose" a large number of black people whose assumed inferiority and "savage instincts" would constitute a threat to society. As Thomas Jefferson put it in 1820, the South had "the wolf by the ears" and could not let it go.[4]

One popular solution to this dilemma was the idea of gradual emancipation coupled with "colonization"—the settlement of freed blacks in their African "homeland." In 1817 a number of prominent Americans, including Henry Clay and Bushrod Washington (nephew of George Washington), formed the American Colonization Society. The society acquired land in West Africa and founded the country of Liberia as a haven for free black Americans whose transportation and settlement there the society financed. Begun with high hopes, the American Colonization Society did

---

[1] Quoted in David Brion Davis, *The Problem of Slavery in the Age of Revolution 1770-1823* (Ithaca, 1975), p. 352.

[2] Napoleon reinstated slavery in French possessions in 1803.

[3] Probably fewer than one thousand annually.

[4] Jefferson to John Holmes, April 22, 1820, in H. A. Washington (ed.), *The Writings of Thomas Jefferson*, 9 vols. (New York, 1853-1854), VII, 159.

nothing to solve the problems of slavery and race. Although Liberia became an independent republic in 1847, the society and its state auxiliaries managed to send fewer than ten thousand blacks there by 1860—about 0.3 percent of the increase in the American black population during that period.

Opposition to the American Colonization Society came from three principal sources: proslavery advocates in the lower South, who resented any effort, however moderate, to interfere with bondage; most free blacks, especially in the North, who considered themselves Americans, not Africans; and the post-1830 abolitionist movement, which denounced the colonization society as racist for its assumption that the race problem could be solved only by sending black people out of the country.

Militant Abolitionism

The most important underlying cause for the emergence of militant abolitionism after 1830 was the religious phenomenon known as the Second Great Awakening. The revisionist Calvinists who led this movement in the North emphasized the free will of anyone to choose the path to salvation. God's grace was available not just to the predestined elect, but to all who experienced conversion, abjured sin, and placed themselves in a state of belief and behavior to receive his grace. This was an activist faith. It spawned a host of reform crusades against "sin"—the sin of infidelity, of Sabbath-breaking, of prostitution, of intemperance, and of enslaving human beings. These crusades inherited the Puritan doctrine of collective accountability and collective judgment. Every man *was* his brother's keeper. All Americans were therefore accountable for the sin of slavery so long as one American held slaves.

The principal evangelical preacher of the Second Great Awakening was Charles Grandison Finney. Among his followers were the eloquent lecturer Theodore Weld and the wealthy merchant brothers Arthur and Lewis Tappan. Along with William Lloyd Garrison, these men became the principal founders of the American Anti-Slavery Society in 1833. The next few years saw a remarkable growth of this organization and its state and local auxiliaries. By 1838, there were 1,350 such auxiliaries with a total claimed membership of 250,000. These societies published pamphlets and newspapers, sponsored lectures, and gathered signatures on petitions to Congress calling for action against slavery.

The scope and fervor of this crusade were unprecedented. The abolitionists of the 1830s spurned the moderation and gradualism of their predecessors. They rejected colonization as a proslavery trick to strengthen the institution by merely appearing to ameliorate it. There must be no compromise with slavery, they insisted: one does not compromise with sin, one vanquishes it. William Lloyd Garrison published the manifesto of the new militancy in the first issue of his famous newspaper, the *Liberator*, on January 1, 1831:

> I *will* be as harsh as truth, and as uncompromising as justice. On this subject, I do not wish to think, or speak, or write, with moderation. No! No! Tell a man whose house is on fire to give a moderate alarm; tell him to moderately rescue his wife from the hands of the ravisher; tell the mother to gradually extricate her babe from the fire into which it has fallen;—but urge me not to use moderation in a cause like the present. I am in earnest—I will not equivocate—I will not excuse—I will not retreat a single inch— AND I WILL BE HEARD.

In the 1830s, abolitionists had two primary goals: to convert Americans, including Southerners and slaveholders, to a belief that slaveholding was a sin; and to win equal rights for free blacks. These goals, and the methods to achieve them, were modeled on the religious crusades, or "revivals," of the Second Great Awakening. Having themselves experienced "conversion" to abolitionism, the reformers hoped to convert others. Once convinced that slavery and racial discrimination were sins against God and man, Americans would cease sinning, surmount racism, abolish slavery, and grant equal rights to the freed people.

But these hopes were doomed to failure. The South closed its mind to the abolitionists. Some Southern states and cities put a price on the head of Garrison and other leading reformers. Intrepid abolitionists who ventured into the South were mobbed and driven out or imprisoned. Mobs broke into Southern post offices and seized and burned abolitionist pamphlets. President Andrew Jackson approved of this type of action and ordered his postmaster general to ban abolitionist literature from the mails, on the ground that it might incite a slave rebellion. Those few Southern whites who did become abolitionists—such as the Kentuckian James G. Birney and the South Carolina sisters Angelina and Sarah Grimké—had to move to the North to proclaim their beliefs.

Nor did most Northerners accept the abolitionist message of total emancipation and equal rights. Such objectives threatened too many economic and racial interests. Northern mobs attacked abolitionist lecturers, destroyed printing presses, and burned abolitionist property in the 1830s. Some of these mobs also attacked free blacks. The mobs consisted mainly of lower-class whites, who feared that emancipation would loose a horde of blacks to come north and compete with them for jobs and social equality. But some mobs included "gentlemen of property and standing"— merchants or lawyers who had business connections with the South, or conservative men who believed that abolitionist radicalism threatened the Union and the very basis of the social order itself.

The Politics of Abolitionism

The failure of moral suasion to convert the nation to abolition prompted some abolitionists to go into politics. In 1839 they founded the Liberty party, which nominated James G. Birney for president in 1840. But Birney received a mere seven thousand votes—0.3 percent of the total.

The formation of the Liberty party was one of several factors that caused a split in the antislavery movement. William Lloyd Garrison led a faction of abolitionists who opposed political action, arguing that it would lead to compromises of principle. The Garrisonians refused to vote under the U.S. Constitution, which they branded as a proslavery document. Several Garrisonians even called for the withdrawal of free states from a Union that sanctioned slavery (or "man-stealing"). In their disappointment with the refusal of major church denominations to endorse militant abolitionism, some followers of Garrison attacked organized religion as a "den of thieves." This angered evangelical abolitionists. The Garrisonians also endorsed equal rights for women, which offended some male abolitionists who, though they believed in equality for black men, could not bring themselves to support equality for women. The women's rights movement grew out of women's participation in abolitionist organizations. As female abolitionists wrote and spoke about the sin of racial subordi-

WILLIAM LLOYD GARRISON.
The scholarly countenance that gazes out from this photograph gives little evidence of the fire of Garrison's rhetoric that seared slaveholders and their allies. Something of a universal reformer, Garrison also embraced women's rights, pacifism, temperance, Indian rights, diet reform, and opposition to capital punishment.

nation, some of them also began to speak out against their own subordination to men. This growing feminist consciousness helped spark the movement that resulted in the first national women's rights convention at Seneca Falls in 1848. Eight years earlier, the Garrisonians' success in electing a woman to the executive board of the American Anti-Slavery Society had provoked a schism in the society. Those who withdrew—including Finney and the Tappan brothers—supported the Liberty party and founded other antislavery societies in the 1840s.

The most important of these was the American Missionary Association. This organization grew out of a successful effort by the Tappan brothers to win the freedom of Africans who had captured the slave ship *Amistad,* which was carrying them to slavery in Cuba. They steered it to Long Island instead, where abolitionists took up their cause and carried the case to the Supreme Court. The Court declared the Africans to be free, and the abolitionists repatriated them to their homeland. The American Missionary Assocation, founded in 1846 to bring Christianity to these and other Africans, became, two decades later, the principal agency for bringing education to freed slaves in the American South.

Although split, the abolitionist movement remained active and important after 1840. Indeed it broadened its impulse: as events unfolded, the widening gulf between free and slave states won more converts to antislavery politics than abolitionists ever did. But as Garrisonians had predicted, this broadening of the movement diluted its religious and humanitarian thrust. Although some political abolitionists continued to support the ultimate goals of total emancipation and equal rights, they and their less radical colleagues focused primarily on restricting the further spread of slavery and pledged not to interfere with it in the states where it already existed. This represented *antislavery* sentiment, but not abolition. It considered slavery wrong but proposed to take no direct action against the institution in the states. Instead, antislavery hoped that restrictions against expansion of slavery into the territories would produce a slow decline of the institution, leading to its gradual extinction at some future date. In the meantime, the territories and new states would fill up with free labor and replicate the social and economic institutions of the free states. This antislavery impulse became politically institutionalized in the Free Soil party of 1848 and in the more powerful Republican party in 1854. Most Free Soilers, in contrast to most abolitionists, cared more about the rights of white men than about the rights of black people. "There are Republicans who are Abolitionists; there are others who anxiously desire and labor for the good of the slave," explained the *New York Tribune* in 1856, "but there are many more whose main impulse is to secure the new Territories for Free White Labor, with little or no regard for the interests of negroes, free or slave."[5]

★ Antislavery and Modernization

Both abolition and antislavery took deepest root in New England and in areas of the North settled by New Englanders. All of the principal founders and leaders of the movement—Finney, Weld, the Tappan brothers, Garrison, and Wendell Phillips—were natives of Massachusetts or Connecticut. Salmon P. Chase, the Ohioan who took over leadership of the Liberty party in the 1840s and helped to broaden it into the Free Soil party in 1848, was born and raised in New Hampshire. Of 567 abolitionist leaders, 63 percent were born in New England—at a time when that region contained but 21 percent of the country's population. Studies of counties in upstate New York and Ohio where abolitionism was strongest have found a significant correlation between Yankee settlement, evangelical revivals, and antislavery organizations.[6]

A similarity existed in the social origins of entrepreneurial and abolitionist leaders—both in Britain and in the United States. Quakers, especially in England, were prominent among both groups. English Quaker families, such as the Darbys, the Lloyds, the Barclays, and the Wedgwoods, formed the vanguard of the industrial revolution and furnished many eighteenth-century British antislavery leaders. Likewise, Quakers were prominent in eighteenth-century American commercial enterprises and dominated the early antislavery societies. After 1830, abolitionist leadership in the United States passed to the evangelical Protestants and Unitarians in New England—at precisely the time these groups and this region were forging the most modernized sector of the economy. Table 3.1 illustrates the similarities between

[5]October 15, 1856.

[6]Data on the birthplace of abolitionist leaders are from the author's research. For studies of New York and Ohio counties, see Whitney R. Cross, *The Burned-over District: The Social and Intellectual History of Enthusiastic Religion in Western New York, 1800-1850* (Ithaca, 1950); Alan M. Kraut, "The Forgotten Reformers: A Profile of Third Party Abolitionists in Antebellum New York," in Lewis Perry and Michael Fellman (eds.), *Antislavery Reconsidered: New Perspectives on the Abolitionists* (Baton Rouge, 1979), pp. 119-145; Gerald Sorin, *The New York Abolitionists: A Case Study of Political Radicalism* (Westport, Conn., 1971); and John L. Hammond, "Revival Religion and Antislavery Politics," *American Sociological Review*, 39 (April 1974), 175-186.

Table 3.1 **ORIGINS OF ABOLITIONISTS AND ENTREPRENEURS**

	Abolitionist Leaders		Ratio to Population*		Entrepreneurs		Ratio to Population*	
New England–born	63%		3:1		51%		3:1	
Congregational	34 ⎤		7:1 ⎤		22 ⎤		5:1 ⎤	
Unitarian	13 ⎬ 67%		13:1 ⎬10:1		10 ⎬ 40%		10:1 ⎬6:1	
Quaker	20 ⎦		20:1 ⎦		8 ⎦		8:1 ⎦	

*This ratio expresses the relationship between the percentage of abolitionist leaders or entrepreneurs and the percentage of the whole American population in these categories. That is, the proportion of all Americans living in New England at the median birth date of the abolitionist leaders (1805) was 21 percent, hence the proportion of abolitionists born in New England was three times that of the whole population. The proportion of Americans living in New England at the median birth date of entrepreneurs (1825) was about 18 percent. The church affiliation ratios are calculated for the 1840s. The size of the samples was:

Abolitionist birthplace: $N = 567$	Entrepreneur birthplace: $N = 247$
Abolitionist religious affiliation: $N = 504$	Entrepreneur religious affiliation: $N = 144$

abolitionist and industrial leadership in the mid-nineteenth-century United States.[7] In an occupational survey of abolitionist leaders ($N = 622$), the proportion of business-men (21 percent) was exceeded only by clergymen (34 percent).

The Free-Labor Ideology

The abolitionist-entrepreneur correlation was no coincidence. The capitalist ideology was a free-labor ideology. It held that the internalized self-discipline of the Protestant ethic created more efficient workers than the coercive external discipline of slavery. The positive incentives of wages or advancement and the negative incentive of poverty provided stronger motivation than the lash. "The whip," said an abolitionist, "only stimulates the flesh on which it is laid. It does not reach the parts of the man where lie the springs of action." "Enslave a man," wrote the antislavery Whig editor Horace Greeley, "and you destroy his ambition, his enterprise, his capacity. In the constitution of human nature, the desire of bettering one's condition is the main-spring of effort."[8]

The ideal of upward social mobility was central to the free-labor ideology. "Our paupers to-day, thanks to free labor, are our yeomen and merchants of to-morrow," said the *New York Times,* in a typical glorification of the Northern free-labor system. "I am not ashamed to confess," said Abraham Lincoln in 1860—then a successful lawyer—"that twenty-five years ago I was a hired laborer, mauling rails, at work on a

[7]The data for abolitionists in Table 3.1 are based on the author's research. For other studies of abolitionist leaders and rank and file that come up with roughly similar data, see Lawrence J. Friedman, *Gregarious Saints: Self and Community in American Abolitionism, 1830–1870* (Cambridge, 1982); Edward Magdol, *The Antislavery Rank and File: A Social Profile of the Abolitionists' Constituency* (Westport, Conn., 1986); and John R. McKivigan, "Schism: The Non-Ideological Factors Underlying the Factionalization of the American Antislavery Movement," unpublished paper, 1985, made available by the author. Data for entrepreneurs and the data for the estimated ratio to the religious affiliations of the whole population are based on the sources cited in Chapter 1, note 10.

[8]Lewis C. Gray, *History of Agriculture in the Southern United States to 1860,* 2 vols. (Washington, D.C., 1933), I, 463; Eric Foner, *Free Soil, Free Labor, Free Men* (New York, 1970), p. 46.

flat-boat." But "free society" enables the poor man "to better his condition; he knows that there is no fixed condition of labor, for his whole life." This principle, "that *all* should have an equal chance," wrote Lincoln, was "the principle that clears the *path* for all, gives hope to all, and, by consequence, *enterprize,* and *industry,* to all."[9]

Because slaves were, in Lincoln's words, "fatally fixed in that condition for life," the free-labor ideology portrayed the South as a region in which the masses were mired in backwardness and poverty while their labor piled up wealth for the privileged few. Although Southerners could point to numerous examples of white men who had risen from poverty to prominence, Free Soilers nevertheless insisted that "slavery withers and blights all it touches. . . . It is a curse upon the poor, free, laboring white [men]. . . . They are depressed, poor, impoverished, degraded in caste, because labor is disgraceful." Wherever slavery goes, said a New York congressman in 1849, "there is in substance no middle class. Great wealth or hopeless poverty is the settled condition."[10]

In short, slavery and modernizing capitalism were irreconcilable. After a trip through Virginia in 1835, the future Whig and Republican leader William H. Seward wrote of "an exhausted soil, old and decaying towns, wretchedly-neglected roads . . . an absence of enterprise and improvement. . . . Such has been the effect of slavery." The institution undermined "intelligence, vigor, and energy," said Seward, and was therefore "incompatible with all . . . the elements of the security, welfare, and greatness of nations."[11] Just as European capitalism had to liberate itself from the outworn restrictions of feudalism, so a dynamic American capitalism could no longer coexist with the outworn institution of slavery.

This view of Northern virtues and Southern vices was of course distorted. Nevertheless, as the conflict over the expansion of slavery into new territories heated up after 1845, an increasing number of Northerners adopted this viewpoint. Those in the antislavery camp regarded the conflict as no less than a contest over the future of America. "We are opposed to the extension of slavery because . . . it diminishes the productive power of its population," declared a Free Soil newspaper. "It is an obstacle to compact settlements, and to every general system of public instruction. [If slavery goes into the territories,] the free labor of all the states will not. . . . If the free labor of the states goes there, the slave labor of the southern states will not, and in a few years the country will teem with an active and energetic population."[12]

★ The Proslavery Counterattack

From Necessary Evil to Positive Good

The antislavery movement struck a raw nerve in the South. As heirs of the Revolutionary tradition, Southern leaders at first recognized the incompatibility of slavery with the ideals of liberty for which Americans of 1776 had fought. For nearly half a century after the Revolution, most Southerners apologized for slavery as a "necessary evil." As an evil, it would eventually die out under the beneficent influences of time and

[9]Foner, *Free Soil,* p. 16; Roy P. Basler (ed.), *The Collected Works of Abraham Lincoln,* 9 vols. (New Brunswick, N.J., 1953–1955), IV, 24, II, 364, IV, 169.
[10]Basler, *Works of Lincoln,* III, 478; Foner, *Free Soil,* pp. 42, 47.
[11]Foner, *Free Soil,* pp. 41, 51.
[12]*New York Evening Post,* November 8, 1847, April 14, 1857.

progress. But as a *necessary* evil, it could not be abolished precipitously, for if it were the South might be plunged into chaos. Hence the popularity in the upper South of colonization, which looked toward the ultimate elimination of the evil by gradual, ameliorative means.

Two developments undermined the necessary evil viewpoint by the 1830s. One was the phenomenal growth of the cotton kingdom, which seemed to make slavery more necessary than ever to the Southern economy. The second was the abolitionist movement, which placed the South on the defensive and provoked a sweeping ideological counterattack that took the form of an assertion that slavery, far from being a necessary evil, was in fact a "positive good." All great societies in history, went the argument, rested on slavery or serfdom—ancient Egypt, biblical Israel, Greece, Rome, the France of Charlemagne, the England of the Magna Charta. "There is not a respectable system of civilization known to history," said Senator R. M. T. Hunter of Virginia, "whose foundations were not laid in the institution of domestic slavery."[13] Even the Bible sanctioned bondage: the apostle Paul urged slaves to obey their masters and advised an escaped slave to return to his master. In 1850 a Southern clergyman wrote a pamphlet, typical of many similar publications, whose title summed up the positive good thesis: *A Defense of the South Against the Reproaches and Encroachments of the North: In Which Slavery Is Shown to Be an Institution of God Intended to Form the Basis of the Best Social State and the Only Safeguard to the Permanence of a Republican Government.*

The proponents of the positive good thesis were confident that they had won the argument, at least in their own section. "Many in the South once believed that slavery was a moral and political evil," said John C. Calhoun in 1838. "That folly and delusion are gone. We see it now in its true light, and regard it as the most safe and stable basis for free institutions in the world." Two decades later, Senator James H. Hammond, also from South Carolina, recalled the days when misguided Southerners:

> . . . believed slavery to be an evil—weakness—disgrace—nay a sin . . . and in fear and trembling [they] awaited a doom that seemed inevitable. But a few bold spirits took the question up—they compelled the South to investigate it anew and thoroughly, and what is the result? Why, it would be difficult to find a Southern man who feels the system to be the slightest burthen on his conscience.[14]

To achieve this result, the South spurned outside criticism and suppressed internal dissent. The section developed a siege mentality: unity in the face of external attack and vigilance against the internal threat of slave insurrections became mandatory. After the Nat Turner revolt in 1831,[15] Southern states imposed new restrictions on both blacks and whites, in the name of preserving order. Nearly every state passed laws limiting freedom of speech. Louisiana, for example, legislated penalties— ranging from twenty-one years at hard labor to death—for speeches or writings "having a tendency to promote discontent among free colored people, or insubordi-

[13]Quoted in David Donald, *Charles Sumner and the Coming of the Civil War* (New York, 1960), p. 349.

[14]Calhoun in *Congressional Globe*, 25th Cong., 2nd sess. (1838), Appendix, 61–62; Hammond quoted in William W. Freehling, *Prelude to Civil War: The Nullification Controversy in South Carolina, 1816-1836* (New York, 1966), p. 299.

[15]Inspired by apocalyptic religious visions, Nat Turner led a group of his fellow Virginia slaves in an uprising in August 1831 that killed at least fifty-five whites and produced a wave of terror and reprisals throughout the South.

nation among slaves." Several states empowered justices of the peace or other officials to confiscate objectionable material sent through the mails. In some communities a "vigilance committee" or a "committee of public safety" was established to employ "all energetic means in ferreting out, and detecting any person or persons that may attempt to circulate among the community, any pamphlet, tract, or other seditious publication of any kind whatever, or tampering with slaves, with a view to excite insurrection." Strangers, especially Yankees, were objects of suspicion and scrutiny. Vigilance committees sometimes inspected hotel registers and searched travelers' luggage. Numerous outsiders fell victim to mob violence—which ranged from tarring and feathering to lynching.[16]

Proslavery spokesmen expressed pride in the South's conservative social order, which resisted the "isms" that convulsed Northern society—not only abolitionism, but feminism, socialism, utopianism, transcendentalism, and millennialism, among a host of others. The slave states, declared a South Carolinian, were "the breakwater" which was "to stay that furious tide of social and political heresies." Only two of more than a hundred utopian communities in the antebellum United States were located in the South. The women's rights movement made no headway south of the Potomac, where white women remained safely on the pedestal that elevated them above the man's world of politics and public affairs. A Southern editor pointed with horror to the "ism-smitten people of Massachusetts," who "crowd to hear a Bloomer-clad unsexed lecturer, who has left her husband at home to take care of the children." Such things could never happen in a slave society, where "the bondsmen, as a lower class, as the substratum of society, constitute an always reliable, never wavering foundation whereon the social fabric rests securely, rooted and grounded in stability, and entirely beyond the reach of agitation."[17]

The South must insulate itself from heresy by shunning Northern magazines and books, said a Richmond newspaper in 1855. It must keep its young men at home instead of sending them to college in the North, where "every village has its press and its lecture room, and each lecturer and editor, unchecked by a healthy public opinion, opens up for discussion all the received dogmas of faith," where unwary youth are "exposed to the danger of imbibing doctrines subversive of all old institutions, and of all the established tenets respecting religion, law, morality, property, and government." Young men should be educated in the South, where "their training would be moral, religious, and conservative, and they would never learn, or read a word in school or out of school, inconsistent with orthodox Christianity, pure morality, the right of property, the sacredness of marriage."[18]

The Wage-Slavery Theme

In their war of words against outside critics, proslavery protagonists soon learned that the best defense was a good offense. "In the Northern states," said a New Orleans newspaper in 1856, "free society has proved a failure. It is rotten to the core." Southerners wrote numerous pamphlets to prove that black slaves on the plantations

---

[16]Russel B. Nye, *Fettered Freedom: Civil Liberties and the Slavery Controversy, 1830–1860* (East Lansing, Mich., 1949), pp. 175, 178, 182–193.

[17]Clement Eaton, *The Freedom-of-Thought Struggle in the Old South* (New York, 1964), p. 350; Avery Craven, *The Coming of the Civil War*, 2d ed. (Chicago, 1957), p. 300.

[18]Craven, *Coming of the Civil War*, pp. 301–302.

enjoyed a higher living standard than "wage slaves" in the factories. Southern slaves never suffered from unemployment or wage cuts; they received free medical care; they were taken care of in old age, rather than cast out to starve or depend on charity. Nowhere in the South did one see such "scenes of beggary, squalid poverty, and wretchedness" as one could find in any Northern city. The South Carolinian William Grayson published a long poem in 1855, *The Hireling and the Slave*, which pungently expressed the wage-slavery theme:

> *The Hireling*
>   Free but in name—the slaves of endless toil . . .
> In squalid hut—a kennel for the poor,
> Or noisome cellar, stretched upon the floor,
> His clothing rags, of filthy straw his bed,
> With offal from the gutter daily fed. . . .
>   These are the miseries, such the wants, the cares,
> The bliss that freedom for the serf prepares. . . .
>
> *The Slave*
>   Taught by the master's efforts, by his care
> Fed, clothed, protected many a patient year,
> From trivial numbers now to millions grown,
> With all the white man's useful arts their own,
> Industrious, docile, skilled in wood and field,
> To guide the plow, the sturdy axe to wield. . . .
> Guarded from want, from beggary secure,
> He never feels what hireling crowds endure,
> Nor knows, like them, in hopeless want to crave,
> For wife and child, the comforts of the slave,
> Or the sad thought that, when about to die,
> He leaves them to the cold world's charity.[19]

The titles of some of the novels written in response to Harriet Beecher Stowe's *Uncle Tom's Cabin* illustrate the same theme; for example, *Uncle Robin in His Cabin in Virginia and Tom Without One in Boston.* So did the title of the most extreme proslavery indictment of free society, George Fitzhugh's *Cannibals All! Or Slaves Without Masters.* By 1852, the wage-slavery theme so pervaded Southern literature that one partisan could write: "It is needless to repeat the evidence that the average condition of the slave at the South is infinitely superior, morally and materially, in all respects, to that of the labouring class under any other circumstances in any other part of the world."[20]

★ The Cavalier Image

Many planters conceived of their class as an aristocracy. "Slavery does indeed create an aristocracy," said James Hammond, "an aristocracy of talents, of virtue, of generos-

---

[19]Allan Nevins, *Ordeal of the Union*, 2 vols. (New York, 1947), I, 515; Eric McKitrick (ed.), *Slavery Defended: The View of the Old South* (Englewood Cliffs, N.J., 1963), pp. 58–59, 66–67.
[20]McKitrick, *Slavery Defended*, pp. 109–110.

ity and courage."[21] The habit of command was instilled into the youth of slaveholding families almost from birth. Planters subscribed to the code of chivalry with its requirements of honor, courtesy, gallantry toward women, and *noblesse oblige.* This helps to explain the popularity of Sir Walter Scott's novels in the South: the planter class could identify with the knights of *Ivanhoe* and the Scottish aristocrats of the *Waverly* novels. As Southern nationalism waxed in the 1850s, some residents of Dixie began to call themselves "Southrons," a term borrowed from Scott. The Southern upper class delighted in jousting tournaments, at which young men designated as the Knight of Malvern, the Knight of the Old Dominion, and the like, competed for the favor of fair maidens before crowds of thousands.

From this self-image arose the notion that Southern planters were descended from the seventeenth-century English Cavaliers, while Yankees were descended from the Roundheads, or Puritans. The Cavaliers, in this theory, were in turn descended from the Norman knights who had conquered Saxon England in the eleventh century, while the Puritans were descended from those conquered Saxons. "The Norman Cavalier of the South cannot brook the vulgar familiarity of the Saxon Yankee," remarked a Kentucky editor in a typical comment. In 1860, the *Southern Literary Messenger* published an article entitled "The Difference of Race Between the Northern People and the Southern People." This difference was none other than that between Cavalier and Puritan, Norman and Saxon. The Southern colonies, the article claimed, had been settled by:

> . . . persons belonging to the blood and race of the reigning family . . . recognized as Cavaliers . . . directly descended from the Norman-Barons of William the Conqueror, a race distinguished in its earliest history for its warlike and fearless character, a race in all times since renowned for its gallantry, chivalry, honor, gentleness, and intellect. . . . The Southern people come of that race.[22]

The reference to "warlike and fearless character" in this quotation pointed to an aspect of Southern life more real than the mythical descent from Cavaliers and Normans. Contemporary observers—Southern, Northern, and foreign alike—agreed that familiarity with weapons and the habit of using them were more common in the South than in the North. The homicide rate was higher below the Mason-Dixon line than above it. Dueling became rare in the North after Aaron Burr killed Alexander Hamilton in 1804, but it persisted in the South until the Civil War.

Dueling was linked to the South's aristocratic code of honor and to the Southerner's reliance on personal action, rather than law, to avenge insult. Many prominent Southern statesmen fought duels. Andrew Jackson killed one of his antagonists, and a South Carolina governor reputedly fought fourteen duels and wounded his man every time. As sectional tensions escalated after 1830, Southern congressmen occasionally challenged their Northern counterparts to duels. The latter usually refused (though in 1838 a Maine congressman was killed by a Kentucky representative in a duel), which tended to confirm the Southern stereotype of Yankees as poltroons.

The martial spirit appeared to be stronger in the South than in the North. More Southern than Northern volunteers fought in the Mexican War, where the principal generals were also Southerners. From 1841 to 1861 the general in chief of the U.S.

---

[21]William S. Jenkins, *Pro-Slavery Thought in the Old South* (Chapel Hill, N.C., 1935), p. 289.

[22]Rollin G. Osterweis, *Romanticism and Nationalism in the Old South* (New Haven, 1949), p. 101; *Southern Literary Messenger,* 30 (June 1860), 401–409.

army was a Southerner. During the 1850s, two of the three brigadier generals and all but one commander of the army's geographical divisions were natives of the South. All four secretaries of war from 1849 to 1860 were Southerners. The proportion of Southerners admitted to West Point, and of regular army officers from the South, was 30 percent greater than the section's proportion of the nation's white population. The camaraderie among Southerners at the Point became important in 1861: eleven of the cadets who had been there together in 1828 and 1829 became top generals or leaders in the Confederacy, including Robert E. Lee, Albert Sidney Johnston, Joseph E. Johnston, and Jefferson Davis.

Perhaps even more significant than the Southern presence at West Point was the large number of military schools in the South. The best known were Virginia Military Institute and the Citadel; but by the 1850s, nearly every Southern state had its military institute. The census of 1860 listed five times as many military colleges in the South as in the North (the North had more than twice as many colleges and professional schools of other types). This too became important when the fighting began in 1861.

Volunteer military companies were popular in both North and South. Some of them were social organizations whose training in military drill was indifferent at best. But others were genuine armed units that took their duties seriously. Although the evidence is inconclusive, the latter seem to have been more numerous in the South

THE RICHMOND GRAYS IN 1859. *Note the healthy appearance and self-confident mien of these men and boys. By 1865 several would be maimed for life, and one-third of them would be dead.*

COOK COLLECTION, VALENTINE MUSEUM

than in the North, in proportion to population, especially by the late 1850s.[23] Charleston, South Carolina, had no fewer than twenty-two such companies—at a time when its white male population of military age numbered about four thousand. In 1859, a Savannah lawyer wrote an account of a trip that his artillery company had taken to Nashville and back:

> At Macon we were received with a salute from the artillery company newly formed, were escorted by the Macon Volunteers, the Floyd Rifles, and the Bibb County Cavalry. . . . Midway between Macon and Atlanta we were met by a delegation from the Gate City Guards. . . . As we passed through Marietta the cadets from the military institute gave us a salute with a small battery of six-pounders. . . . [In Nashville] we were received by the German *Yagers,* the Shelby Guards, and the cadets from the military institute. . . . [Upon our return to Savannah] the Guards, the Blues, the Oglethorpe Light Infantry, and the Irish Jasper Greens were all out in full ranks to meet us.[24]

An important purpose of the South's armed readiness was the control of slaves. A central feature of Southern life was the slave patrol, a mounted detachment of three or four white men under a captain that patrolled its "beat" each night to apprehend slaves without passes and to prevent secret gatherings of bondsmen. Since each patrol rode about once every two weeks, some fifty or more white men in each beat performed this duty. The patrols included nonslaveholders and formed another link that bound them to the system.

Although large-scale slave insurrections occurred rarely in the United States, Southern whites lived in constant fear of an uprising. It took only a few such examples—Nat Turner's revolt in 1831, or the aborted conspiracies of Gabriel Prosser and Denmark Vesey, the first near Richmond in 1800, the second in Charleston in 1822—to keep alive that dread. One function of the volunteer military companies was preparedness "to quell sudden insurrection." As the Savannah lawyer quoted above put it in 1856: "I think it a duty which every citizen owes in our citizen-soldier state of society . . . to connect himself if possible with one of these military companies. It is certainly a police service very necessary in its character."[25]

★ Slavery and National Politics

Slavery was the main issue in national politics from 1844 to the outbreak of the Civil War. And many times before 1844 this vexed question burst through the crust of other issues to set section against section, as in the Missouri debates of 1819–1820. Even the nullification crisis of 1832, ostensibly over the tariff, had slavery as its underlying cause. The South Carolina nullifiers feared that the centralization of government power, as manifested by the tariff, might eventually threaten slavery

---

[23]Marcus Cunliffe, in *Soldiers and Civilians: The Martial Spirit in America, 1775–1865* (Boston, 1968), maintains that the military ethos was equally vigorous in North and South. In particular, he argues that the volunteer companies were if anything more common in the North than in the South. But much of his own evidence demonstrates the contrary. Cunliffe sometimes fails to interpret the evidence on a per capita basis: that is, with less than half the North's white population, the South could have fewer West Point alumni or fewer volunteer companies than the North but still have a larger number in proportion to population.

[24]Robert Manson Myers (ed.), *The Children of Pride* (New York, 1972), pp. 489–494.

[25]Ibid., pp. 211–212.

itself. Nullification was the most extreme assertion of states' rights—a constitutional theory whose fundamental purpose was to protect slavery against potential federal interference.

The Democratic party served as the main political bulwark of slavery. The South formed the backbone of the Jacksonian Democratic coalition. In 1828, Andrew Jackson won 71 percent of the popular vote in the slave states, compared with only 50 percent in the free states. Three-fifths of his electoral votes came from the South. Four years later, Jackson carried 70 percent of the popular vote in the slave states and 51 percent in the North. The Jacksonians rewarded their Southern support. Three of Jackson's four appointees to the Supreme Court were Southerners. President Martin Van Buren, Jackson's hand-picked successor, appointed two more Southern justices but no Northerners to the Court. Jackson's veto of bills to recharter the Second Bank of the United States and to appropriate funds for road construction pleased Southern proponents of states' rights. So did the administration's willingness to ban antislavery materials from the Southern mails. And congressional Democrats supplied most of the votes for the "gag rule"—a resolution that barred the reception of antislavery petitions in the House from 1836 to 1844.

Despite Van Buren's reputation as a "doughface" (a Northern man with Southern principles), many Southerners did not trust the New Yorker. Although Van Buren won the presidency in 1836, the newly organized Whig party (whose principal leader was Henry Clay of Kentucky) carried a slight majority of the Southern popular vote that year. For the next fifteen years, the Democratic and Whig parties remained evenly balanced in both the North and the South. Party leaders strove to keep the divisive slavery issue out of national politics. But this effort succeeded for only a few years. The annexation of Texas and the subsequent war with Mexico pushed the question of slavery's expansion to the forefront of national politics and divided both parties along sectional lines.

FOUR

Texas, Mexico, and the Compromise of 1850

*W*e must *"satisfy the northern people . . . that we are not to extend the institution of slavery as a result of this war."*

—Gideon Welles, Connecticut Democrat, 1846

★ The Annexation of Texas

Americans began migrating to Texas in the 1820s at the invitation of a Mexican government that had just won its independence from Spain. By 1830, however, Mexico was alarmed at the influx of a population alien in language and culture, suspect in political allegiance, and committed to slavery in defiance of Mexico's recent abolition of the institution. The growing number of American settlers produced controversies over land claims and political rights. In 1836, tensions between Texans and the central government in Mexico City reached the breaking point. The Texans proclaimed their independence and, after suffering the massacre of the defenders of the Alamo, won the decisive battle of San Jacinto on April 21, 1836. They also captured the Mexican leader Antonio Lopez de Santa Anna. In return for his release, Santa Anna signed a treaty granting Texas independence. Although the Mexican Congress repudiated the treaty, joyful Texans established the Lone Star Republic and petitioned for annexation to the United States.

But this request ran into a snag in Washington, where antislavery Whigs charged collusion between Southern Democrats and Texans to foment revolution and annexation in the hope of expanding slave territory. Several Northern Democrats also opposed annexation. To preserve peace with Mexico and harmony in the Democratic party, Presidents Andrew Jackson and Martin Van Buren kept Texas at arm's length. The disappointed Texans turned their energies to strengthening their republic, and the Texas issue subsided in American politics.

It did not subside for long. The death, from pneumonia, of the first Whig President, William Henry Harrison, one month after his inauguration in 1841 brought John Tyler into the White House. A Virginia Whig who opposed much of his party's legislative program for higher tariffs, a new national bank, and federal aid for roads and waterways, Tyler broke with congressional Whigs on these issues and soon found himself a president without a party. He turned to Southern Democrats for support, appointed several Southerners to his cabinet—including fellow Virginian Abel Upshur as secretary of state—and cast about for an issue on which he might win the 1844 election. He settled on the annexation of Texas as "the only matter, that will take sufficient hold of the feelings of the South to rally it on a southern candidate."[1]

Upshur opened secret negotiations with Texas for a treaty of annexation. At the same time, pro-administration newspapers began to point with alarm at alleged maneuvering by the British government in Texas. Britain had negotiated a treaty of recognition and commerce with the republic. English abolitionists expressed hope that their country's expected influence in Texas would promote emancipation there. Southerners magnified this into the first stage of a British plot to set up satellite free states in the Western Hemisphere as barriers to further American expansion and as beachheads for an assault, in alliance with Northern abolitionists, on slavery in the United States itself.

This made good propaganda. Anglophobia was still a potent force in American politics. Southerners feared that the confinement of slavery to its present boundaries would mean ultimate asphyxiation. Unless they could increase the number of slave states, the South would become a helpless minority in the national government. Southerners must "*demand* . . . the admission of Texas . . . as indispensable to their security," wrote Secretary of State Upshur to John C. Calhoun, the South's foremost partisan. "Both parties [in the South] may unite on that, for it is a *Southern* question, and not one of whiggism and democracy."[2]

When an accident killed Upshur in February 1844, his successor was none other than Calhoun, who completed the annexation treaty and submitted it to the Senate in April. At the same time, Calhoun publicly informed the British minister that annexation was necessary to forestall abolitionist plots against slavery, an institution "essential to the peace, safety, and prosperity" of the United States.[3] This open avowal of a proslavery purpose did not sit well with Northern senators. Nor did Southern Whigs wish to support the renegade Tyler and risk war with Mexico by approving annexation. They joined Northern Whigs and several Northern Democrats to defeat the treaty in June. But even before this happened, Texas had become the chief issue in the presidential campaign.

The two leading presidential contenders, Henry Clay and Martin Van Buren, were wounded by the Texas whiplash. Both of them had come out against annexation in letters published simultaneously on April 27. Clay's position was standard Whig doctrine, even in the South, and the party nominated him unanimously four days later. But Van Buren's letter sent shock waves among Southern Democrats. It accelerated the drive by Calhoun Democrats to defeat the New Yorker's nomination. This drive succeeded because of the Democratic rule requiring a two-thirds majority at national conventions to name a candidate. Southern delegations used the rule through eight ballots to block Van Buren's nomination, even though he had received a simple majority on the first ballot. On the ninth ballot, the exhausted Democrats finally nominated dark horse James K. Polk of Tennessee, an ardent annexationist. "We have

[1]Charles Sellers, "Election of 1844," in Arthur M. Schlesinger, Jr. (ed.), *History of American Presidential Elections,* 4 vols. (New York, 1971), I, 760.
[2]Frederick Merk, *Slavery and the Annexation of Texas* (New York, 1972), p. 20.
[3]Sellers, "Election of 1844," p. 821.

triumphed," exulted one of Calhoun's allies. "Polk is nearer to *us* than any public man who was named. He is a large Slave holder and [is for] Texas—States rights *out & out*."[4]

Polk's success undercut Tyler's forlorn hope to be a third-party candidate, and the President withdrew from the race. "Texas fever" swept the South as the campaign warmed up. "The people seem literally to have taken fire on this subject of Texas," wrote a Virginian, "& nothing short of *immediate annexation* will serve them." Clay was alarmed by the slippage of his strength among Southern Whigs vulnerable to the annexation pressure. In July he wrote two public letters explaining that while he still opposed annexation if it would mean war with Mexico, "I should be glad to see it, without dishonor, without war, with the common consent of the Union."[5] This provoked anger among antislavery Whigs, some of whom vowed to vote for Liberty party candidate James G. Birney. In the end, Clay's equivocation on Texas won back few votes in the South while losing perhaps decisive votes to the Liberty party in New York. That state went for Polk by a margin of only five thousand votes and thereby gave him the presidency.

Polk carried all but two of the future Confederate states. At the same time, the Liberty party vote in the North increased ninefold from 1840. Although the Liberty ballots added up to no more than 3 percent of the Northern total, the 1844 election drove in the thin edge of the wedge that would eventually split the intersectional two-party system into predominantly sectional parties.

★ Manifest Destiny and the Mexican War

Although Polk's margin of victory was narrow (49.6 percent of the popular vote to Clay's 48.1 percent), annexationists chose to consider the outcome a mandate. Hoping to acquire Texas as the crowning achievement of his administration, Tyler in December 1844 outflanked the required two-thirds Senate majority for approval of treaties by submitting to Congress a joint resolution of annexation, which required a simple majority of both houses. Despite the doubtful constitutionality of this procedure, both houses passed the joint resolution on the eve of Tyler's retirement from office in March 1845. Although several Northern Democrats broke ranks to vote initially against the joint resolution, these dissenters wheeled into line on the final vote to adopt annexation as a party measure. Texas came in as a state at the end of 1845.

Northern Democrats were willing to swallow Texas because in return they expected Southern support for the acquisition of an equally large slice of territory in the Pacific Northwest. The 1844 Democratic platform had pledged the party to acquire "the whole of the territory of Oregon" as well as Texas. Both the United States and Britain claimed Oregon, which then stretched all the way from the northern borders of present-day California and Nevada to the southern border of Russian Alaska. Since 1818, the two countries had by agreement jointly occupied this huge area. But in the 1840s American settlers began pouring into the fertile valleys of the Columbia and Willamette rivers. Like the Texans, they wanted to become part of the United States. In 1845, President Polk recommended termination of the joint

[4]William J. Cooper, *The South and the Politics of Slavery, 1828-1856* (Baton Rouge, 1978), p. 206.
[5]Sellers, "Election of 1844," pp. 762, 855-856.

Anglo-American occupation agreement and reasserted the American claim to the whole territory—stretching north to the latitude of 54°40′. Inspired by the bombastic eloquence of Democratic orators, who announced America's "manifest destiny" to acquire the whole continent, Democrats proclaimed the slogan "Fifty-four forty or fight!" To Northern Democrats, Oregon became a test of whether their Southern colleagues would support the expansion of free territory as vigorously as they supported the expansion of slave territory. The Tennessean Polk failed the test. While he was willing to provoke war with Mexico to obtain the Southwest, he was unwilling to risk war with Britain to acquire all of Oregon. But this did not become clear until the Mexican War was already under way.

Relations with Mexico deteriorated from the outset of Polk's administration. Three issues divided the two countries. The first was American annexation of Texas. This was probably negotiable, because Texas had maintained its independence for a decade and Mexico had no realistic hope of regaining it. The second was the Texas border. As a Mexican province, Texas's southern border had been the Nueces River. The Texans, backed by the Polk administration, claimed an area more than twice as large, with the Rio Grande as the border. The third issue was the future of sparsely populated California and New Mexico, which Polk had determined to acquire in one way or another.

The President employed a carrot-and-stick approach in 1845. He sent the Louisianian John Slidell to Mexico City as a "minister plenipotentiary" empowered to offer up to $30 million for California and New Mexico, as well as the U.S. assumption of Mexican debts to American citizens in return for Mexican acceptance of the Rio Grande boundary. At the same time, Polk ordered American troops under General Zachary Taylor into the disputed territory south of the Nueces and dispatched a naval squadron to patrol the Mexican coast. He authorized the American consul in Monterey, California, to act as a secret agent to stir up pro-American sentiment among the local population, which included several hundred American settlers. The administration also sent secret contingency orders to the Pacific fleet to seize California ports if war broke out between Mexico and the United States.

The Mexican government refused to receive Slidell. Soon thereafter a revolution in Mexico City brought a militant anti-American regime into power, which vowed to recover the "stolen province" of Texas. In response, Polk in January 1846 ordered Taylor's troops to the Rio Grande while American ships blockaded the river. A Mexican army camped across the river from Taylor. Hoping for an incident that would justify a declaration of war, the impatient Polk was ready by May 9 to send a war message to Congress even without an incident when word arrived that Mexicans had killed several American soldiers north of the Rio Grande in a skirmish on April 25. Polk dispatched his war message on May 11. "Notwithstanding all our efforts to avoid it," said the President disingenuously, war "exists by the act of Mexico herself, [for she has] invaded our territory and shed American blood upon American soil."[6]

Since Mexico's claim to the disputed territory was at least as strong as the American claim, it would have been equally true to say that the United States had started the war by shedding Mexican blood on Mexican soil. This was the view of abolitionists, antislavery Whigs, and even many Southern Whigs. A Whig senator from Ohio created a sensation when he declared: "If I were a Mexican, I would tell you,

[6]James D. Richardson (comp.), *Messages and Papers of the Presidents, 1789–1897,* 20 vols. (Washington, D.C., 1897–1913), V, 2292.

'Have you not room in your own country to bury your dead men? If you come into mine we will greet you with bloody hands, and welcome you to hospitable graves.' "
The abolitionists won new converts to their belief that Texas and the Mexican War were steps in a nefarious "slave power conspiracy" to expand slave territory. James Russell Lowell's antiwar dialect poems, supposedly written by the Yankee rustic Hosea Biglow, achieved a wide popularity in New England:

> They jest want this Californy
>> So's to lug new slave-states in
> To abuse ye, an' to scorn ye,
>> And to plunder ye like sin.

The Massachusetts legislature agreed with Lowell: in 1847 it resolved that this "unconstitutional" war was being waged for "the triple object of extending slavery, of strengthening the slave power, and of obtaining control of the free states."[7]

The demand for "all Oregon" became one of the war's first casualties. Not wanting to fight two wars at the same time, Polk retreated from "fifty-four forty" and negotiated a compromise with Britain on the 49th parallel. Twelve Northern Democratic senators rebelled and voted against this treaty. Only the unanimous support of the Whigs, who were cool toward Manifest Destiny and desirous of peace with Britain, permitted ratification of the treaty. Bitter Northern Democrats accused their Southern colleagues of bad faith: "Texas and Oregon were born in the same instant, nursed and cradled in the same cradle," but having used Northern votes to get Texas, "the peculiar friends of Texas turned and were doing all they could to strangle Oregon."[8] Nevertheless, most Northern Democrats continued to support the administration's war policy.

Despite Whig dislike of "Mr. Polk's War," few congressmen were willing to risk political suicide by voting against a war that was popular in most parts of the country. Some Whigs remembered that opposition to the War of 1812 had killed the Federalist party. Only fourteen Whigs in the House and two in the Senate voted against the declaration of war. Most Whigs voted appropriations for troops and supplies. But in preliminary roll calls on this legislation and in congressional votes on auxiliary legislation connected with the war, a clear antiwar faction emerged, consisting of nearly all Northern Whigs, plus several Southern Whigs and a few Northern Democrats. Antiwar sentiment was partly responsible for a Whig gain of thirty-eight House seats in 1846 and 1847, most of them in the Northeastern states.

Had the American forces not enjoyed such remarkable success in Mexico, the antiwar opposition might have evolved into a powerful coalition. But mixed armies of regulars and volunteers led by Generals Zachary Taylor and Winfield Scott won a string of stunning victories over numerically larger Mexican forces that resulted in the capture of Mexico City itself in September 1847. A small American army also captured Santa Fe, New Mexico, and then marched overland to help the Pacific naval squadron and volunteer units of American settlers subdue Mexican resistance in California.

American armies in Mexico owed their success to excellent artillery, the élan of the infantry, the low morale of Mexican soldiers, and especially to the superiority of

---

[7]Louis Filler, *The Crusade against Slavery 1830-1860* (New York, 1960), p. 186; *The Works of James Russell Lowell,* Standard Library ed., 11 vols. (Boston, 1890), VIII, 46–47; H. V. Ames (ed.), *State Documents on Federal Relations* (Philadelphia, 1906), pp. 241–242.

[8]Chaplain W. Morrison, *Democratic Politics and Sectionalism: The Wilmot Proviso Controversy* (Chapel Hill, N.C., 1967), pp. 11–12.

American officers—from Scott and Taylor down to the lieutenants. The roster of junior officers included men who would play the leading roles in a far bloodier conflict fifteen years later: Robert E. Lee, Ulysses S. Grant, Thomas J. Jackson, Albert S. and Joseph E. Johnston, George B. McClellan, Pierre G. T. Beauregard, James Longstreet, Braxton Bragg, Joseph Hooker, George Gordon Meade, George H. Thomas, and Jefferson Davis.

American conquests whetted the appetite of expansionists for an additional slice of Mexico south of the Rio Grande. This desire prompted Polk in October 1847 to recall his peace negotiator Nicholas Trist, who seemed too willing to compromise with the Mexicans. Trist ignored the recall, negotiated the Treaty of Guadalupe Hidalgo, and sent it to Washington in February 1848. By this treaty Mexico gave up all claim to Texas north of the Rio Grande and, in return for a payment of $15 million and assumption of Mexican debts to Americans, ceded New Mexico and California to the United States. (This territory included present-day California, Nevada, Utah; most of Arizona and New Mexico; and part of Oklahoma, Colorado, and Wyoming.) In the Senate, seven Whigs who wanted no Mexican territory and five Democrats who wanted more voted against the treaty, but the remaining votes were sufficient to approve it on March 10.

In the preceding three years, the United States had acquired a million and a quarter square miles of new territory. Nearly half of it lay south of the old Missouri Compromise line of 36°30′. It had been won largely by the exertions of two Southern presidents and of armies commanded by Southern generals (Scott was a Virginian and Taylor a Louisianian) in which two-thirds of the volunteer soldiers were from slave states. One can thus readily imagine the shock and anger of Southerners when Northern congressmen tried to exclude slavery from the territory won in the Mexican War.

★ The Wilmot Proviso

On August 8, 1846, when the war was barely three months old, an obscure first-term Democratic congressman from Pennsylvania named David Wilmot offered an amendment to an appropriations bill: "that, as an express and fundamental condition to the acquisition of any territory from the Republic of Mexico . . . neither slavery nor involuntary servitude shall ever exist in any part of said territory."[9] The principle embodied in this amendment—the Wilmot Proviso, as it came to be known— remained the lodestone of sectional conflict for the next fifteen years.

Wilmot acted in behalf of a group of Northern Democrats whose grievances had reached the boiling point. Some of these grievances concerned economic legislation. The Polk administration came into power pledged to dismantle the last vestiges of Whig programs for federal aid to economic development. Most Northern Democrats approved of this, but significant blocs were alienated by two actions: the Walker Tariff of 1846, which reduced duties for many commodities below the level of a supposed administration commitment to Democratic congressmen from tariff-conscious Pennsylvania; and Polk's veto of a rivers and harbors improvements bill supported by Midwestern Democrats—the same Democrats who were angered by the administration's compromise with Britain on the Oregon question. Other grievances were

[9]*Congressional Globe*, 29th Cong., 1st sess. (1846), 1217.

political. Van Buren's supporters had not forgotten the denial of the 1844 presidential nomination to their leader. Polk added insult to injury by refusing to appoint any Van Buren Democrats to his cabinet and by turning the rich federal patronage in New York over to Van Buren's factional enemies.

Underlying all these grievances was a burgeoning resentment at Southern domination of the party. It had been Southern Democrats who had sabotaged Van Buren in 1844, and it was they who had formulated the Walker Tariff and sustained the rivers and harbors veto; it was a Southern president who had conceded away half of Oregon while insisting on all of Texas, and who had provoked Mexico into a war that a growing number of Northerners regarded as wicked aggression to expand slavery. Northern Democrats feared punishment at the polls if they appeared to support the war for proslavery purposes. "There have been enough northern democrats who have sacrificed themselves to southern interests and I do not wish to see any more," said a New York party leader. "The South has never yielded anything to conciliate the North, [and] we have yielded too much to conciliate the South," wrote Connecticut Democrat Gideon Welles in July 1846. We must "satisfy the northern people . . . that we are not to extend the institution of slavery as a result of this war."[10] Antislavery Whigs shared these sentiments. The South, wrote one, "[has] trampled on the rights and just claims of the North sufficiently long and have fairly shit upon all our Northern statesmen and are now trying to rub it in and I think now is the time and just the time for the North to take a stand."[11]

Northern Whigs voted unanimously for Wilmot's proviso; so did all but four Northern Democrats, while every Southern Democrat and all but two Southern Whigs voted against it. Having passed the House, the proviso failed to come to a vote in the Senate at this session. At the next session, in February 1847, the House repassed the proviso; but the Senate, with five Northern Democrats joining the Southerners, passed the appropriations bill without the antislavery amendment. Under heavy administration pressure, twenty-three Northern House Democrats then receded from the proviso and cast the necessary votes to pass the bill unamended.

Parties Split along Sectional Lines

Despite this victory for the South, the political system had experienced an ominous wrenching of the normal party division of congressional votes into an almost completely sectional division. This was an ill omen for the future of the parties and of the Union itself. Before the Wilmot Proviso, the political system had been able to accommodate sectional differences because slavery was a state institution beyond the power of Congress. But with the imminent acquisition of territory whose status was a matter for congressional legislation, the question of slavery exploded beyond party lines and became an arena for sectional conflict.

Every Northern state legislature but one endorsed the Wilmot Proviso. Southern legislatures responded with pledges of "determined resistance [at] all hazards and to the last extremity." The proviso affronted the South with regard to its most cherished value—honor. To prevent slave owners from taking their property into the territories was to stigmatize them. It was an imputation of "degrading inequality . . . which says

[10]Eric Foner, "The Wilmot Proviso Revisited," *Journal of American History,* 61 (September 1969), 270, 277, and 277n.
[11]Michael F. Holt, *The Political Crisis of the 1850s* (New York, 1978), p. 51.

to the Southern man, Avaunt! you are not my equal, and hence are to be excluded as carrying a moral taint." The South could not accept such "degradation," said dozens of spokesmen. "Death is preferable to acknowledged inferiority."[12]

Most of all, Southerners feared encirclement by free territory that, like a boa constrictor, would slowly squeeze slavery to death. Some antislavery men avowed precisely this purpose. "If you drive on this bloody war of conquest to annexation," warned an Ohio Whig congressman, "we will establish a cordon of free States that will surround you; and then we will light up the fires of liberty on every side, until they melt your present chains, and render all your people free." Such statements reinforced Southern fears. James H. Hammond of South Carolina warned that adoption of the Wilmot Proviso would insure ten new free states west of the Mississippi. "Long before the North gets this vast accession of strength she will ride over us rough shod, proclaim freedom or something equivalent to it to our Slaves and reduce us to the condition of Hayti. . . . If we do not act now, we deliberately consign our children, not our posterity, but *our children* to the flames."[13] One after another, Southern congressmen invoked the threat of disunion as the inevitable consequence of the Wilmot Proviso.

As he had often done before, John C. Calhoun made the formal presentation of the Southern position. And as before, Calhoun based his presentation on a rigorous exegesis of constitutional rights. The territories, he said in a series of resolutions introduced in the Senate on February 19, 1847, were the "common property" of the several states; as the "joint agent" of the states, Congress had no power to deny the citizens of any state the right to take their property into a territory; therefore slavery was legal in all of the territories. If the institution was "entirely excluded from the territories," said Calhoun in a speech supporting his resolutions, the balance of fifteen slave and fifteen free states would be destroyed and the former would be "at the entire mercy of the non-slaveholding States." "If this scheme should be carried out— if we are to be reduced to a mere handful . . . wo, wo, I say to this Union." In a private letter written the same day, Calhoun told a friend: "You will see that I have made up the issue between North and South. If we flinch we are gone, but if we stand fast on it, we shall triumph either by compelling the North to yield to our terms, or declaring our independence of them."[14]

Between the polar opposites of the Wilmot and Calhoun positions ranged a spectrum of opinions that seemed to offer room for compromise. One compromise proposal, supported by Polk and his cabinet and backed by a coalition of moderate Whigs and Democrats, was to extend the Missouri Compromise line of 36°30' to the Pacific. Thus Oregon territory (present-day Oregon, Washington, and Idaho) plus the area now comprising Utah, Nevada, western Colorado, and the northern half of California would have been organized without slavery; the area now comprising Oklahoma, New Mexico, Arizona, and southern California would have been organized with no restrictions against slavery. This compromise attracted some antislavery Northerners, who believed that climate and geography would prevent slavery from

---

[12]Cooper, *The South and the Politics of Slavery*, pp. 235, 239; Holt, *Political Crisis of the 1850s*, p. 54.

[13]*Congressional Globe*, 29th Cong., 2nd sess. (1847), Appendix, 281; William L. Barney, *The Road to Secession: A New Perspective on the Old South* (New York, 1972), pp. 105–106.

[14]*Congressional Globe*, 29th Cong., 2nd sess. (1847), 454–455; Morrison, *Democratic Politics and Sectionalism*, p. 35.

taking root in the new Southwest. But most antislavery people were concerned not only about these territories but also about additional territory the United States might acquire in the future. The hard-line supporters of both the Wilmot Proviso and the Calhoun resolutions refused to recede from their positions.

Failure of the 36°30′ solution opened the way for another possible compromise, which became known as "popular sovereignty." The early champion of this approach was Michigan Democrat Lewis Cass, an aspirant for his party's presidential nomination in 1848 (Polk was not a candidate for reelection). At the end of 1847, Cass proposed "leaving to the people of the territory to be acquired the business of settling the matter for themselves." This was consistent with democracy and self-government. It also had the political virtue of ambiguity. Nowhere did Cass specify at what stage the people of a territory would be empowered to regulate slavery. Could a territorial legislature prohibit slavery if it wished? Northern Democrats understood popular sovereignty to mean that it could. Or did the Cass formula mean that the people of a territory would be empowered to decide on slavery only when they applied for statehood? Southern Democrats, who believed that nothing less sovereign than a state could legislate against property in slaves, interpreted popular sovereignty in this way. Thus slavery might gain a legal foothold in territories where it was economically feasible, and one or more of the new states might come into the Union with slavery. Although aware of these opposing sectional interpretations, most Northern and Southern Democrats endorsed popular sovereignty and tacitly agreed to preserve the ambiguity for the sake of harmony in the forthcoming presidential campaign.

★ The Election of 1848

But the Democratic national convention could not prevent the slavery-extension issue from splitting the party. The issue first confronted the convention in the form of rival delegations from New York. The Van Burenites (or "Barnburners" in the political lexicon of the time) were pledged to the Wilmot Proviso, while the "Hunkers" were willing to conciliate the South.[15] The Barnburners rejected a compromise proposal to seat both delegations and stomped out of the convention to nominate Van Buren on a splinter ticket. A combination of Southern and Western Democrats nominated Cass, on a platform whose vague references to slavery failed to satisfy Southern Calhounites. William Lowndes Yancey of Alabama offered a resolution affirming the Calhoun position on slavery in the territories. When a six-to-one majority voted it down, Yancey walked out of the convention. Although only one other delegate followed him, this symbolic gesture portended trouble in the future.

The Whigs attempted to minimize sectional damage to their party by adopting no platform at all and by nominating a nonpolitician for President. The party passed over its two venerable leaders, Henry Clay and Daniel Webster, to nominate war hero Zachery Taylor, who had never voted in his life and was not even sure until 1848 that he was a Whig. The nomination of a Mexican War general by the antiwar party provided one more illustration of the strange convolutions of American politics.

[15]The Barnburners were the progressive wing of the New York Democrats. They resented Southern domination of the national Democratic party and patronage-machine control of the state party. Like the proverbial Dutchman who burned his barn to rid it of rats, they were said to be willing to bolt the party (and therefore to cripple it) in order to punish the opposing faction. The Hunkers were said to be men without principle who only hankered or "hunkered" for office.

Taylor owned many slaves. Although this did not prevent most Northern Whigs from supporting him, a vigorous antislavery minority refused to do so. The nomination brought to a boil the long-simmering dispute between "Conscience" and "Cotton" Whigs in Massachusetts. The former consisted of younger men influenced by the antislavery movement. They resented the domination of the state's Whig party by textile manufacturers who were economically dependent on Southern cotton. Although these Cotton Whigs had opposed the annexation of Texas and had supported the Wilmot Proviso, they sought a détente with Southern Whigs in 1848. In response, the Conscience faction under the leadership of Charles Francis Adams and Charles Sumner denounced Taylor's nomination as the product of an unholy alliance between "the Lords of the Lash" and "the Lords of the Loom." They bolted the party and prepared to join a third-party coalition.

The time appeared to be ripe for such a coalition. "The whole country seems to be arousing at last!" wrote Charles Sumner to Salmon P. Chase of Ohio in July 1848. "The spirit of Freedom is spreading in Massachusetts now as in the days of the earlier Revolution."[16] Chase headed a group within the Liberty party working for a fusion with antislavery defectors from the major parties. Since 1844 the Liberty party had suffered its own defection—of a minority who interpreted the Constitution as authorizing the federal government to abolish slavery in the states. Since few abolitionists took this extreme position, these Liberty purists found themselves as isolated on one wing of the antislavery movement as were the Garrisonians—who believed that the Constitution should be repudiated as a proslavery document—on the other. The mainstream Liberty men followed Chase's lead in late 1847 by nominating Senator John P. Hale of New Hampshire for President, on a platform calling for the prohibition of slavery wherever the national government had the constitutional power to ban it—in the territories, in the District of Columbia, and in all federal installations. This platform paved the way for a coalition with like-minded Whigs and Democrats.

Hale was willing to step aside for a candidate who might be able to mobilize broader support, especially in the key state of New York. Such a candidate was Martin Van Buren, who had already received the Barnburner nomination. During the summer, complicated negotiations between Liberty men, Conscience Whigs, and Barnburner Democrats laid the groundwork for a Free Soil convention at Buffalo in August. The sticking point was Van Buren. It came hard for antislavery Whigs and abolitionists to accept this former doughface Democrat. But in return for Barnburner support of a strong antislavery platform, the Liberty men and Conscience Whigs swallowed Van Buren. They also managed to nominate Charles Francis Adams as his running mate. Choosing as its slogan "Free Soil, Free Speech, Free Labor, and Free Men," the Free Soil party was born.

Its birth upset the Whig and Democratic strategy of trying to keep the slavery issue out of the campaign. In the North, both major parties were forced to adopt an antislavery stance: Democrats insisted that popular sovereignty would keep the territories free, while Whigs cited their support for the Wilmot Proviso. In the South, however, each party presented a different face: Democrats pointed with pride to their record of territorial expansion as evidence of friendship to Southern interests, while Whigs emphasized that Louisiana slaveholder Taylor would better protect Southern

[16]Kinley J. Brauer, *Cotton versus Conscience: Massachusetts Whig Politics and Southwestern Expansion, 1843–1848* (Lexington, Ky., 1967), p. 240.

rights than Midwesterner Cass. "We prefer Old Zack with his sugar and cotton plantations and four hundred negroes to all their compromises," proclaimed a Richmond newspaper.[17]

Such appeals apparently won votes. The Whig tally in the South increased by 10 percent over 1844 while the Democratic vote declined by 4 percent. Taylor carried eight of the fifteen slave states. He also carried seven of the fifteen free states, including crucial New York, and thereby won a majority in the electoral college. Van Buren carried no states but won 14 percent of the Northern popular vote. His candidacy did not affect the outcome, however; for while he took enough Democratic votes from Cass in New York to put that state in the Whig column, he neutralized this electoral impact by attracting enough Whig voters in Ohio to give that state to the Democrats.

★ The Compromise of 1850

During the lame-duck session of Congress before Taylor's inauguration on March 4, 1849, the smoldering embers of sectionalism flamed up anew. The Northern-controlled House reaffirmed the Wilmot Proviso, passed a resolution condemning the slave trade in the District of Columbia, and came close to passing a bill to abolish slavery itself there. In retaliation, a caucus of Southern congressmen asked Calhoun to draft an address setting forth Southern grievances. Calhoun eagerly seized this opportunity to write a platform for what he hoped would become a new Southern rights party. But fewer than two-thirds of the Southern Democrats signed the address, and Southern Whigs wanted no part of it at all. Having just won the presidential election, Whigs looked forward to a rejuvenation of their fortunes with Taylor in the White House. Alexander Stephens of Georgia expressed this viewpoint: We "feel *secure* under General Taylor."[18]

Once in office, however, Taylor shocked his Southern allies. He considered himself President of the whole country, not merely the South. Forty years in the army had given him a national perspective and an unsuspected distaste for proslavery extremists whom he branded in 1850 as "intolerant and revolutionary."[19] William H. Seward, New York's antislavery senator, became one of Taylor's principal advisers. The President faced an imminent decision on the question of slavery in the territories. The discovery of gold at Sutter's Mill in 1848 brought an avalanche of settlers into California, making it necessary to provide political organization for the region. Taylor's solution was to bypass the aggravating territorial problem by admitting California and New Mexico immediately *as states.* This provoked howls of protest from the South, for under Mexican law slavery had not existed in these areas and they would therefore come in as free states. To many Southerners, Taylor's policy was the Wilmot Proviso in disguise.

The President sent emissaries to San Francisco and Santa Fe to encourage the citizens to adopt state constitutions and to apply for admission. Californians needed no urging. In the fall of 1849 they held a convention and wrote a state constitution—

---

[17]Cooper, *The South and the Politics of Slavery,* p. 265.

[18]Ibid., p. 271.

[19]Thelma Jennings, *The Nashville Convention: Southern Movement for Unity, 1848–1851* (Memphis, 1980), p. 49.

which prohibited slavery. With a population already larger than that of two existing states (Delaware and Florida), California petitioned for admission to statehood. Affairs in sparsely populated New Mexico were too confused for the same thing to happen there. For one thing, a boundary dispute with Texas (which claimed the eastern half of the present state of New Mexico) threatened to break out into a shooting war. For another, the recently established Mormon settlement near the Great Salt Lake had adopted a constitution for a proposed new state named Deseret. Although slavery did not exist in Deseret, polygamy did, and it was equally unacceptable to many congressmen. Statehood would have to wait until these problems could be sorted out.

The question of California became a touchstone of Southern rights and power. Its admission as a free state would set a fatal precedent. Whether or not slavery could be expected to flourish in the Southwest, said Robert Barnwell Rhett of South Carolina, "the right is important because it applies to future acquisitions of territory, and by refusing to acknowledge [the South's rights] you force open the whole question of power." Alexander Stephens insisted: "Principles, sir, are not only outposts, but the bulwarks of all constitutional liberty; and if these be yielded, or taken by superior force, the citadel will soon follow." "Our only safety," said Hammond of South Carolina, "is in *equality* of POWER."[20]

The California controversy pumped new life into Calhoun's Southern rights movement. A ground swell of sentiment led in the fall of 1849 to a call for a convention to meet in Nashville the following June. Southern radicals, soon to be called fire-eaters, began to speak openly of secession. They hoped to use the Nashville convention to promote this cause. The backlash against Taylor in the South weakened the Whigs there. Several state elections in 1849 produced sharp declines in the Whig vote. In self-defense, Whigs began to vie with Democrats in protestations of loyalty to Southern rights. Secession rhetoric became commonplace. Calhoun observed that Southern senators and representatives were "more determined and bold than I ever saw them. Many avow themselves disunionists, and a still greater number admit, that there is little hope of any remedy short of it." If the North did not allow the South permanent equality in the Senate, said James Hammond to Calhoun, "we should kick them out of the Capitol & set it on fire."[21] Such violent rhetoric was matched by physical violence, as several fistfights broke out in Congress. On April 17, 1850, Senator Henry S. Foote of Mississippi pulled a revolver against a colleague on the Senate floor.

In 1850 the republic faced a crisis of the first order. To the center of the stage in this high drama strode three of the country's foremost statesmen, for their last appearance before the footlights of history: Senators Henry Clay, Daniel Webster, and John C. Calhoun. All three had been born during the Revolution and had been in public life for nearly half a century. All three had tried without success for the country's highest office. Their crucial roles in the great debate of 1850 marked the passing of leadership to the next generation. Calhoun would die in the midst of the debate; Clay and Webster would follow him to the grave two years later. Four junior senators who played a prominent role in the debate—Stephen A. Douglas, William H.

---

[20]Barney, *The Road to Secession*, pp. 106–107, 110.

[21]J. Franklin Jameson (ed.), *Correspondence of John C. Calhoun*, in American Historical Association, *Annual Report, 1899* (Washington, D.C., 1900), II, 780; Holman Hamilton, *Prologue to Conflict: The Crisis and Compromise of 1850* (New York, 1964), p. 74.

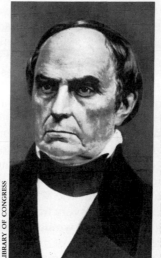

HENRY CLAY, DANIEL WEBSTER, AND JOHN C. CALHOUN

Seward, Jefferson Davis, and Salmon P. Chase—would emerge as four of the most influential politicians of the next decade.

In 1820 and 1833 Henry Clay had earned a reputation as "the Great Pacificator" by constructing compromises to prevent disunion. In 1850 he stepped forward once more to propose compromise. On January 29, 1850, Clay presented eight resolutions to the Senate. The first six were paired in groups of two, each pair offering something to each section. California would be admitted with its free-state constitution, but the remainder of the Mexican cession would be organized as territories "without the adoption of any restriction or condition on the subject of slavery"; the Texas boundary dispute would be settled in favor of New Mexico, but Texas would be compensated by federal assumption of its public debt; the slave trade in the District of Columbia would be abolished, but slavery there would itself be guaranteed against federal interference. These six resolutions perhaps conceded more to the North than to the South. All of California would be free, and New Mexico probably would be. The area of slavery would be scaled down by the reduction of Texas' size, thereby putting a crimp in Southern hopes for the division of Texas into two or more slave states. But the reaffirmation of slavery in the District would be a Southern gain, and the rejection of the Wilmot Proviso would be an antislavery defeat. The last two resolutions offered concessions to the South. One declared that Congress had no authority to interfere with the interstate slave trade, the other called for a stronger federal law to help slave owners recover fugitive slaves who had escaped to the North.

Clay's eloquent plea for his resolutions was followed by some of the great set speeches in the history of the Senate. On March 4, Calhoun, ill and soon to die, sat wrapped in flannels while a Virginia senator read aloud his speech. Opposing the compromise, Calhoun warned that the Union was in danger. National institutions had already been split or gravely weakened by the sectional conflict: the Methodist and Baptist churches had divided into Northern and Southern branches over such questions as whether a slaveholder could be a bishop or a missionary; voluntary associations were splitting over the issue of slavery; political parties themselves were going the same way. In each of these schisms, said Calhoun, the North had been the aggressive party. The only hope for preserving the Union was to adopt a constitutional amendment restoring to the South "the power she possessed of protecting herself before the equilibrium between the sections was destroyed." Calhoun probably had in mind his proposal for a "concurrent majority," by which the country would have two presidents, one from each section, each having veto power over national legislation.[22]

Three days later, Daniel Webster rose to deliver what many would later refer to as his "Seventh of March" address. "I wish to speak to-day," he began, "not as a Massachusetts man, nor as a Northern man, but as an American. . . . I speak to-day for the preservation of the Union. 'Hear me for my cause.' " Despite his antislavery constituency and his previous support for the Wilmot Proviso, Webster now spoke for compromise. Nature would exclude slavery from the Mexican cession; why insult Southern honor by legislating exclusion? "I would not take pains uselessly to reaffirm an act of nature, nor to reenact the will of God."[23] But such an assertion was unacceptable to Free Soilers, who were by no means certain that God would exclude slavery from New Mexico. Webster compounded his sin in their eyes by endorsing the proposed fugitive slave law. Although Webster's speech won praise from conservatives in both North and South, it earned him obloquy among antislavery people, whose anguish was best captured by John Greenleaf Whittier's poem "Ichabod":

> So fallen! so lost! the light withdrawn
> > Which once he wore!
> The glory from his gray hairs gone
> > Forevermore! . . .
>
> All else is gone; from those great eyes
> > The soul has fled:
> When faith is lost, when honor dies,
> > The man is dead!

Much more to abolitionist taste was Seward's "Higher Law" address on March 11. "Under the steady action of moral, social, and political causes . . . emancipation is inevitable," said Seward. "Whether it shall be peaceful or violent depends on the question whether it be hastened or hindered. . . . All measures which fortify slavery, or extend it, tend to the consummation of violence; all that check its extension and abate its strength tend to its peaceful extirpation." Clay's compromise was therefore "radically wrong and essentially vicious." Not only did the Constitution justify the prohibition of slavery in the territories, "but there is a higher law than the Constitution," the law of God; under it, all men are free and equal in his sight. The South pronounced Seward's speech "monstrous and diabolical"; Clay condemned the higher law doctrine as "wild, reckless, and abominable."[24]

After the oratory was over, the Senate in April created a "committee of thirteen," with Clay as chairman, to fashion his resolutions into legislation. By this time a discernible bloc of compromise supporters had emerged, consisting mainly of

---

[22]*Congressional Globe,* 31st Cong., 1st sess. (1850), Appendix, 451–455. Calhoun outlined his proposal for a concurrent majority in his posthumously published *Disquisition on Government.*

[23]*Congressional Globe,* 31st Cong., 1st sess. (1850), Appendix, 269–276.

[24]Ibid., pp. 260–269; Allan Nevins, *Ordeal of the Union,* 2 vols. (New York, 1947), I, 301.

Midwestern Democrats and upper-South Whigs. This bloc constituted less than a quarter of all senators and representatives, however, for Northern Whigs (and some Northern Democrats) opposed those parts of the compromise they considered proslavery, while Southern Democrats and lower-South Whigs opposed those they considered antislavery. Clay agreed to report the various components of the compromise as a package, in the hope that this would induce a majority from both sections to vote for the whole bill in order to get the parts of it they favored. But this strategy backfired. Instead, the opponents of each part voted against the whole in order to defeat the part they opposed. Clay introduced his "omnibus bill"[25] in May; but after nearly three months of complex maneuvering, in which party and sectional coalitions formed and dissolved in kaleidoscopic fashion, the Senate killed the measure on July 31. An exhausted and disheartened Clay left steaming Washington for the sea breezes of Newport.

Stephen A. Douglas of Illinois replaced Clay as the leader of the procompromise forces. A pragmatic Democrat and a skilled parliamentarian, who said later that he cared not whether slavery in the territories was voted up or down, Douglas had never believed in the omnibus approach. He was confident that he could put together separate coalitions in favor of each part of the compromise. During the next two months, aided by his lieutenants in the House, he did exactly that.

Two events during the summer assisted Douglas's efforts. In June the Nashville convention, billed in advance as a conclave of fire-eaters, had failed to ignite. So long as compromise proposals remained before Congress, most Southerners favored deferral of extreme actions. The delegates from nine Southern states adopted restrained resolutions and adjourned to await events. One month later, sudden death from gastroenteritis removed President Taylor from the scene. To the end, Taylor had insisted on his plan for the admission of California and New Mexico as states, with no quid pro quo for the South. The new President, Millard Fillmore of New York, favored the compromise. Fillmore used his influence to persuade several Whig congressmen to abstain from roll calls on compromise measures distasteful to them, which reduced the number of opposition votes.

From mid-August to mid-September of 1850 Congress passed five separate bills: the admission of California; the adjustment of the Texas border; the organization of the New Mexico and Utah territories with the provision that when admitted as states they "shall be received into the Union, with or without slavery, as their constitution may prescribe at the time of their admission"; the enactment of a stringent fugitive slave law; and the abolition of the slave trade in the District of Columbia.

This, then, was the "compromise" of 1850. But if a compromise is "an agreement among adversaries, by which each consents to certain terms desired by the other," one may question whether this was a genuine compromise. In no case did a majority of the "adversaries" on either side consent to the terms desired by the other side; on the contrary, a majority of Northerners voted against those measures they considered proslavery, and a majority of Southerners voted against those they considered antislavery. The bills passed only because the procompromise bloc of Northern Democrats and upper-South Whigs supported each one, and a large number of Northern

---

[25]The bill admitted California as a state, organized New Mexico and Utah as territories without reference to slavery, adjusted the Texas boundary in New Mexico's favor, and compensated Texas with $10 million to finance its public debt. A fugitive slave law and a bill to abolish the slave trade in the District of Columbia were separately reported.

congressmen abstained on the bills pertaining to Utah, New Mexico, and fugitive slaves. Because of this, and because of events that followed ten years later, historian David Potter's appellation, "the Armistice of 1850," seems more appropriate.[26]

In any event, the consequences of some parts of the 1850 settlement turned out to be different from those anticipated. Although California came in as a free state, its voters sent mostly proslavery representatives and senators to Washington. California could scarcely have given the South more aid and comfort in national politics if it had been a slave state. On the other hand, the territorial provisions for New Mexico and Utah proved to be a hollow victory for the South. Although Utah adopted a slave code in 1852, the territory contained only twenty-nine slaves by 1860. Southerners took a few slaves to New Mexico and pushed through a slave code in 1859, but the 1860 census found no slaves in the territory. While the District of Columbia bill ended the transportation of slaves into the District for purposes of sale and transfer, it did not end the buying and selling of slaves within the District itself. And the Fugitive Slave Law, which had been one of the least-debated parts of the Compromise of 1850, turned out to be its most explosive feature.[27]

Whatever the ambiguities and ironies of the Compromise, it did avert a grave crisis in 1850—or at least postponed it. Most Americans—even those who disliked the Compromise—breathed a sigh of relief. Moderates in both parties and in both sections took their cue from President Fillmore, who announced that the Compromise was "a final and irrevocable settlement" of sectional differences. Acceptance of the Compromise was more hearty in the South than in the North. Most Southerners, especially Whigs, regarded it as a Southern victory. "We of the South had a new lease for slave property," wrote a North Carolina Whig. "It was more secure than it had been for the last quarter of a century."[28]

These sentiments blunted the fire-eaters' drive to keep disunionism alive. In four lower-South states—South Carolina, Georgia, Alabama, and Mississippi—Unionist coalitions of Whigs and moderate Democrats defeated efforts by Southern Rights Democrats to win control of the state governments and to call secession conventions. The Georgia Unionists in December 1850 adopted resolutions that furnished the standard platform for the South during the next decade. It was a platform of conditional Unionism. Although Georgia did "not wholly approve" of the Compromise, she would "abide by it as a permanent adjustment of this sectional controversy." But if Congress or the North took any of certain actions, Georgia would be obliged to resist even to the point of secession. Those actions were abolition of slavery in the District of Columbia, repeal or nonenforcement of the Fugitive Slave Law, prohibition of slavery in the territories of Utah or New Mexico, refusal to admit a new slave state, or suppression of the interstate slave trade. Since these were precisely the policies advocated by Free Soilers and a growing number of Northern Whigs, antislavery men viewed the Georgia platform as a species of political blackmail.

As moderates and Unionists, Southern Whigs stood to gain by their section's acceptance of the 1850 Compromise. But the Democrats ultimately reaped most of the benefits. Indeed, by 1852 the Whig party was in serious trouble in the South, for three reasons: (1) The memory of the late President Taylor's "betrayal" of the South remained fresh; (2) the Democrats had proven themselves to be stronger Southern

---

[26]David Potter, *The Impending Crisis 1848–1861* (New York, 1976), pp. 90, 113.
[27]For an account of the law and its consequences, see pages 79 to 84.
[28]Cooper, *The South and the Politics of Slavery*, p. 301.

rights advocates than the Whigs, and thus the first hint of renewed Northern aggression was sure to cause Whig defections to the Democrats; and (3) a ground swell of Northern hostility to the Fugitive Slave Law produced resistance to its enforcement and strengthened the antislavery wing of the Whig party in the North. Several antislavery radicals had recently been elected to Congress: John P. Hale of New Hampshire, Salmon Chase and Benjamin Wade of Ohio, Seward of New York, and Sumner of Massachusetts to the Senate; Thaddeus Stevens of Pennsylvania and George W. Julian of Indiana to the House, where they joined the doughty veteran Joshua Giddings of Ohio, who had battled the "slave power" in Congress for many years. Nearly all of these men were of New England birth or parentage. Most of them were Whigs. Southern Whigs therefore suffered at home from their party affiliation with these Yankee "fanatics."

★ The Election of 1852

The 1848 Barnburners had been an aberration caused more by intraparty Democratic factionalism than by genuine antislavery convictions. By 1851 most Barnburners had tamely returned to the party, leaving their Wilmot Proviso principles behind them. In 1852 the Democrats nominated dark horse Franklin Pierce of New Hampshire for President on a states' rights platform that denounced abolitionists and reaffirmed the Compromise of 1850. Despite his Yankee heritage, Pierce had a safe proslavery record. The Democrats became again a united, intersectional party.

Northern Whigs remained divided between a pro-Compromise Fillmore faction and an antislavery Seward faction, while Southern Whigs determined to bolt the party if the latter prevailed. The Whig national convention of 1852 illustrated the sectional tensions and paradoxes that were crippling the party. Northern antislavery Whigs supported the nomination of Winfield Scott, the Southern general who had conquered Mexico. Southern Whigs backed Fillmore, a New Yorker. The convention managed to adopt a platform that "acquiesced in" the Compromise of 1850. But half of Scott's delegates voted against this plank, and many of the remainder supported it only as part of an implicit bargain to secure conservative support for Scott. Through fifty-two ballots, the convention deadlocked between the two candidates, with 96 percent of Scott's votes coming from free states and 85 percent of Fillmore's from slave states. A handful of Webster delegates held the balance of power. On the fifty-third ballot, Scott picked up enough Fillmore support to win the nomination, but he received only one-tenth of his votes from the South.

The Free Soilers nominated John P. Hale on an unequivocal platform that denounced the Compromise of 1850, demanded the repeal of the Fugitive Slave Law, opposed any future admission of slave states, and branded slavery "a sin against God and a crime against man. . . . Christianity, humanity, and patriotism, alike demand its abolition."[29]

Southern Whigs knew that more than a few of their Northern brethren harbored similar sentiments. They suspected that Scott, like Taylor before him, would become prey to Seward's wiles. Believing that the South "must not *offer Bounties for Anti-Slavery Agitation and Aggression* by supporting a candidate forced upon her by

[29]Roy and Jeannette Nichols, "Election of 1852," in Arthur M. Schlesinger, Jr. (ed.), *History of American Presidential Elections,* 4 vols. (New York, 1960), II, 954.

abolition influences," several prominent Southern Whigs repudiated the ticket and went over to the Democrats.[30] In six states of the lower South, Scott won only 35 percent of the popular vote, compared with 50 percent for Taylor in 1848. Scott carried only two of the fifteen slave states. He also carried just two free states, but the Whig popular vote in the North declined only slightly from 1848. The Free Soil vote dropped to 6 percent of the Northern total, as the Barnburners' return to the Democratic fold swelled Pierce's victory margin.

In the South, as Alexander Stephens, the former Whig party leader, bluntly phrased it, "the Whig party is dead."[31] By 1853 the Democrats controlled every one of the future Confederate states. The Whigs elected only fourteen of the sixty-five congressmen from these states. For all practical purposes, the Whigs had become a Northern party, with Northern Whigs badly divided among themselves. The intersectional two-party system tottered on the edge of the grave.

[30]Cooper, *The South and the Politics of Slavery,* p. 330.
[31]Ibid., p. 343.

FIVE

Filibusterers, Fugitives, and Nativists

I want Cuba. . . . I want Tamaulipas, Potosi, and one or two other Mexican States . . . and a foothold in Central America. . . . Yes, I want these Countries for the spread of slavery. —Albert Gallatin Brown, senator from Mississippi, 1850s

★ Manifest Destiny and Slavery in the 1850s

An exasperated Southern congressman complained in 1850 that the conflict over slavery in the territories was a quarrel about "an imaginary negro in an impossible place." Many contemporaries echoed Daniel Webster's contention that Nature would ban slavery from the Mexican cession. "The right to carry slaves to New Mexico or California is no very great matter, whether granted or denied," wrote the Kentuckian John J. Crittenden in 1848, "the more especially when it seems to be agreed that no sensible man would carry his slaves there if he could."[1] If this was true, then the Civil War was indeed caused by fanatics on each side who tore the country apart over a "pernicious abstraction."

But it was by no means certain that Nature would keep slavery out of the Southwest. While it was true that, given the existing level of agricultural technology, the cultivation of cotton and tobacco had almost reached its western limits by the 1850s, this did not necessarily mean that slavery was unfeasible in the new territories. Slave labor had proved successful in mining and other industries in the South and in Latin America. In a Senate speech opposing the Compromise of 1850, Jefferson Davis insisted that slavery could flourish in the California gold mines. The *Southern Quarterly* maintained that "California is by nature peculiarly a slaveholding State." If the government had not interfered, "thousands of young, intelligent, active men would have been in that region, having each carried with them from one to five slaves." Several hundred slaves did work in the California mines before the state constitution prohibited slavery. Some of them even continued to work as slaves after 1850, under

---

[1] Harold M. Hyman and William M. Ciecek, *Equal Justice under Law: Constitutional Development 1835-1875* (New York, 1982), p. 134; Michael F. Holt, *The Political Crisis of the 1850s* (New York, 1978), p. 77.

court decisions allowing the temporary residence of slaveholders in the state. Noting the mineral resources of New Mexico, the *Charleston Mercury* declared: "The right to have property protected in the territory is not a mere abstraction. . . . There is no vocation in the world in which slavery can be more useful and profitable than in mining."[2]

The real crux of the issue, however, was not the territories already owned but those likely to be acquired in the future. In 1850, an American aged sixty-five had seen the country quadruple in size during his adult life. There was little reason for him to expect this process to stop. President Pierce's inaugural address pledged further annexations. Since a strong power (Britain) controlled the land to the north, the obvious direction for expansion was to the south. Antislavery congressmen, therefore, felt apprehension not only about slavery in existing territories but even more about slavery in future territories.

There was good reason for their apprehension. Proslavery expansionists were casting covetous eyes on Cuba, Central America, and Mexico. Jefferson Davis pressed for the acquisition of Cuba and of additional Mexican territory to "increase the number of slave-holding constituencies." His Mississippi Senate colleague, Albert Gallatin Brown, declared: "I want Cuba. . . . I want Tamaulipas, Potosi, and one or two other Mexican States . . . and a foothold in Central America. . . . Yes, I want these Countries for the spread of slavery." Many Southern voices echoed these sentiments: "I look to the acquisition of Cuba as of great importance to the South"; "Our destiny is intertwined with that of Cuba. . . . The safety of the South is to be found only in the extension of its peculiar institutions"; "The desire that Cuba should be acquired as a Southern conquest, is almost unanimous among Southern men." The South's leading monthly, *DeBow's Review,* hammered away in almost every issue on the need to expand southward: "We have a destiny to perform a manifest destiny over all Mexico, over South America, over the West Indies."[3]

The fulfillment of this destiny was the goal of a shadowy, fantastic organization known as the Knights of the Golden Circle, founded at Louisville in 1854 by a Virginian named George Bickley. A fraternal organization with elaborate rituals and regalia, the Knights proposed a scheme to establish a "golden circle" of slave states starting in the South and extending in a wide arc through Mexico, Central America, northern South America, and the West Indies. This would add twenty-five new slave states to the Union, said Bickley. If Congress refused to admit them, the South could secede and become the center of a vast new slave empire that would produce most of the world's cotton, tobacco, sugar, and coffee. Although Bickley was something of a charlatan and his organization accomplished little, the Knights did manage to provoke controversy. During the Civil War, Bickley tried to organize antiwar groups in the North.

Realistic American expansion efforts after the Mexican War focused mainly on Cuba. In 1848 the Polk administration offered Spain $100 million for the island. When

---

[2]Davis and the *Mercury* quoted in Robert S. Starobin, *Industrial Slavery in the Old South* (New York, 1970), pp. 219-220; *Southern Quarterly* quoted in William R. Brock, *Parties and Political Conscience: American Dilemmas 1840-1850* (Millwood, N.Y., 1979), p. 319.

[3]Davis and Brown quoted in Robert E. May, *The Southern Dream of a Caribbean Empire, 1854-1861* (Baton Rouge, 1973), pp. 11, 9; many Southern voices quoted in John McCardell, *The Idea of a Southern Nation: Southern Nationalists and Southern Nationalism, 1830-1860* (New York, 1979), pp. 248, 258-259; *DeBow's Review* quoted in John Hope Franklin, *The Militant South* (Cambridge, Mass., 1956), p. 99.

the Spanish government indignantly refused, Southerners tried other means. They hoped to foment a Texas-style revolution among dissident Cuban sugar planters who wanted American annexation. For this purpose they supported Narciso Lopez, a Venezuelan-born Cuban adventurer who had fled the island in 1848 after an abortive uprising. Lopez recruited American volunteers to invade Cuba. This was the first of many American filibustering[4] expeditions after the Mexican War.

The unsympathetic Taylor administration ordered the navy to seize the ships of the Lopez expedition before they could sail. The undaunted Lopez reorganized a force of several hundred men and slipped out of New Orleans in 1850. He captured Cardenas and burned the governor's mansion, but the Cubans failed to rise and a Spanish counterattack forced the filibusterers to scurry for Key West. The U.S. government prosecuted the leaders for violation of neutrality laws, but New Orleans juries failed to convict. Instead, the city treated Lopez as a hero. Prominent Southerners helped him raise men and money for a third attempt. With five hundred men Lopez again invaded Cuba in August 1851. But once more the expected uprising failed to materialize. Many of Lopez's troops were cut off and killed; more than fifty were captured and executed as pirates, including Lopez and young William Crittenden of Kentucky, nephew of the U.S. attorney general. This put a temporary damper on filibustering.

But it did not discourage American efforts to acquire Cuba. The Pierce administration made acquisition of Cuba a primary goal of its foreign policy. The President appointed the flamboyant Pierre Soulé of Louisiana as minister to Spain. Within months of his arrival in Madrid, Soulé offended the Spaniards with his denunciations of monarchy, wounded the French ambassador in a duel, and tried to present an ultimatum to the Spanish government over an incident concerning an American merchant ship in the Havana harbor. In the spring of 1854, Secretary of State William Marcy instructed Soulé to offer Spain $130 million for Cuba and, if this failed, to "direct your efforts to the next desirable object, which is to detach that island from Spanish dominion." When the Spanish government refused to sell, Soulé began intriguing with revolutionary groups bent on overthrowing the government. Meanwhile, Marcy authorized Soulé and the U.S. ministers to Paris and London—John Mason and James Buchanan—to meet at Ostend, Belgium, to exchange views concerning the acquisition of Cuba. The three ministers sent to Washington a remarkable memorandum written by Soulé and revised by Buchanan. "Cuba is as necessary to the North American republic as any of its present . . . family of states," they declared. If Spain refused to sell and if the United States considered Cuba essential to its security, then "by every law, human and Divine, we shall be justified in wresting it from Spain."[5]

When this "Ostend Manifesto" was leaked to the press, it produced an uproar in both Europe and America. Antislavery groups denounced it as a "manifesto of the Brigands," which proposed "to grasp, to rob, to murder, to grow rich on the spoils of provinces and toils of slaves."[6] The House subpoenaed the diplomatic correspon-

---

[4]From the Spanish *filibustero*, meaning freebooter or pirate.

[5]William R. Manning (ed.), *Diplomatic Correspondence of the United States: Inter-American Affairs, 1831–1860,* 12 vols. (Washington, D.C., 1932–1939), XI, 175–178, 193–194.

[6]Allan Nevins, *Ordeal of the Union,* 2 vols. (New York, 1947), II, 362.

dence and published it. Already in political trouble over the Kansas-Nebraska act,[7] the Pierce administration recalled Soulé and gave up the Cuba project.[8]

In 1854 a major filibustering enterprise overlapped the official efforts to buy Cuba. The leader of this venture was former Governor John A. Quitman of Mississippi. With the support of Cuban exiles in New York, Quitman raised money and recruited volunteers for an invasion of the island. Numerous public men in the South openly aided the undertaking. Through his friendship with Secretary of War Jefferson Davis, Quitman thought he had obtained the administration's tacit support for the venture. Senator John Slidell of Louisiana even introduced a motion on May 1, 1854, to suspend the neutrality laws. But Quitman failed to strike while the iron was hot. By the fall of 1854 the backlash against the Kansas-Nebraska Act and the Ostend Manifesto caused Pierce to announce that he would enforce the neutrality laws. Quitman finally called off the invasion in April 1855.

These failures caused expansionist attention to shift toward Mexico and Central America. The minister to Mexico, James Gadsden, tried in 1853 to purchase an additional 250,000 square miles of the country. The ostensible purpose was to obtain land for a railroad to the Pacific. But Northern senators suspected, with good reason, that a supplemental hidden purpose was to gain potential slave territory. Mexico refused to sell this much territory and reduced the purchase to 54,000 square miles; Northern senators cut out another 9,000 miles before approving in 1854 the Gadsden Purchase—which resulted in the acquisition of what is now southern Arizona and New Mexico.

During the 1850s American filibusterers, mostly from Texas and California, launched dozens of raids into Mexico. Some of them had simple plunder as their goal; others were part of a sporadic border warfare that continued for years after the Mexican War. But some were animated by a desire to create "a chain of slave states from the Atlantic to the Pacific" across northern Mexico.[9] None of these raids succeeded; some turned out disastrously for the invaders—particularly the Crabb expedition of 1857. Henry Crabb, a Tennessee-born Californian, led an army of ninety men into the province of Sonora, where they were surrounded and all executed in cold blood after surrendering to Mexican authorities.

Crabb's boyhood friend William Walker eventually met the same fate, but not until he had won a reputation as the greatest of all filibusterers, "the grey-eyed man of destiny." A restless native of Tennessee who had moved to California, Walker recruited other footloose men for an invasion of Baja California in 1853. After some initial success, they were driven back across the border to stand trial in San Francisco for violation of the neutrality laws. A sympathetic jury acquitted Walker after deliberating for eight minutes. Two years later, Walker went after bigger game. With a small army he invaded Nicaragua; in alliance with local rebels, he overthrew the government and in June 1856 proclaimed himself president. Walker pronounced his conquest to be the first step toward "regeneration" of the Central American republics by Anglo-Saxon settlers. Many of Walker's predominantly Southern backers also saw it as

---

[7]See pages 90 to 95.

[8]This did not end official efforts to obtain Cuba, however. After his election as President in 1856, Buchanan tried to buy the island; and as late as 1860, the Democratic platform pledged the party to further efforts in that direction.

[9]John R. Wells to John Quitman, April 26, 1856, in May, *Southern Dream of a Caribbean Empire*, p. 137.

the first step toward the reintroduction of slavery in Central America and the creation of several new slave states.

But the other Central American republics had different ideas. They formed an alliance to invade Nicaragua and expel Walker. To rally support and recruits from the South to meet this threat, Walker in September 1856 issued a decree reinstituting slavery in Nicaragua. This elicited enthusiasm and some recruits from the South, but they were too late to save Walker's regime. The remnants of the defeated and cholera-decimated filibusterers were rescued by a U.S. naval vessel in May 1857.

Walker returned to a hero's welcome in the South, which furnished men and supplies for a second invasion of Nicaragua. But the American navy stepped in to prevent it. Southerners in Congress denounced the naval commander who detained Walker. A hung jury in New Orleans voted 10 to 2 to acquit him of violating the neutrality laws. Walker made a triumphal tour of the South. He wrote a book about his experiences in which he urged Southern backing for another invasion. "If the South wishes to get her institutions into tropical America she must do so before treaties are made to embarrass her action," wrote Walker. "The hearts of Southern youth answer the call of honor. . . . The true field for the exertion of slavery is in tropical America."[10] He received enough encouragement to launch a new filibustering expedition. But this time his luck ran out. The Honduras militia stopped his small force, and on September 12, 1860, Walker's remarkable career came to an end before a Honduran firing squad.

Southern support for these efforts to acquire new slave territory did much to undermine the fragile sectional armistice that followed the Compromise of 1850. So did Northern reaction to the Fugitive Slave Law.

★ The Fugitive Slave Law

The issue of fugitive slaves went back to the framing of the Constitution. Article IV, Section 2, specified that persons "held to Service or Labour in one State" who escaped to another "shall be delivered up on Claim of the Party to whom such Service or Labour may be due." In plain English, this meant that slaves who fled to a free state were still slaves and liable to be returned to bondage. In 1793, Congress enacted a fugitive slave law that authorized slave owners to recapture their escaped slaves beyond state lines and bring them before any state or federal court to establish proof of ownership. This procedure worked well enough for a time. But with the emergence of militant abolitionism in the 1830s, the fugitive slave question became a major controversy.

For Northerners, the escaped bondsman transformed slavery from an abstraction into a flesh-and-blood reality. The antislavery press publicized stories about the heroic flights of fugitives who outwitted the bloodhounds and followed the North Star to freedom. Abolitionists found that escaped slaves made the most effective antislavery lecturers. The autobiographies of fugitives (sometimes ghost-written) became the most effective antislavery literature. The organization of an "underground railroad" to help fugitives on their way gave antislavery Yankees an opportunity to do something practical against slavery. Although the underground railroad was never as extensive in fact as in legend, the exaggerated rumors about it inflamed Southern anger and

[10]William Walker, *The War in Nicaragua* (New York, 1860), pp. 278-280.

exacerbated sectional tensions. And although the number of slaves who escaped to the North was a tiny fraction of the total (probably fewer than a thousand per year), their symbolic importance magnified the issue out of proportion to their numbers.

What made it worse, in Southern eyes, was the enactment by several Northern states of "personal liberty laws." The main purpose of these statutes was to prevent the kidnapping of free blacks for sale into slavery. The personal liberty laws of some states also prohibited state officials from participating in the recapture of slaves and assured fugitives the rights of habeas corpus and trial by jury.

The constitutionality of these laws came before the U.S. Supreme Court in *Prigg v. Pennsylvania* (1842), a case that concerned a Maryland slave owner convicted in Pennsylvania of kidnapping after he had forcibly carried his runaway slave back to Maryland. In a divided decision, the Court overturned the conviction and ruled the Pennsylvania antikidnapping statute unconstitutional. At the same time, however, the Court also ruled that enforcement of the fugitive slave clause of the Constitution was entirely a federal responsibility. Pennsylvania's law prohibiting state officers from enforcing the 1793 federal statute was therefore valid. This complex decision produced a new wave of personal liberty laws in the 1840s, by which seven states prohibited their officials from taking part in the recapture of fugitives or forbade the use of state and local jails to hold fugitives pending a decision on their return. These laws provoked Southern demands for a new federal statute to put teeth into the fugitive slave clause.

The 1850 Fugitive Slave Act did just that. In fact, it was one of the strongest national laws yet enacted by Congress. The act included the following provisions: (1) a category of U.S. commissioners was created who were empowered to issue warrants for the arrest and return of fugitives to slavery; (2) an affidavit by the claimant was to be sufficient evidence of ownership, and the fugitive was to be denied the right to testify in his or her own behalf; (3) the commissioner was to be granted a fee of $10 if he found for the claimant but only $5 if he released the fugitive; and (4) the commissioner was authorized to deputize any citizen to serve as a member of a posse to aid in enforcement of the law, and stiff fines or jail sentences could be meted out to those who refused such orders or who resisted the law. Attempts by Northern congressmen to mandate a jury trial for fugitives were defeated.

This law proved to be the most consequential product of the Compromise of 1850. Southerners insisted that its enforcement was the *sine qua non* of union. Antislavery Northerners denounced it. In Ralph Waldo Emerson's words, it was "a filthy law" that no one could obey "without loss of self-respect." Although supporters of the statute claimed that the extra paperwork involved if a commissioner remanded a fugitive to slavery justified the doubled fee, opponents regarded this fee as a shameless bribe. As one Free Soiler put it, the law fixed the price of a slave at a thousand dollars and the price of a Yankee soul at five. Many Northerners considered the prohibitions against fugitive testimony and jury trials to be denials of due process. Worst of all was the provision authorizing federal commissioners to deputize citizens, which might compel anyone to become a slave catcher. Many Yankees vowed civil disobedience. Congressman Joshua Giddings predicted that even the army could not enforce the statute: "Let the President . . . drench our land of freedom in blood; but he will never make us obey that law."[11]

---

[11]Emerson quoted in James Ford Rhodes, *History of the United States from the Compromise of 1850 . . . ,* 7 vols. (New York, 1893–1906), I, 207–208; Giddings quoted in Frederick J. Blue, *The Free Soilers: Third Party Politics 1848–54* (Urbana, Ill., 1973), p. 204.

BETTMANN ARCHIVE

HARRIET TUBMAN. Known as "the Moses of her people," Tubman was the most famous "conductor" on the underground railroad. She is shown here on the far left with a group of ex-slaves she had led northward to freedom. After escaping from Maryland herself in 1849, Tubman risked recapture by returning numerous times to help at least sixty slaves escape along a network of "stations" maintained by Quakers and free blacks in Delaware and Pennsylvania.

Northern anger was intensified by a sharp increase in attempts to recapture fugitives during the first year of the law's operation. A class of professional slave catchers came into existence. Ostensibly the agents of Southern owners, some of them were no better than kidnappers bearing forged affidavits who saw a chance to make a tidy sum by selling captured free blacks to the South. In February 1851 a black man in Madison, Indiana, was seized in front of his wife and children and returned to an owner who claimed that he had run away nineteen years earlier. Slave catchers grabbed a hard-working black Methodist in New York and spirited him away to Baltimore before his wife and children knew what had happened. A black tailor who had lived in Poughkeepsie for many years was arrested and carried to South Carolina, where he was held for a price of $1,750. A black woman who said she had lived in Philadelphia all her life was claimed by a Maryland man who insisted that she had run away twenty-two years earlier. The Marylander also claimed ownership of her six children, all born in Philadelphia. In this case, the commissioner ruled against the claimant. In the cases of the New York Methodist and Poughkeepsie tailor, local blacks and whites raised funds to buy their freedom. But no such ransoms redeemed most of the other eighty-one fugitives whose return from the North to slavery in 1850–1851 was recorded—not to mention an unknown number of unrecorded cases.

Nor was there a happy ending to the most tragic fugitive slave case of the decade—the Margaret Garner affair. Margaret Garner and her four children escaped with three other slaves across the Ohio River to Cincinnati in January 1856. The owner traced them and obtained a warrant for their arrest. As the fugitives were about to be captured by a U.S. marshal's posse, Margaret Garner tried to kill her children to prevent their return to slavery. She managed to cut her daughter's throat but was stopped before she could do the same to her sons. Ohio courts tried to retain custody in order to try her for murder, but the federal commissioner overrode the state and ordered Garner and her children returned to their Kentucky owner, who promptly sold them down the river. A steamboat accident killed Garner's infant child before she and her two surviving sons were finally sold in the New Orleans slave market.

The Fugitive Slave Law had a devastating impact on Northern black communities. Many "free" blacks were in fact escaped slaves; even if they were not, their inability to testify in their own behalf left them helpless in the face of an affidavit certified by a Southern court. Thousands of Northern blacks fled to Canada. The law pumped new life into black nationalism in the North by seeming to provide new evidence that blacks could never live safely in the United States. Projects for emigration to Haiti, Central America, and Africa gained momentum during the 1850s.

But flight was not the only response to the Fugitive Slave Law. Blacks and whites in several Northern cities formed vigilance committees to hide or protect fugitives from slave catchers, and to give them legal assistance if arrested. People holding a variety of antislavery opinions came together on these committees, along with others who had not previously professed any such opinions. The vigilance committees urged nonviolent resistance. But many members did not shrink from violence. The black leader and one-time fugitive slave Frederick Douglass said that the best way to make the Fugitive Slave Law a dead letter was "to make a dozen or more dead kid-nappers."[12]

Vigilance committees played a role in some of the spectacular fugitive rescues of the decade. In October 1850 the Boston committee spirited away two famous fugitives, William and Ellen Craft, from under the nose of a Georgia jailer who had come to claim them. Four months later a black waiter named Fred Wilkins, who was known to his friends as Shadrach, was arrested in Boston as a fugitive. While he was being held in the federal courthouse, a crowd of black men burst through the door and snatched him away before the astonished deputy marshal realized what was happening. In April 1851 the government managed to foil another attempt in Boston to rescue a fugitive, Thomas Sims, only by guarding him with three hundred soldiers and taking him away at four o'clock in the morning for shipment South. In September 1851 a group of black men in the Quaker community of Christiana, Pennsylvania, shot it out with a Maryland slave owner and his allies who had come to arrest two fugitives. The slave owner was killed and his son severely wounded in the affray. The following month a group of black and white abolitionists broke into a Syracuse police station, carried off the arrested fugitive William McHenry (alias Jerry), and sent him across Lake Ontario to Canada.

The Millard Fillmore administration, committed to making the Compromise of 1850 work, was determined to punish these violations of the Fugitive Slave Law. The government indicted several dozen men involved in the Shadrach, Christiana, and

[12]Philip Foner (ed.), *The Life and Writings of Frederick Douglass,* 4 vols. (New York, 1950–1955), II, 207.

McHenry rescues. But with the exception of one man convicted in the William McHenry case, all the defendants were acquitted or released after mistrials by hung juries. Northern juries would no more convict violators of the Fugitive Slave Law than Southern juries would convict violators of the neutrality laws.

Perhaps because most available fugitives had gone into hiding or fled to Canada, the number of arrests and returns—as well as of rescues—decreased after 1851. Excitement over the fugitive slave issue cooled down in 1852. Moderates in the North and in the South seemed to gain control of affairs with their affirmations of support for all parts of the Compromise of 1850, including the Fugitive Slave Law.

But beneath this surface calm the volcano of Northern discontent continued to rumble. The astounding popularity of Harriet Beecher Stowe's novel, *Uncle Tom's Cabin,* both reflected and reinforced the North's feelings of guilt and revulsion toward the hunting down of slaves on its own soil. Although the book's plot and subplots are contrived and its prose seems sentimental to the modern reader, *Uncle Tom's Cabin* was—and still is—a powerful novel. Mrs. Stowe was moved to write it by her own anguish at the Fugitive Slave Law. The story ran serially in an antislavery newspaper for nearly a year, beginning in the spring of 1851, and was published as a book in the spring of 1852. Within months it became one of the best-sellers of all time. It provoked tears in the North and angry rebuttals in the South. A decade later, when Mrs. Stowe was introduced to Abraham Lincoln, the President reportedly said: "So you're the little woman who wrote the book that made this great war."

Two events in the spring of 1854 rekindled Northern defiance of the Fugitive Slave Law. The first was the passage of the Kansas-Nebraska Act, which repealed the Missouri Compromise's ban on slavery in the Louisiana Purchase territory north of 36°30′ (see pages 90 to 93). The Kansas-Nebraska Act served to outrage many Northern moderates who had previously urged obedience to the Fugitive Slave Law. Since the South had repudiated one key sectional compromise, they felt no obligation to respect the other. A second jarring event in 1854 was the Anthony Burns affair.

The Burns Affair, Ableman v. Booth

Anthony Burns was a Virginia slave who had escaped to Boston and gone to work in a clothing store, where he was suddenly seized on May 24. News of the arrest spread quickly. The vigilance committee organized mass rallies; antislavery protesters poured into Boston from surrounding areas; black and white abolitionists mounted an ill-coordinated assault on the federal courthouse that killed one of the deputies guarding Burns but failed to rescue the fugitive. Determined to make an example of this case and to prove that the law could be enforced "even in Boston," the Pierce administration refused an offer from the city's leaders to purchase Burns's freedom at three times his market value. Instead, the government sent in federal troops. They marched Burns to the harbor, where a ship waited to carry him back to Virginia, while tens of thousands of bitter Yankees looked on and bells tolled the death of liberty in the cradle of the American Revolution.

It is impossible to exaggerate the impact of this event. "When it was all over," wrote a conservative Boston attorney who had previously counseled obedience to the law, "and I was left alone in my office, I put my face in my hands and wept. I could do nothing less." Another conservative, Edward Everett, commented that "a change has taken place in this community within three weeks such as the 30 preceding years had not produced." And Amos A. Lawrence, formerly a leader of the Cotton Whigs, said that "we went to bed one night old fashioned, conservative, Compromise Union Whigs & waked up stark mad Abolitionists."[13]

Anthony Burns (whose freedom a Boston committee later managed to buy) was the last fugitive returned from Boston—or from anywhere in New England. Nine Northern states passed new personal liberty laws in the wake of the Burns affair. These laws included one or more of the following provisions: the appointment of state attorneys to defend fugitives, state payment for all defense costs, the denial of the use of any public building for the detention of fugitives, new and stringent antikidnapping statutes, and jury trials in state courts for accused fugitives. The purpose of these laws was to harass slave catchers and to make their enterprise so costly, time-consuming, and precarious that they would give it up. In this the laws were successful, for the number of fugitives returned from states that had passed new personal liberty laws declined after 1854.[14]

The personal liberty laws of some states virtually nullified federal law. Inevitably, therefore, the issue came before the U.S. Supreme Court, in *Ableman v. Booth* (1859). This case arose when a Wisconsin abolitionist named Sherman Booth was convicted by a federal court and imprisoned for leading a raid in 1854 that had freed a fugitive held in custody. The Wisconsin Supreme Court ruled the Fugitive Slave Law unconstitutional and ordered Booth's release. The federal attorney appealed to the U.S. Supreme Court, where Chief Justice Roger Taney spoke for the majority in ruling the Fugitive Slave Law constitutional and declaring any state interference with its enforcement unconstitutional. Booth went back to prison. Thus the supremacy of federal law, supported by the South, was upheld, and state sovereignty, supported by the North, was struck down—indeed an ironic commentary on the South's traditional commitment to states' rights.

★ Free Soilers and Free Blacks

Although the personal liberty laws might seem to have indicated a liberalization of Northern racial attitudes, that interpretation would be an oversimplification. Indeed, in some parts of the North the opposite was true. While several Northern states were passing personal liberty laws, others were adopting new "black laws" that imposed degrading restrictions on free blacks. Most of the legislation to protect fugitives came out of the upper North (New England, upstate New York, Michigan, Wisconsin, and Minnesota), while several lower-North states and the new Western states of California and Oregon retained or passed black laws.

The Indiana constitutional convention of 1851 adopted a provision forbidding black migration into the state. This supplemented the state's laws barring blacks already there from voting, serving on juries or in the militia, testifying against whites in court, marrying whites, or going to school with whites. Iowa and Illinois had similar laws on the books and banned black immigration by statute in 1851 and 1853, respectively. These measures reflected the racist sentiments of most whites in those states. The exclusion laws were also passed as a conciliatory assurance to the South

---

[13]Attorney quoted in Nevins, *Ordeal of the Union*, II, 151–152; Everett and Lawrence quoted in Jane H. and William H. Pease (eds.), *The Fugitive Slave Law and Anthony Burns* (Philadelphia, 1975), pp. 51, 43.

[14]In these states during the 1850s, sixty-two slaves were returned before passage of new laws, and twenty-seven afterwards.

that no fugitives would be welcomed in these states. There was little likelihood of black migration to Oregon, but upon admission to the Union in 1859, that state also adopted the full range of black laws—among them an exclusion statute. A decade earlier, California had refrained from excluding blacks by law only because it feared this might harm the state's chances for admission. But the Golden State adopted all the other discriminatory legislation that prevailed in the lower North. Even the territory of Kansas, a Free Soil stronghold by the end of the decade, voted at one point for a constitutional clause excluding blacks, though this provision was dropped before Kansas came in as a state in 1861. Most Western settlers clearly wanted no black people in their midst—slave *or* free.

This antiblack animus infected even a portion of the Free Soil movement. David Wilmot himself insisted that his proviso did not arise from any "squeamish sensitiveness upon the subject of slavery, nor morbid sympathy for the slave. . . . The negro race already occupy enough of this fair continent." Wilmot was perfectly willing to call his resolution "the white man's proviso."[15]

This sentiment was identified mainly with the Democratic or "Barnburner" constituency of the Free Soil party. Liberty men and Conscience Whigs expressed more liberal attitudes. The 1844 Liberty party platform contained several planks affirming equal rights and pledging to work for the removal of racial discrimination in Northern states. In Massachusetts, where blacks enjoyed almost full civil and political equality, a coalition of Liberty men, Garrisonian abolitionists, and Conscience Whigs worked to remove the last vestiges of legal discrimination. They managed to repeal the anti-intermarriage law in 1843 but failed in their attempts to remove the ban on blacks in the militia. In 1855 they finally won passage of a law prohibiting school segregation. In 1846 an effort by Liberty men and antislavery Whigs in New York to abolish the discriminatory $250 property qualification for black voters was defeated by Democrats, including many Barnburners who voted Free Soil two years later. The Free Soilers achieved one of their greatest successes in Ohio, whose black laws until 1849 were the most restrictive in the North. The election of 1848 gave the Free Soilers the balance of power in Ohio politics. They used this leverage to strike a bargain with the Democrats whereby the latter grudgingly voted to elect Salmon P. Chase to the Senate and to repeal laws prohibiting black migration into the state, testimony against whites in court, and attendance at public schools. These concessions were made in return for Free Soil votes that would enable the Democrats to control the legislature.

Before the Civil War, only the New England states (except Connecticut) allowed blacks to vote on equal terms with whites. During the 1850s, the Free Soilers and Republicans tried to enact black suffrage in a few other Northern states, but failed. Democrats made much political capital by calling their opponents the "nigger party" or "amalgamation party." So pervasive was racism in many parts of the North that no party could win if it endorsed full racial equality. Thus the Free Soil platforms of 1848 and 1852 failed to include the earlier Liberty party planks demanding equal rights. Free Soil and Republican campaigns for state black suffrage laws in the 1850s sometimes seemed half-hearted.

Quite apart from the question of political expediency, many Free Soilers also harbored prejudices and stereotypes that inhibited a commitment to racial equality. They could hate slavery and sympathize with fugitive slaves but at the same time favor the colonization abroad of black people in order to preserve America as a white man's

[15]*Congressional Globe*, 29th Cong., 2nd sess. (1847), Appendix, 317.

country. The ambivalence of the Free Soil party—and later of the Republican party—toward racial equality was one reason why some abolitionists remained aloof from these parties. For instance, the wealthy New York abolitionist Gerrit Smith and a handful of followers actively supported the Radical Abolitionist party, a Liberty party splinter group, through the 1850s.

★ Nativism and the Rise of the Know-Nothings

For a few years in the 1850s, ethnic conflict among whites rivaled sectional conflict as a major political issue. The immediate origins of this phenomenon lay in the spectacular increase of immigration after 1845. In the 1820s, the number of immigrants had averaged fewer than 13,000 per year. The average quadrupled in the 1830s. But even this paled in comparison with the immigration of the late 1840s. Land shortages and labor surpluses in Europe, plus the potato blight in Ireland and the revolutions of 1848 on the Continent, caused millions to emigrate. High wages, cheap land, and the booming American economy attracted most of them to the United States. During the decade 1846–1855, more than three million immigrants entered the United States—equivalent to 15 percent of the 1845 population. This was the largest proportional increase in the foreign-born population for any ten-year period in American history. Because 87 percent of the immigrants settled in free states, their impact was felt mainly in the North, where several cities by 1855 had a foreign-born population approaching or exceeding half of the total population.

Equal in significance to the increase in the foreign-born population were changes in its composition. Before 1840, three-quarters of the immigrants were Protestants, mostly from the British Isles. Only one-fifth of them became unskilled laborers or servants, while the remainder were farmers, skilled workers, and white-collar or professional men. In the 1840s and 1850s, however, more than half of the immigrants were Catholics, two-thirds of whom came from Ireland and most of the rest from German-speaking countries. Moreover, the proportion of unskilled laborers among this much larger wave of immigration was double that among the earlier immigrants. Irish Catholics, who settled primarily in the large cities of the Northeast, became the poorest, most concentrated, and most visible of the immigrants.

Anti-immigrant sentiment, or "nativism," manifested itself less against the foreign-born in general than against Roman Catholics in particular. Indeed, some of the fiercest nativists were Scots-Irish Presbyterians and Welsh or English Methodists, who brought their anti-Catholic feelings with them from the old country. Anti-Catholicism had deep roots in Britain and in America. Bloody Mary, Guy Fawkes Day, the Glorious Revolution, and similar memories formed part of the cultural baggage of Anglo-American Protestantism. British Catholics had suffered deprivation of certain civil and political rights even after the Catholic Emancipation Act of 1829. In the United States, the Protestant evangelicalism of the Second Great Awakening produced a heightened anti-Catholicism. Protestant perceptions of Irish and German drinking habits, the Irish and German tendency to vote for the Democratic party and to oppose equal rights for blacks, and the resistance of Catholics to the Protestant-dominated public schools further intensified the prejudices of evangelical Protestants and reformers.

Even before the post-1845 increase in immigration, ethnic and religious tensions had sometimes burst into violence: a Protestant mob destroyed a convent in Charlestown, Massachusetts, in 1834; riots between Protestants (including Scots-

IMMIGRATION TO THE UNITED STATES

(From Division and the Stresses of Reunion *1845–1876, by David M. Potter. Copyright © 1973 Scott, Foresman and Company. Reprinted by permission.)*

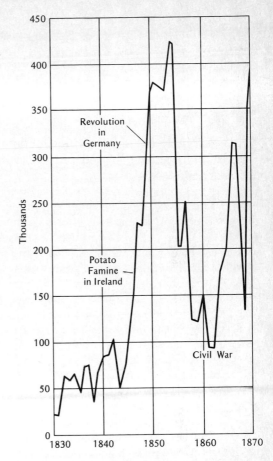

Irish) and Catholics in Philadelphia in 1844 left at least sixteen dead, hundreds injured, and two Catholic churches as well as thirty other buildings destroyed. Increased immigration exacerbated these tensions. Seventeen people were killed and fifty wounded in an 1854 election-day clash between Protestant gangs and Catholic Democrats in Baltimore; an election riot the same year killed ten in St. Louis; a similar combat between natives and Irish immigrants in Louisville in 1855 left twenty-two dead.

Election-day riots were one outcome of nativism's having entered the realm of politics. In 1843 and 1844, so-called American parties had contested local elections in New York and Philadelphia. Several secret fraternal organizations of a nativist hue had been founded in the 1840s. One of these was the Order of the Star Spangled Banner, organized in New York in 1849. When questioned about this order, members replied, "I know nothing." By 1854 the "Know-Nothings" had achieved national prominence and had an estimated membership of a million. Their main goal was to restrain the growing political power of immigrants. Several states allowed foreign-born men to vote even before they were naturalized; in other states, the short five-year wait for naturalization meant that by the early 1850s the heavy immigration of the late 1840s was showing up on the voting rolls. Angry nativists charged that Democratic machines in several cities were illegally enrolling alien voters prior to naturalization—

and there was much truth in the charge. In Boston, the number of foreign-born voters increased by 200 percent from 1850 to 1855 while the number of native-born voters increased by only 14 percent. To counter this development, the Know-Nothings went into politics themselves, organizing under the American party name. They proposed to lengthen the naturalization period from five to fourteen years—or even twenty-one years; to permit only citizens to vote; and to restrict officeholding to native-born citizens.

The temperance and education issues became linked to nativism (see pages 15 to 18). Maine's passage of a law banning the manufacture and sale of liquor set off a "Maine law" crusade that produced similar statutes in several other states during the 1850s. Many Irish and German Americans considered these laws an attack on their cultural autonomy. At the same time, a drive by Catholic leaders in some states to end the reading of the King James Bible in public schools and to secure tax support for parochial schools aroused fears of a Roman threat to American institutions. This "despotic faith," charged one nativist, intended to "substitute the mitre for our liberty cap, and blend the crozier with the stars and stripes." Since Romanism was "diametrically opposed to the genius of American republicanism," the election of "true Americans" was necessary to "guarantee the three vital principles of Republican Government—*Spiritual Freedom, Free Bible, and Free Schools.*"[16]

The Know-Nothings capitalized on this nativist ferment in the 1854 state and local elections. Old-line party leaders were dumbfounded by what they described as a "hurricane," a "tornado," "a freak of political insanity." A baffled Pennsylvania Democrat declared that "nearly everybody appears to have gone altogether deranged on Nativism here." A despairing Whig leader in New York confessed that "the new questions have destroyed everything like party discipline, and many staunch old Whigs are floating off they don't know where."[17] The Know-Nothing hurricane swept away the old parties in Massachusetts, winning 63 percent of the vote and electing all the state officers, all the congressmen, and all but two members of the legislature. The new party polled more than 40 percent of the vote in Pennsylvania and 25 percent in New York. The next year it won control of three more New England states, made further gains in the Mid-Atlantic states, and moved southward to carry Maryland, Kentucky, and Texas, and to become the main rival of the Democrats in several other Southern states.

In the border states and in the South, Know-Nothings recruited former Whigs looking for a new political home. In the Northeast, they drew voters from both major parties but cut more into Whig than Democratic strength. While some native-born Democrats bolted their party because of resentment at its increasingly immigrant cast, the Whigs, having traditionally attracted the majority of middle-class and skilled working-class Protestants, were most susceptible to nativist appeals. Already crippled by the sectional conflict over slavery, the Whigs suffered a mortal blow in the nativist defections of 1854–1855.

Nativists and Free Soilers maintained an ambivalent relationship. On the one hand, the antislavery movement grew out of the same milieu of evangelical Protestantism as did nativism. The ideology of free-labor capitalism viewed both Catholicism and slavery as symbolic of backward, autocratic, and repressive social systems. "The Catholic press upholds the slave power," noted a Free Soil paper. "These two malign

---

[16]Holt, *Political Crisis of the 1850s,* p. 162.
[17]Ibid., pp. 157–158.

powers have a natural affinity for each other." A Know-Nothing convention in Massachusetts resolved that since "Roman Catholicism and slavery" were both "founded and supported on the basis of ignorance and tyranny . . . there can exist no real hostility to Roman Catholicism which does not [also] embrace slavery."[18] Many Free Soilers voted for Know-Nothing candidates in 1854. And in some states, the "anti-Nebraska" parties that sprang up in reaction to the Kansas-Nebraska Act entered into coalitions with nativist parties. Most of the congressmen elected on antislavery tickets in the 1854 elections also received some degree of nativist support, and vice versa.

On the other hand most abolitionists, Free Soil leaders, and antislavery Whigs denounced nativism both as a form of bigotry and as a red herring that distracted attention from the main goal of restricting slavery. "Neither the Pope nor the foreigners ever can govern the country or endanger its liberties," said one Republican, "but the slave-breeders and slavetraders do govern it." The editor of the Free Soil *National Era* (the newspaper in which *Uncle Tom's Cabin* was first serialized) described the Know-Nothings as a "detestable organization . . . as repugnant to the doctrine of equal rights, as Slavery. . . . You have no more right to disfranchise your brother man, seeking a home in this country, than you have to disfranchise your colored neighbor."[19] In New York, William H. Seward had been fighting nativists for a decade or more. And from the Illinois prairie came some pertinent words from an antislavery Whig who was soon to join the Republican party. "I am not a Know-Nothing," said Abraham Lincoln.

> How can any one who abhors the oppression of negroes, be in favor of degrading classes of white people? Our progress in degeneracy appears to me to be pretty rapid. As a nation, we began by declaring that *"all men are created equal."* We now practically read it "all men are created equal, *except negroes."* When the Know-Nothings get control, it will read "all men are created equal, except negroes, *and foreigners, and catholics."* When it comes to this I should prefer emigrating to some country where they make no pretense of loving liberty—to Russia, for instance, where despotism can be taken pure, and without the base alloy of hypocrisy.[20]

For reasons to be narrated in the next chapter, the political power of the Know-Nothings in the North collapsed in 1856. By that year the American party was mainly a Southern party, a way station for Southern Whigs who did not yet know where else to go. But while it lasted, the Know-Nothing phenomenon had wrenched the normal patterns of politics in the Northeast completely out of shape. It gave the *coup de grâce* to the Whig party. In the long run, however, the Kansas-Nebraska Act proved to be more important than nativism in producing a fundamental political realignment, for it gave birth to an antislavery party that soon became the dominant political force in the North.

[18]Eric Foner, *Free Soil, Free Labor, Free Men* (New York, 1970), p. 231; Ray Allen Billington, *The Protestant Crusade 1800-1860: A Study of the Origins of American Nativism* (New York, 1938), p. 425.

[19]Foner, *Free Soil,* p. 234; Richard H. Sewell, *Ballots for Freedom: Antislavery Politics in the United States 1837-1860* (New York, 1976), p. 268.

[20]Lincoln to Joshua Speed, August 24, 1855, in Roy P. Basler (ed.), *The Collected Works of Abraham Lincoln,* 9 vols. (New Brunswick, N.J., 1953-1955), II, 323.

SIX

Kansas and the Rise of
the Republican Party

We are playing for a mighty stake; if we win we carry slavery to the Pacific Ocean, if we fail we lose Missouri, Arkansas, and Texas and all the territories; the game must be played boldly.

—David R. Atchison, senator from Missouri, 1854

★ *The Kansas-Nebraska Act*

On January 4, 1854, Senator Stephen A. Douglas, chairman of the Committee on Territories, reported a bill to organize the area west and northwest of Missouri as Nebraska territory. This action set off a new and fateful controversy over slavery in the territories.

The origins of the Nebraska bill stretched back nearly a decade. Land-hungry pioneers pressed for territorial organization to extinguish Indian titles and to open the fertile acres for settlement. Interests supporting a railroad from the Midwest to California likewise clamored for establishment of a territory, to facilitate surveys and the acquisition of a right of way. In February 1853 the House passed a territorial bill. Since Nebraska was north of 36°30′, the Missouri Compromise banned slavery there. The Southern faction in the Senate therefore killed the bill. Missourians were particularly sensitive on this matter, for "if Nebraska be made a free Territory," explained a St. Louis newspaper, "then will Missouri be surrounded on three sides by free territory, where there will always be men and means to assist in the escape of our slaves. . . . This species of property would become insecure, if not valueless in Missouri." A meeting of Missouri slaveholders resolved: "If the Territory shall be opened to settlement, we pledge ourselves to each other to extend the institutions of Missouri over the Territory at whatever sacrifice of blood or treasure." Missouri's Senator David Atchison vowed that he would see Nebraska "sink in hell" before it became a free territory.[1]

Atchison had the power to make his threat good. As president pro tem of the Senate, he was next in line for the presidency, the vice president having died in 1853.

---

[1] Allan Nevins, *Ordeal of the Union*, 2 vols. (New York, 1947), II, 92-93.

Atchison boarded at a house on F Street in Washington with a trio of other powerful Southern senators: James M. Mason and Robert M. T. Hunter of Virginia and Andrew P. Butler of South Carolina, chairmen respectively of the Foreign Relations, Finance, and Judiciary committees. This "F Street Mess," as they called themselves, exerted potent pressure for repeal of the Missouri Compromise as a prerequisite for the organization of Nebraska.

Recognizing the potential for a Northern backlash if the ban on slavery north of 36°30' was repealed, Stephen Douglas initially tried to circumvent this pressure by equivocation. Contemporaries and historians have ascribed various motives to Douglas in this matter: sympathy for the expansion of slavery, or at least indifference toward its expansion; an eagerness to win Southern support for the Democratic presidential nomination in 1856; a desire to promote the building of a trans-continental railroad with its eastern terminus in his own state of Illinois. Whatever the weight of these factors, Douglas's chief motive probably grew out of his belief in Manifest Destiny. He wanted to organize Nebraska territory in order to speed Ameri-can westward expansion. To prevent further delay, he hoped to bypass the trou-blesome slavery question. His original version of the Nebraska bill in 1854 merely copied the language of the 1850 Utah and New Mexico bills. Douglas's draft specified that when admitted as a state, Nebraska would come in "with or without slavery as its constitution may prescribe." This was not good enough for the Southerners, how-ever, because by banning slavery during the territorial stage, the Missouri Compro-mise would guarantee a free state. So Douglas tried another tactic. Discovering that a "clerical error" had omitted a key section of the bill, he added it: "All questions pertaining to slavery in the Territories, and in the new States to be formed therefrom, are to be left to the people residing therein, through their appropriate representa-tives." This was popular sovereignty, which Douglas had championed since 1848. Although it was an implied repeal of the Missouri Compromise, it still did not go far enough for Southern senators.

At this point a Whig senator from Kentucky, eager to rehabilitate his party's Southern rights image, introduced an amendment explicitly repealing the part of the Missouri Compromise that prohibited slavery north of 36°30'. Douglas at first resisted this amendment, which he knew would provoke outrage in the North. But after a private conference with the Kentucky senator, Douglas reportedly capitulated with the words: "By God, Sir, you are right. I will incorporate it in my bill, though I know it will raise a hell of a storm."[2]

Douglas and a delegation of Southern senators persuaded a reluctant but weak-willed President Pierce to endorse repeal, thereby making it a Democratic party measure with the lever of patronage to prod reluctant Northern Democrats into line. When Douglas introduced his revised bill on January 23, it contained an additional feature dividing the territory in two: Kansas immediately to the west of Missouri, and Nebraska to the north of Kansas. Observers interpreted this as marking out Kansas for slavery and Nebraska for freedom. The question of *when* the inhabitants of these territories would be able to decide on slavery—at the time of the first territorial legislature, as Northern Democrats believed, or not until statehood, as Southerners insisted—was deliberately left unresolved, to preserve the precarious intersectional Democratic support for the measure.

Douglas's action certainly did raise a hell of a storm. The first thunderclap was

2David M. Potter, *The Impending Crisis 1848-1861* (New York, 1976), p. 160.

LIBRARY OF CONGRESS

STEPHEN A. DOUGLAS. One of the most talented men in public life, the 5-foot, 4-inch Douglas was called "the Little Giant." Combative in his public style, he was skilled at behind-the-scenes political compromise. He attained national leadership of the Democratic party by the mid-1850s, but his ambition for the presidency was thwarted by Southern opposition and by his fellow Illinoisian Abraham Lincoln. Douglas was a hard drinker as well as a hard worker; the combination killed him at the age of forty-eight in 1861.

an *Appeal of the Independent Democrats*[3] written by Salmon P. Chase and Joshua Giddings, signed by the leading Free Soilers in Congress, and published in the *National Era* on January 24. The *Appeal* arraigned the Kansas-Nebraska bill as "a gross violation of a sacred pledge" (the Missouri Compromise); as a "criminal betrayal of precious rights; as part and parcel of an atrocious plot to exclude from the vast unoccupied region immigrants from the Old World and free laborers from our own States, and convert it into a dreary region of despotism, inhabited by masters and slaves."[4] This became the Free Soil theme in the bitter congressional debates that followed and in hundreds of protest rallies held throughout the North.

With energy and skill, Douglas piloted the Kansas-Nebraska bill through the Senate. He maintained that the Compromise of 1850, by introducing popular sovereignty in territory north of 36°30′, had implicitly repealed the Missouri Compromise. Although this was a specious argument—the 1850 legislation applied only to territory acquired from Mexico, not to the Louisiana Purchase, and no one had then believed that this legislation affected the Missouri Compromise—it was to become Southern

---

[3]Something of a misnomer, since nearly all the signers were former Whigs.
[4]Nevins, *Ordeal*, II, 112.

and Democratic orthodoxy. Douglas also insisted—as he had in 1850—that Nature would prevent slavery from gaining a foothold in the new territory. This was questionable, for the eastern third of present-day Kansas possesses about the same climate and soil conditions as the Missouri River basin in Missouri, where most of that state's slaves resided and raised hemp and tobacco, which could also be grown in Kansas.

The quintessence of the Senate debate was captured in an exchange between George Badger of North Carolina and Benjamin Wade of Ohio. Badger: "If some Southern gentleman wishes to take the . . . old woman who nursed him in childhood, and whom he called 'Mammy' . . . into one of these new Territories for the betterment of the fortunes of his whole family—why, in the name of God, should anybody prevent it?" Wade: "We have not the least objection . . . to the senator's migrating to Kansas and taking his old 'Mammy' along with him. We only insist that he shall not be empowered to sell her after taking her there."[5]

Douglas drove the bill to Senate passage on March 3 by a vote of 37 to 14. Northern Democratic senators voted 14 to 5 for the bill. The struggle in the House was harsher and more prolonged, for Northern Democrats there had to face the voters in November. At one point in the House debate some congressmen drew weapons, and bloodshed was narrowly avoided. The House finally passed the bill on May 22 by a vote of 113 to 100. Northern Democrats divided 44 to 44 on the measure, a sure sign of trouble for the party in the North. In the combined vote of both houses, Southerners provided 61 percent of the aye votes and Northerners 91 percent of the nay votes. It was clearly a Southern victory, a "triumph of Slavery [and] Aristocracy over Liberty and Republicanism," in the bitter words of a Northern newspaper.[6]

But it was an expensive triumph. As Horace Greeley later remarked, the bill created more abolitionists in two months than William Lloyd Garrison and Wendell Phillips had created in twenty years.

★ The Rise of the Republican Party

Throughout the North during the spring and summer of 1854, angry meetings protested the "Nebraska outrage" and organized new political coalitions. In some states Free Soilers took the lead; in others, antislavery Whigs. Anti-Nebraska Democrats in the Northwest and nativists in the Northeast contributed significant strength to these coalitions. The new organizations took various names: Anti-Nebraska; Fusion; People's; Independent. But the name that caught on was Republican, which linked the struggle of 1854 with the country's first battle for freedom in 1776. Many towns later claimed credit for having held the first "Republican" meeting. The honor seems to belong to Ripon, Wisconsin, where an anti-Nebraska rally in the Congregational church on February 28, 1854, adopted the name Republican. A meeting of about thirty antislavery congressmen in Washington on May 9 suggested that the anti-Nebraska coalition appropriate this name. A state convention in Michigan on July 6 officially chose the name Republican for the state party.

Several other state organizations also adopted the name in 1854. In some states,

---

[5]James Ford Rhodes, *History of the United States from the Compromise of 1850 . . .* , 7 vols. (New York, 1893–1906), I, 452–453.

[6]James A. Rawley, *Race and Politics: "Bleeding Kansas" and the Coming of the Civil War* (Philadelphia, 1969), p. 36.

however, Whig leaders refused to give up their old allegiance and still hoped to turn their party into the vehicle of the Northern political revolution. William Seward's Whigs fought the 1854 campaign under their own name in New York. In Illinois, Abraham Lincoln stayed with the Whig party. But the Whigs faced two handicaps in their efforts to control the anti-Nebraska movement: in some states the conservative, "cotton" wing of the party wanted no part of a coalition with Free Soilers and bolting Democrats; in others, the latter groups refused to subsume themselves under the name of Whig. Although former Whigs would eventually become the dominant element in the Republican party, they would lose their identity as Whigs in the process. By the end of 1855 the Whig party had quietly expired.

Under whatever name, the anti-Nebraska parties reaped rewards from the political realignment of 1854. The elections that fall were a disaster for the Democrats. Perhaps as many as a quarter of the Northern Democratic voters deserted their party. A startling sixty-six of the ninety-one free-state Democratic incumbents went down to defeat in the congressional elections. Only seven of the forty-four representatives who had voted for the Kansas-Nebraska bill won reelection. Having carried all but two Northern states in 1852, the Democrats lost all but two in 1854. As a result, the party became even more a Southern party. In the next Congress, Southern Democrats would outnumber their Northern colleagues by two to one. With the exception of the abnormal years of the Civil War and Reconstruction, Northern Democrats did not again reach parity with their Southern colleagues in Congress until 1930.

The new Republican party was the chief beneficiary of the Democratic disaster. But this was not immediately apparent. Not all anti-Nebraska men were yet Republicans. In several states the Know-Nothings won more votes than the Republicans. But in 1855–1856, the latter scored a major coup by outmaneuvering the Know-Nothings to gain most of their antislavery adherents. Some antislavery men who had supported the Know-Nothings in 1854, especially in Massachusetts, had done so with the intention of taking over the movement and converting it into a new antislavery party. A meeting of the National Council of the American party in June 1855 gave them a chance to take the first step in that direction. Delegates from twelve free states walked out after the meeting adopted resolutions endorsing the Kansas-Nebraska Act. In February 1856, a second Northern bolt took place when another American party convention voted down a resolution calling for repeal of the Kansas-Nebraska Act.

Meanwhile in the winter of 1855–1856, a protracted struggle over the election of a Speaker of the House further strengthened the Republicans at the expense of the Know-Nothings. About two-thirds of the one hundred or so anti-Nebraska congressmen elected in 1854 now classified themselves as Republicans, though some of these had been elected with Know-Nothing support. The Republican caucus nominated Nathaniel P. Banks of Massachusetts for Speaker. Banks, formerly a Know-Nothing, was now a Republican. Since neither the Republicans nor the Democrats had a majority in the House, the Know-Nothings held the balance of power and prevented either party from winning a majority. Day after day, week after week, the balloting dragged on. Finally the House changed its rules to allow election of a Speaker by a plurality. Banks thereupon won on the 133rd ballot with 103 votes. About 30 of these votes came from Northern Know-Nothings, who thereby declared themselves Republicans. This marriage was consummated in June 1856 when the "North Americans" endorsed the Republican presidential nominee, John C. Frémont. For them, slavery had proved to be a more potent negative image than immigration. The Republicans thereby absorbed most Northern nativists into their ranks.

In the process, Republicanism took on some of the cultural baggage of nativism. The Republicans became the party of reformist, antislavery Protestantism. They also became the party of dynamic, innovative capitalism, whose ideology of modernization attracted mainly the native-born Yankees of the upper North. A map of Republican strength in the 1856 presidential election (see page 100) is remarkably congruent with a map of New England settlement patterns, of antislavery and temperance societies, of a high density of public schools and literacy, and of areas that opposed black laws and favored black suffrage but contained few if any black residents. Although the Republicans officially spurned nativism, many party members inherited a hostile view of slavery and Catholicism as dual manifestations of repression, ignorance, and backwardness.

Southerners and Catholics returned the hostility. Their epithets of "Black Republicans," "Yankees," and the "Puritan party" summed up in turn a host of negative symbols associated with the Republicans: abolitionism and racial equality, material acquisitiveness and sharp practice, hypocrisy, bigotry, and an offensive eagerness to reform other people's morals or to interfere with their property. The Butternuts of the southern Midwest (see pages 22 to 24) shared these anti-Republican attitudes. Most of the Democrats who left their party after Kansas-Nebraska and eventually became Republicans lived in the upper North; the Butternuts remained loyal Democrats and along with Catholics and Southerners continued to form the backbone of the party.

★ Bleeding Kansas

The Republicans took over the Free Soil commitment to the principle of the Wilmot Proviso as their central tenet: no slavery in the territories, no more slave states. When the antislavery forces lost the congressional battle for a free Kansas, they vowed to carry the struggle to the territory itself. "Since there is no escaping your challenge," Senator Seward told his Southern colleagues, "I accept it in behalf of the cause of freedom. We will engage in competition for the virgin soil of Kansas, and God give the victory to the side which is stronger in numbers as it is in right." On the other side, Senator Atchison of Missouri wrote: "We are playing for a mighty stake; if we win we carry slavery to the Pacific Ocean, if we fail we lose Missouri, Arkansas, and Texas and all the territories; the game must be played boldly."[7]

And boldly did he play. Although the Free Soil forces organized first, forming the New England Emigrant Aid Company in the summer of 1854 to finance settlements in Kansas, it was Atchison's people who did the first settling. Most of the early settlers in Kansas came from Missouri. Some brought their slaves with them. Most of the Free Soil settlers came from Midwestern states. Only a sprinkling of New Englanders migrated to Kansas, but the publicity surrounding the New England Emigrant Aid Company provoked proslavery partisans to portray a Yankee conspiracy to abolitionize the West. Much of the subsequent conflict between Free Soil and proslavery settlers was of the sort typical in frontier communities: clashes over land claims or town sites or water rights, and the inevitable violence of settlements without established institutions of law and order. But because Kansas was the national cockpit of the slavery question, all conflicts became polarized around this issue.

[7]Seward quoted in *Congressional Globe*, 33rd Cong., 1st sess. (1854), Appendix, 769; Atchison quoted in Rawley, *Race and Politics*, p. 81.

In the fall of 1854, Andrew Reeder, a Pennsylvania Democrat, arrived in Kansas to begin his duties as territorial governor. His first task was to supervise an election for the territory's delegate to Congress. The proslavery men were determined to make this initial test of popular sovereignty come out in their favor. On election day, 1,700 armed Missourians crossed the border to vote in Kansas. These "border ruffians," as the antislavery press dubbed them, swelled the overwhelming majority that sent a proslavery delegate to Washington.

The border ruffians repeated their tactics in the election of a territorial legislature in March 1855. This time, four or five thousand of them swarmed across the border. Atchison returned home from the Senate to lead the invasion. "There are eleven hundred coming over from Platte County to vote," he told his followers, "and if that ain't enough we can send five thousand—enough to kill every God-damned abolitionist in the Territory."[8] Although by this time bona fide settlers from free states were in the majority, the proslavery voters cast 5,247 ballots, the Free Soilers 791. A congressional investigation later concluded that 4,968 of the proslavery votes were fraudulent. But Governor Reeder, intimidated by the Missourians, refused to order a new election. Although urged to take corrective action, President Pierce did nothing. The Southern press applauded. "Missourians have nobly defended *our* rights," declared an Alabama newspaper.[9] The legislature (or "bogus legislature," as antislavery men called it) passed a draconian slave code. It restricted officeholding to avowed proslavery men. Anyone who questioned the legality of slavery in Kansas could be imprisoned, and anyone who advocated a slave rebellion or aided the escape of fugitive slaves could be put to death.

Outraged free-state settlers began to organize in self-defense. They turned the town of Lawrence into an antislavery stronghold and began arming themselves with "Beecher's Bibles" (so called because antislavery clergyman Henry Ward Beecher had said that Sharps rifles would do more than Bibles just then to enforce morality in Kansas). They organized a free-state party, held an election for a constitutional convention (boycotted by the proslavery voters), met in Topeka to draw up a constitution prohibiting slavery, and established their own legislature in the winter of 1855–1856. To prove that they were not the "abolitionist fanatics" portrayed by the proslavery press, the free-staters adopted an ordinance banning the entry of free blacks as well as of slaves.[10]

Kansas now had two territorial governments—one legal but fraudulent, the other illegal but representing a majority of settlers. In Washington, the President and the Democratic-controlled Senate recognized the former, while the Republican-organized House favored the latter. When Governor Reeder declared his sympathy with the free-staters, Pierce replaced him with a solid proslavery man, Wilson Shannon. The Republican party benefited from Northern anger at the border ruffians, whose buccaneering practices the antislavery press played up for all they were worth.

Meanwhile in Kansas the sporadic violence took more organized form. In November 1855, each side mobilized several hundred armed men along the Wakarusa River.

---

[8]William E. Gienapp, *The Origins of the Republican Party 1852–1856* (New York, 1987), p. 170.
[9]Rawley, *Race and Politics,* p. 89.
[10]Of the thirty-seven delegates who signed the Topeka constitution, thirteen had been born in the South and twenty-one were former Democrats. These were the elements that supported black exclusion. In the referendum on this provision, the New England settlers voted against it but were overwhelmed by the more numerous Midwesterners.

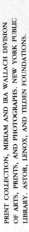

SOUTHERN CHIVALRY — ARGUMENT VERSUS CLUB'S.

SOUTHERN CHIVALRY: ARGUMENT VERSUS CLUBS.
This Northern cartoon depicts Preston Brooks's assault on Senator Charles Sumner on May 22, 1856. The pen in Sumner's hand symbolizes the words of "truth," to which the only Southern response was the brutality of the cane wielded as a club. Note other Southern senators in the background smiling on the scene or preventing Northern senators from coming to Sumner's aid. Reaction to this incident intensified sectional polarization.

The Missourians prepared to attack Lawrence, but at the last minute Governor Shannon persuaded them to desist. This "Wakarusa War" amounted to nothing more than a few skirmishes. The harsh winter that followed kept everyone indoors for several months. But with the coming of spring, violence burst forth once again. On May 21 an army of seven hundred proslavery men rode into Lawrence, destroyed the offices of two newspapers and threw their presses into the river, burned down the hotel and the house of the free-state "governor," and pillaged the stores.

Even before news of this affair reached the East, acts of verbal and physical violence in Washington had inflamed sectional passions. On May 19 and 20, Charles Sumner of Massachusetts delivered a long philippic in the Senate entitled "The Crime Against Kansas." Given to florid rhetoric and provocative assertions of superior Northern morality, Sumner lashed the South with sexual metaphors about the "rape" of Kansas. Included in his speech were several abusive references to Senator Andrew Butler of South Carolina. Two days later Butler's cousin, Representative Preston Brooks, entered the Senate chamber after adjournment, walked over to Sumner's desk, and began beating him over the head with a cane. His legs trapped under the desk, Sumner was unable to defend himself. Trying to stand up, he finally wrenched the bolted desk from the floor, stumbled forward and collapsed, while the enraged Brooks continued to hit him until pulled away by other congressmen who had rushed to the scene. Suffering from shock as well as from his injuries, Sumner did not return to the Senate for three years. But the Massachusetts legislature reelected him in 1857 and kept his seat vacant as a silent but eloquent symbol of martyrdom to the "barbarism" of slavery.

Brooks's act provoked wrath in the North. "Bleeding Sumner" along with "Bleeding Kansas" became potent Republican rallying cries. Southern moderates deplored Brooks's caning of Sumner. But their voices were decidedly in the minority. "Every Southern man is delighted," Brooks wrote the day after the event. "The fragments of the stick are begged for as sacred relics."[11] The *Richmond Whig* expressed the opinion of many Southern newspapers when it endorsed "this elegant and effectual caning. . . . The only regret we feel is that Mr. Brooks did not employ a horsewhip or cowhide upon his slanderous back instead of a cane." A solid Southern vote against the expulsion of Brooks by the House prevented the necessary two-thirds majority. Brooks resigned anyway, won unanimous reelection in his district, and returned triumphantly to Washington. While Brooks was in South Carolina, the mayor of Columbia gave him a fine new hickory cane with a gold head. From all over the South Brooks received canes; one presented by the city of Charleston bore the inscription "Hit Him Again"; his own constituents gave him one inscribed "Use Knock-Down Arguments."[12]

Thus far, Southerners had committed most of the violence in the Kansas controversy. But out in Kansas was a man who believed in an eye for an eye. John Brown looked and acted like an Old Testament prophet. A Connecticut-born abolitionist who had failed in most of his business and farming enterprises, Brown had drifted west and in 1855 settled in Kansas with several of his sons. He commanded a free-state military company that participated in the Wakarusa War. In May 1856, this company was on its way to defend Lawrence when word reached it that the town had already been sacked. When he heard this news Brown was seized with "frenzy." It was time to "fight fire with fire," he said, to "strike terror in the hearts of the proslavery people." When the company learned the next day about the caning of Sumner, Brown "went crazy—*crazy*," according to witnesses. "It seemed to be the finishing, decisive touch."[13] Brown led a party containing four of his sons and two other men on a nighttime raid along Pottawatomie Creek. They seized five proslavery settlers from their cabins and murdered them in cold blood by splitting their skulls with broadswords.

This butchery launched full-scale guerrilla war in Kansas. Although shocked antislavery people in the East denied—or chose not to believe—the truth about these killings,[14] most Kansans knew who had done them. For the next four months, hit-and-run attacks by both sides raged in Kansas and were exaggerated by the national press into full-scale battles. Several newspapers had a standing headline for news from Kansas: "Progress of the Civil War." John Brown participated in these skirmishes, and one of his sons was killed. About two hundred other men died in the Kansas fighting during 1856. In September, President Pierce finally replaced the ineffective Governor Shannon with John Geary, a tough but fair-minded Pennsylvanian who had won his spurs as a captain in the Mexican War and as San Francisco's first mayor. Combining persuasion with a skillful deployment of federal troops, Geary imposed a truce on the two sides and brought an uneasy peace to Kansas in the fall of 1856. By this time the

---

[11]Robert L. Meriwether (ed.), "Preston S. Brooks on the Caning of Charles Sumner," *The South Carolina Historical and Genealogical Magazine*, 52 (January 1951), 3.

[12]Nevins, *Ordeal*, II, 446–447; John Hope Franklin, *The Militant South 1800–1861* (Cambridge, Mass., 1956), pp. 54–55.

[13]Stephen B. Oates, *To Purge This Land With Blood: A Biography of John Brown* (New York, 1970), pp. 128–129, 133.

[14]Proof of Brown's responsibility did not come out until years later.

larger question of which Kansas was a part—slavery in the territories—was the focus of the presidential election.

★ The Election of 1856

The Republicans were the first entirely sectional major party in American history. Although a few delegates from four upper-South states attended the national convention, the party had no hope of carrying a single county in the slave states. The Republican platform called for a free Kansas, denounced Democratic efforts to acquire Cuba, and affirmed the duty of Congress "to prohibit in the Territories those twin relics of barbarism—Polygamy, and Slavery." Although four-fifths of the platform dealt with slavery, the party also endorsed government aid for the construction of a transcontinental railroad and for rivers and harbors improvements—measures that had been blocked by Southern congressmen or vetoed by President Pierce.

By nominating John C. Frémont—whose father was a Catholic and who had himself been married by a Catholic priest—the Republicans dismayed some of their nativist supporters. But Frémont's nomination was a calculated gamble to attract ex-Democrats. The established Republican leaders, Seward and Chase, were radicals whose notoriety might offend timid voters. The dashing young Frémont, by contrast, had little political experience but had won popularity by his explorations in the West and his role in the California Bear Flag Revolt against Mexican rule.[15]

"Availability" also dictated the Democratic nomination of James Buchanan. The incumbent, Pierce, and the party's most prominent leader, Douglas, were too closely identified with the Kansas-Nebraska Act. Buchanan had the good fortune to have been out of the country as minister to Britain during the previous three years. After sixteen deadlocked ballots at the Democratic convention, Douglas withdrew in favor of Buchanan. The platform reiterated all the Jeffersonian-Jacksonian states' rights planks, coming out against any government role in the economy or in social reform. It also reaffirmed the Fugitive Slave Law, denounced the Republicans as abolitionists in disguise, and endorsed popular sovereignty in the territories.

What was left of the American party nominated Millard Fillmore, who also received the endorsement of the remnant of Whigs who vainly hoped to revive their moribund party. The 1856 contest was really two elections: between Buchanan and Fillmore in the South, and between Buchanan and Frémont in the North. Although Fillmore ran well in the upper South and in former Whig strongholds of the lower South, he carried only Maryland. Frémont won the upper North—Wisconsin, Michigan, all of New England, and New York (where heavy upstate majorities outweighed a dismal showing in New York City). Large pluralities in the "Yankee" areas of Ohio and Iowa gave the Republicans these states also. But the crucial struggle took place in the lower North—New Jersey, Pennsylvania, Indiana, and Illinois. Whoever could

[15]When war broke out between Mexico and the United States in 1846, a group of American settlers in California's Sacramento Valley, aided by Captain Frémont of the U.S. Topographical Corps who happened to be there mapping the country, captured the headquarters of the Mexican commandant at Sonoma. They raised a flag bearing a grizzly bear facing a red star and proclaimed the independent Bear Flag Republic. Three weeks later, American troops entered California and the joyful settlers lowered their bear flag in favor of the stars and stripes.

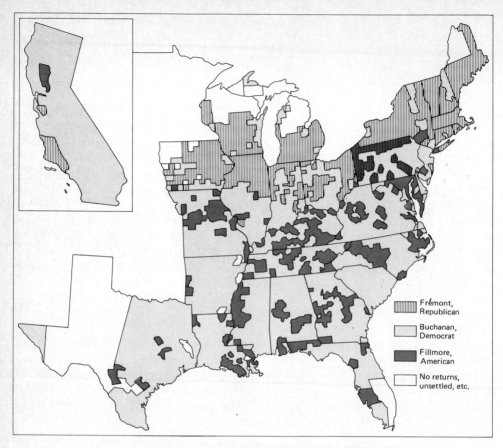

**COUNTIES CARRIED BY CANDIDATES
IN THE 1856 PRESIDENTIAL ELECTION**

carry Pennsylvania plus any one of the others would be elected. Both sides concentrated most of their efforts in these states.

On the Republican side the campaign evoked a moral fervor unprecedented in American politics. "The process now going on in the politics of the United States," wrote a Republican journalist, "is a *Revolution.*" Young Republicans organized Wide Awake clubs and marched in huge torchlight parades. They chanted the slogan "Free Soil, Free Labor, Free Men, Frémont." Republican rhetoric presented the election as a struggle between democracy and aristocracy, progress and reaction. "We require for our country a government of the people, instead of a government by an oligarchy; a government maintaining before the world the rights of men rather than the privilege of masters," declared a Republican meeting in Buffalo. "The contest ought not to be considered a *sectional* one but the war of a *class*—the slaveholders—against the laboring people of *all classes.*"[16]

[16]Roy F. Nichols and Philip S. Klein, "Election of 1856," in Arthur M. Schlesinger, Jr., *History of American Presidential Elections,* 4 vols. (New York, 1971), II, 1031; Michael F. Holt, *The Political Crisis of the 1850s* (New York, 1978), pp. 196-197.

Southern rhetoric seemed to confirm this Republican argument. "The great evil of Northern *free* society is that it is burdened with a *servile class of mechanics and laborers,* unfit for self-government," declared a South Carolina newspaper. A Virginia editor explained that "we have got to hating everything with the prefix *free,* from free negroes up and down the whole catalogue—*free farms, free labor, free society, free will, free thinking, free children, and free schools*—all belonging to the same brood of damnable *isms.*"[17]

Democrats exploited two powerful issues in the lower North—racism and the fear of disunion. "The Black Republicans," a Democratic newspaper informed voters, intended to "turn loose . . . millions of negroes, to elbow you in the workshops, and compete with you in the fields of honest labor." The election would show whether the Northern people preferred "niggers . . . [and] a false, wretched, miserable and resultless philanthropy, to their own race and color and the Union and all its countless blessings." With Southern fire-eaters and even some moderates uttering threats of secession if Frémont won, Buchanan benefited from apprehensions about the future of the Union. After the Republicans carried Maine with 65 percent of the vote in that state's September balloting, Governor Henry A. Wise of Virginia put his militia on alert and wrote that "if Frémont is elected there will be a revolution."[18] Such statements caused many Northern conservatives of Whig background to rally behind Buchanan as the only alternative to disaster. The pacification of Kansas in October also helped the Democrats by robbing the Republicans of their best issue.

Buchanan carried all four of the crucial lower-North states (plus California) and was therefore elected. He won 45 percent of the popular vote nationwide—41 percent in the free states and 56 percent in the slave states. Fillmore won 44 percent of the popular vote in the South but only 13 percent in the North—though this was enough to deny Frémont the lower North. Buchanan carried fourteen of the fifteen slave states but only five of the sixteen free states. He was the first President since 1828 who failed to win a majority in both sections. His election was a Southern victory. But like earlier Southern victories—the annexation of Texas, the Mexican War, and the Kansas-Nebraska Act—it ultimately strengthened the antislavery cause in the North. This paradoxical process was carried a step further by an event that occurred two days after Buchanan's inauguration—the announcement of the Supreme Court's decision in the Dred Scott case.

[17]Nevins, *Ordeal,* II, 498.
[18]Stephen E. Maizlish, *The Triumph of Sectionalism: The Transformation of Ohio Politics, 1844-1856* (Kent, 1983), p. 232; Rawley, *Race and Politics,* p. 162; Roy F. Nichols, *The Disruption of American Democracy* (New York, 1948), p. 44.

SEVEN

The Deepening Crisis, 1857-1859

*Let us discard all this quibbling about this man and the other man, this race and
. . . the other race being inferior . . . and unite as one people throughout this land,
until we once more stand up declaring that all men are created equal.*
—Abraham Lincoln, 1858

★ The Dred Scott Decision

The men who fashioned the Compromise of 1850 hoped that their handiwork would
lay to rest the issue of slavery in the territories. So did proponents of the Kansas-
Nebraska Act. But both measures left unresolved the question of whether a territorial
legislature could prohibit slavery before the territory achieved statehood. And both
had backfired by stirring up rather than calming Northern passions. In 1857 the Dred
Scott decision followed the same pattern. The Supreme Court intended to settle once
and for all the legal status of slavery in the territories. Instead, it inflamed the embers
of sectionalism.

The case followed a long and complex route to the Supreme Court. Dred Scott
was a Missouri slave whose owner, an army surgeon, had taken him to Illinois and to
Wisconsin territory when stationed at army posts there in the 1830s. In 1846, after the
owner's death, Scott sued the heirs for his freedom, on the grounds that residence in a
free state and in a territory made free by the Missouri Compromise had made him a
free man. Scott first lost and then won his suit in a Missouri circuit court, only to see
the state's supreme court overturn the lower courts and deny him freedom in 1852.
The legal owner having meanwhile moved to New York, Scott took his case to the
federal circuit court, under the constitutional clause that allows a citizen of one state
to sue a citizen of another in the federal courts. Scott again lost his bid for freedom
when the federal court upheld the Missouri Supreme Court in 1854, whereupon
Scott's lawyers appealed to the U.S. Supreme Court. The appeal was argued in the
spring of 1856 and held over for reargument in the 1856-1857 term.

By this time, the case had acquired a significance far beyond the issue of Scott's freedom.[1] Three important questions came before the Court. (1) Did prolonged residence in a free state or territory make Scott free? (2) As a slave and a black, was Scott a citizen with the right to sue in federal courts? (3) Was the Missouri Compromise, which had prohibited slavery in the portion of Wisconsin territory where Scott resided, a constitutional law? The first of these questions was the least controversial. Precedents existed for upholding the ruling of the Missouri Supreme Court that Scott had been only a "sojourner" in a free state and territory and therefore remained a slave. The U.S. Supreme Court could have evaded the second and third questions by simply affirming the circuit court's decision. Indeed, on February 14, 1857, a majority of the justices decided to do just that, and Justice Samuel Nelson began to write the opinion.

But a few days later the Court reconsidered and decided to issue a comprehensive ruling covering all aspects of the case. What caused this change of mind? A definitive answer is shrouded in the secrecy of the Court's proceedings. But certain things are clear. For eleven years—ever since the Wilmot Proviso—the legal status of slavery in the territories had been the chief issue before the country. This issue had crippled one political party, given birth to another, and threatened to divide a third—the Democrats—over the question of whether slavery could be excluded by a territory's residents prior to statehood. For years, people had hoped for a judicial resolution of this question. The New Mexico and Utah territorial bills of 1850 and the Kansas-Nebraska Act of 1854 included provisions to expedite an appeal to the Supreme Court on the matter. But no case had arisen from these territories. Now came one from another part of the Louisiana Purchase.

During the winter of 1856–1857, Washington was alive with rumors that the Court would seize this opportunity to resolve the issue of whether slavery could legally be excluded from a territory. Confident that the Court would rule in their favor, Southerners were eager for a comprehensive decision. They had good reason for confidence. Five of the justices, including Chief Justice Roger Taney, were Southern Democrats. Two of the four Northern justices were also Democrats, and one of them, Robert Grier of Pennsylvania, was a proslavery partisan with Southern relatives. The temptation to settle the vexed territorial question by "judicial statesmanship" proved too strong. On a motion of Justice James M. Wayne of Georgia, the Court agreed that Taney, speaking for the majority, should write a decision that denied black citizenship and declared unconstitutional the Missouri Compromise's exclusion of slavery from northern territories.

The five Southern justices wanted to win the support of at least one free-state colleague, to avoid the appearance of a sectional decision. Justice John Catron of Tennessee urged President-elect Buchanan to bring pressure on his fellow Pennsylvanian Grier to concur with the majority. Buchanan needed little urging. Sympathetic to the proslavery position and owing his election mainly to Southern voters, Buchanan also hoped for a judicial resolution of the territorial question to prevent it from damaging his administration as it had his predecessor's. The President used his influence with Grier, who decided to go along with the Southern justices. Apprised of the forthcoming ruling, Buchanan made a disingenuous reference to it in his inaugural

---

[1]Scott would obtain his freedom in any event. Three months after the Supreme Court handed down its negative ruling, his owner manumitted him. Scott died a year later.

ROGER TANEY   *DRED SCOTT*

address: "To their decision. in common with all good citizens, I shall cheerfully submit, whatever this may be."[2]

Two days later, on March 6, the Court spoke. It spoke with many voices, for every justice wrote an opinion. This has made it difficult to know precisely what the Court ruled. Taney wrote the 7-to-2 majority decision; but some of the concurring opinions followed different lines of reasoning to arrive at approximately the same points. Taney ruled as follows: (1) Dred Scott was still a slave. (2) As a slave *and* as a black,[3] he was not a citizen because at the time the Constitution was written, blacks "had for more than a century before been regarded as beings of an inferior order . . . so far inferior, that they had no rights which the white man was bound to respect."[4] By a tendentious process of reasoning, Taney concluded that neither these inferior beings nor their descendants in 1857 were citizens and therefore Scott's suit in federal court should have been denied in the first place. (3) Scott's sojourn in Illinois did not free him, for under interstate comity, Missouri law prevailed. (4) His sojourn in Wisconsin territory did not free him, because Congress had no power to exclude slavery from a territory and the exclusion clause of the Missouri Compromise was therefore unconstitutional.

Taney and the concurring justices based their territorial ruling on several principles: the Calhoun idea that the territories were the joint property of the states, not the creation of Congress; the principle that slave property had the same standing as any other property and that a master's slave could no more be excluded from a territory than could a farmer's horse (thus Taney denied the power of a territorial legislature as well as of Congress to exclude slaves); and the due process clause of the Fifth Amendment, which prohibited the federal government from depriving any person of life, liberty, or property without due process of law. Antislavery people, of course, emphasized the word "liberty" in the Fifth Amendment as the basis for banning

[2]Don E. Fehrenbacher, *The Dred Scott Case: Its Significance in American Law and Politics* (New York, 1978), p. 313.

[3]Three of the concurring opinions stated only that slaves were not citizens, without going into the question of whether free blacks, as the descendants of slaves, were also deprived of citizenship.

[4]Fehrenbacher, *Dred Scott Case*, p. 347.

slavery in all jurisdictions of the federal government. But for Taney, property super-seded liberty, and the clause as a whole outweighed Article IV, Section 3, of the Constitution, which gave Congress the "Power to dispose of and make all needful Rules and Regulations respecting the Territory" of the United States. To Republicans, this section empowered Congress to exclude slavery; to a majority of justices, it did not.

Taney's ruling evoked almost universal praise below the Mason-Dixon line. "Southern opinion upon the subject of southern slavery . . . is now the supreme law of the land," exulted the *Augusta* (Georgia) *Constitutionalist.* "Opposition to south-ern opinion upon this subject is now opposite to the Constitution, and morally treason against the Government." Many Northern Democrats were equally jubilant. A party newspaper in Pennsylvania called the decision "the funeral sermon of Black Republicanism. It . . . crushes into nothingness the whole theory upon which their party is founded."[5]

But the decision was not unanimous, and its obvious partisanship robbed it of respect among Republicans. Justice Nelson of New York submitted a separate opinion that merely affirmed the circuit court ruling and refused to comment on the other issues. Justices John McLean of Ohio (a former Whig turned Republican) and Benjamin Curtis of Massachusetts (who still called himself a Whig) submitted dis-senting opinions that upheld the Missouri Compromise, affirmed black citizenship, and declared that Scott should be freed. Curtis's opinion was a powerful indictment of Taney's reasoning on every crucial point. He demonstrated that blacks were legal citizens of several states in 1787 and later, and that by Article IV, Section 2, of the Constitution ("The Citizens of each State shall be entitled to all Privileges and Immunities of Citizens in the several States"), they were entitled to the rights of U.S. citizens. Curtis riddled Taney's circumlocutions concerning the power of Congress in the territories, and stated that the exclusion of slavery was neither deprivation of property nor denial of due process.

Most modern scholars have judged Curtis's dissent to be better law than Taney's majority opinion. The most recent and thorough study of the case demonstrates that Taney was an "intensely partisan" advocate of Southern rights, a "bitter sectionalist" who disliked the North and held Republicans in contempt. His Dred Scott decision was a calculated attempt to destroy the central principle of the Republican party. It was a ruling of "unmitigated partisanship, polemical in spirit though judicial in language, and more like an ultimatum than a formula for sectional accommodation."[6]

This modern appraisal almost echoes contemporary Republican opinions of the decision. "A wicked and false judgment," "an atrocious doctrine," a "willful perver-sion," a "collation of false statements and shallow sophistries," "the greatest crime in the judicial annals of the Republic," were some of the Republican epithets. Abolitionists condemned in particular the ruling against black citizenship, while Republicans concentrated most of their fire on the abrogation of congressional power over slavery in the territories. Republicans also pointed with alarm to the legal implications of the decision for the free states themselves. If Dred Scott's "sojourn" of two years in Illinois did not free him, what was to prevent slaveholders from bringing their slaves into the free states for two years or even longer? If slaves were no different from other property, what right did a state have to legislate against ownership of such

[5]Ibid., pp. 418–419.
[6]Ibid., pp. 3, 234, 311. See also Don E. Fehrenbacher, "Roger B. Taney and the Sectional Crisis," *Journal of Southern History,* 43 (November 1977), 555–566.

property? Abraham Lincoln warned that Taney's Court would probably soon hand down a decision "declaring that the Constitution of the United States does not permit a *state* to exclude slavery from its limits."[7]

Antislavery people insisted that the Dred Scott ruling was not valid law. "The Decision of the Supreme Court is the Moral Assassination of a Race and Cannot be Obeyed," declared the *New York Independent.* The *Chicago Tribune* maintained that no "Free People can respect or will obey a decision so fraught with disastrous consequences to the People and their Liberties."[8] But such assertions brought Republicans into uncomfortable proximity with the civil disobedience theories of Garrisonian abolitionists. Democrats lost no opportunity to nail the Republicans on this point. The Court's decision, they said, was the law of the land. Defiance of the law was treason to the Constitution. To counter this accusation, Republicans seized upon Justice Curtis's contention that Taney's ruling on slavery in the territories was an *obiter dictum*—a comment in passing that had no direct bearing on the case and was therefore not binding. Since Taney had declared that Scott was not a citizen, his case—and thus the question of slavery in the territories—was not properly before the Court, and any opinion concerning it was a mere *dictum* "entitled to as much moral weight," said the *New York Tribune,* as "the judgment of a majority of those congregated in any Washington bar-room."[9]

The *dictum* thesis was a political godsend to the Republicans. It enabled them to repudiate the decision without acquiring the stigma of lawlessness.[10] The legislature of Maine passed a resolution declaring the Dred Scott decision "not binding in law or conscience." Several other legislatures followed suit. Republicans capitalized on Northern hostility to the decision with a pledge to "reconstitute" the Court and obtain a new ruling. "The remedy is . . . the ballot box," said the *Chicago Tribune.* "Let the next President be Republican, and 1860 will mark an era kindred with that of 1776."[11]

The Dred Scott decision confounded all the hopes of its authors. It did not settle the slavery question. Instead of calming sectional rancor, it served to intensify it. It did not weaken the Republican party; rather, by lending credence to Republican charges of a conspiracy to nationalize slavery, it strengthened the party. Nor did it really establish the right of slavery in the territories, for the decision was not self-enforcing. Southerners therefore began to call for a federal slave code to protect slavery in the territories. Finally, the decision did not resolve the Democrats' intraparty division concerning *when* popular sovereignty became operational. Taney's ruling that a territorial legislature, as the creation of Congress, had no more right to exclude slavery than had Congress itself, conflicted with Stephen Douglas's conception of popular sovereignty. Douglas's efforts to reconcile popular sovereignty with the Dred

[7]Charles Warren, *The Supreme Court in United States History,* rev. ed., 2 vols. (Boston, 1926), II, 302–309; Roy P. Basler (ed.), *The Collected Works of Abraham Lincoln,* 9 vols. (New Brunswick, N.J., 1953–1955), II, 467.

[8]*New York Independent* quoted in Fehrenbacher, *Dred Scott Case,* p. 429; *Chicago Tribune,* March 12, 1857.

[9]*New York Tribune,* March 7, 1857.

[10]For half a century the *dictum* thesis prevailed—even among legal scholars. But historians and jurists now recognize that whatever the legal soundness or political wisdom of Taney's decisions, it was not mere *dictum.* All of the questions on which he ruled, except the power of territorial legislatures over slavery, were legal aspects of the case and therefore properly before the Court.

[11]Fehrenbacher, *Dred Scott Case,* p. 432; *Chicago Tribune,* March 19, 1857.

Scott decision occurred against the backdrop of a new flareup over Kansas that forced Douglas into opposing the Buchanan administration and the Southern wing of his party.

★ *The Lecompton Constitution*

While the Supreme Court was pondering the fate of Dred Scott, affairs in Kansas were building toward a new crisis. Although Governor Geary had pacified the territory, the struggle for power continued. The proslavery forces were clearly losing the population battle. Every observer conceded that the free-staters had at least a two-to-one majority of settlers, and the annual spring migration was expected to enlarge it even more. With a boldness born of desperation, the proslavery territorial legislature in February 1857 called a convention to write a constitution and apply for statehood without submitting the constitution to the voters. The legislature enacted a bill that put the preparation of voting lists and the counting of votes for convention delegates in the hands of proslavery officials. Governor Geary vetoed the bill, but the legislature passed it over his veto. Worn out by overwork and the strain of threats on his life, Geary resigned on March 4. He had survived the Mexican War and San Francisco's hell-roaring gold rush days, but Kansas proved too much for him.

President Buchanan appointed a diminutive but tough Mississippian, Robert J. Walker, to replace Geary. Although Walker was determined to be impartial, the whipsaw of Kansas politics soon cut him to pieces also. Territorial officials gerrymandered election districts to give the proslavery counties a majority of convention delegates. Denouncing the whole proceeding as a farce, free-state voters boycotted the election in June. This gave the slave-state faction control of the convention by default. Walker insisted, however, that any constitution they drew up must be submitted to the voters. For this he was denounced and threatened by his former friends in the South. The Buchanan administration at first backed Walker on this question. But events in the fall of 1857 caused Buchanan to cave in to the Southerners who dominated his administration.

The Kansas constitutional convention that met at Lecompton in September drafted a constitution intended to make Kansas a slave state. But while it was doing so, a new election for a territorial legislature took place in October. Assured by Walker that this would be a fair election, the free-state voters took part. The results at first appeared to give the proslavery candidates a narrow victory. But frauds soon came to light. In one district with 30 legitimate voters, a total of 1,601 names had been copied onto the voting rolls from the Cincinnati city directory. Walker threw out 2,800 fraudulent votes, which gave the Free Soilers a substantial majority in the next territorial legislature.

Although Southerners abused Walker for "going behind the returns," their censure constituted an admission that the Free Soilers had a majority in an honest election—one that would ensure the defeat of the Lecompton constitution in a referendum. Since Congress would almost certainly refuse to sanction statehood without a referendum, the leaders of the Lecompton convention worked out an ingenious method to save the constitution and have a referendum too. They prepared a new article that would guarantee slaveholders' rights to retain ownership of the two hundred slaves (and their progeny) then living in the territory but would prohibit future importations of slaves into Kansas. The voters could then ratify the constitution either including this article ("the constitution *without* slavery") or including the original provision, which allowed the future importation of slaves ("the constitution *with* slavery"). These were the only two choices in the referendum.

Republicans denounced this "Lecompton swindle" as a travesty of popular sovereignty. So did Senator Stephen Douglas and many other Northern Democrats. They saw it as a swindle because: (1) it gave voters no opportunity to reject the constitution outright, even though the document contained several controversial features besides the slavery provisions; (2) the constitution "without slavery" was a subterfuge that, by protecting slave property already in the territory, opened the door for future smuggling of additional slaves into the state despite the ban on importation.

Because they considered both the constitution and the convention that framed it illegitimate, Kansas Free Soilers boycotted the referendum on December 21. The constitution "with slavery" therefore won easy ratification by a vote of 6,226 (of which 2,720 were later declared fraudulent) to 569. Meanwhile, the new Free Soil territorial legislature mandated a second referendum on January 4, 1858, in which voters could accept or reject the constitution outright. The slave-state voters boycotted this election, which resulted in a vote of 138 for the constitution with slavery, 24 for the constitution "without slavery," and 10,226 against the constitution.

The Lecompton constitution became the central issue of an acrimonious congressional session in 1857–1858. Douglas declared political war on the administration over the issue, and led the fight in the Senate against admission of Kansas to statehood under the Lecompton constitution. At one point in February 1858, a wild sectional fistfight broke out among thirty congressmen during an all-night debate on Lecompton. Northern state legislatures denounced the constitution; but several Southern legislatures threatened secession unless Congress admitted Kansas as a state under this "duly ratified" document: "Rather than have Kansas refused admission under the Lecompton constitution," said a South Carolinian, "let [the Union] perish in blood and fire."[12] Frightened by these threats and browbeaten by his Southern advisers, Buchanan reneged on his commitment to a referendum on the whole constitution. He now declared that the December 21 election was a legitimate referendum while the January 4 election—which was in fact more representative of Kansas opinion—was not. In his message transmitting the Lecompton constitution to Congress, the President declared that Kansas "is at this moment as much a slave State as Georgia or South Carolina."

Buchanan made Lecompton a test of party loyalty. During a political career of forty years that included service as a congressman, senator, minister to Russia and to Britain, and secretary of state, the sixty-seven-year-old bachelor President had come to love the Democratic party above all else on earth and to regard faithfulness to its policies as the highest virtue. Buchanan decided to use all of the administration's resources of patronage and power to bring wavering Democratic senators and representatives into line on Lecompton. Despite Douglas's bitter opposition, the Lecompton constitution was accepted by the Senate, where the greater Southern strength plus the proslavery inclinations of several Northern Democrats secured passage of a Kansas statehood bill on March 23. But the House was a different matter. Northern representatives had to face the voters in 1858. Nearly half of the Northern Democrats along with all of the Republicans opposed Lecompton and defeated it in a showdown vote on April 1.

[12]Don E. Fehrenbacher, *The South and Three Sectional Crises* (Baton Rouge, 1980), p. 54.

In Kansas, the aftermath of this affair proved almost anticlimactic. The administration saved face by sponsoring a bill for renewed submission of the Lecompton constitution to the voters under the guise of adjusting the customary federal land grant to new states. Kansans rejected the constitution by a margin of six to one on August 2, 1858. When Kansas finally achieved statehood in 1861, it came in as the most Republican state in the Union.

For the Democratic party, the legacy of Lecompton was bitter. Douglas had broken with a president from his own party and had alienated most of his former supporters in the South, where he was now regarded as no better than a Black Republican. This ensured a divisive Democratic national convention in 1860, when Douglas was certain to command the support of most Northern delegates for the presidential nomination.

The Lecompton struggle also exposed the defects of popular sovereignty in the light of the Dred Scott decision. Even though slavery still existed legally in Kansas territory after 1858, it ceased to exist there in fact because the now overwhelming predominance of Free Soilers created an environment in which it could not survive. In a speech at Springfield, Illinois, back in June 1857, Douglas had tried to reconcile the Dred Scott doctrine with popular sovereignty. Although the right of slave owners to hold their property in the territories was guaranteed by the Constitution, said Douglas on that occasion, "it necessarily remains a barren and worthless right, unless sustained, protected and enforced by appropriate police regulations and local legislation" which "must necessarily depend entirely upon the will and wishes of the people of the Territory."[13] This truism had provoked little controversy at the time. But in the aftermath of Lecompton it became an issue on which Southerners could flail Douglas. Popular sovereignty was ground between the upper millstone of Republican demands for the congressional exclusion of slavery from the territories and the nether millstone of Southern demands for a federal slave code to guarantee its protection there.

★ The Lincoln-Douglas Debates

On June 16, 1858, a convention of Illinois Republicans nominated Abraham Lincoln for the U.S. Senate. This action was almost unprecedented, for senators were then elected by state legislatures and rarely nominated by a party convention prior to the legislative selection. But the unusual circumstances of 1858 called for unusual action. Douglas's break with the Buchanan administration had caused several Eastern Republicans to suggest an endorsement of his reelection to the Senate as the first step toward a broadened antislavery coalition. But Illinois Republicans would have none of this. They had fought Douglas through thick and thin. They knew he was no crypto-Republican. To endorse him would be to commit suicide as a party. Their nomination of Lincoln nailed Republican colors to the mast. It made the senatorship the sole issue in the election of the Illinois legislature. By forcing Douglas to fight for his political life, it cast a long shadow toward 1860. It also produced the most famous debates in American history.

Lincoln set the tone for the campaign with his acceptance speech, which has come down through history as the "House Divided" address. His purpose was to put

---

[13]Fehrenbacher, *Dred Scott Case*, p. 456.

the greatest possible distance between Douglas and the Republicans. Although Douglas had opposed the Lecompton constitution, he did so only on the grounds that Kansans had been denied a fair vote on the measure. Douglas had said repeatedly that he cared not whether slavery was voted up or down. The "care not" policy, said Lincoln, was anathema to Republicans who considered slavery a moral, social, and political evil. This had been the position of the republic's founders, who excluded slavery from the Northwest Territory and the northern part of the Louisiana Purchase, and hoped for its eventual demise everywhere. But in 1854 Douglas had pushed through the repeal of the Missouri Compromise. In 1857 he had supported the Dred Scott decision. Quoting the Bible, Lincoln said that " 'A house divided against itself cannot stand.' I believe this government cannot endure, permanently half *slave* and half *free*. . . . It will become *all* one thing, or *all* the other." Under Democratic leadership, it might become all slave. But the Republicans—true heirs of the founders—intended to "arrest the further spread of it, and place it where the public mind shall rest in the belief that it is in the course of ultimate extinction."[14]

This linkage of Douglas with the most extreme proslavery advocates was a challenge Douglas could not ignore. His campaign speeches lashed out at Lincoln's alleged misrepresentations. Lincoln replied, and for weeks the two candidates followed each other around the state engaging in long-range debates by speaking on the same platform only days apart. Douglas finally agreed to meet Lincoln in seven face-to-face debates. These debates have become part of the folklore of American history. Thousands of farmers crowded into each of the seven towns to listen to three hours of outdoor oratory in weather ranging from stifling heat to cold rain. The campaign took on the character of high drama. It was David versus Goliath—only this time David, at 6 feet 4 inches, was nearly a foot taller than Goliath.

Douglas tried to put Lincoln on the defensive by identifying him with the abolitionists. The country *could* survive half slave and half free, said Douglas. It had done so from the beginning and there was no reason why it could not do so indefinitely. Popular sovereignty gave the residents of territories the choice to have slavery or not. In all remaining territories they were sure to exclude slavery, said Douglas, if given a fair choice. This would achieve what most Northerners wanted without the risk of disunion, which the Black Republicans would provoke with their abolitionist doctrine of "ultimate extinction."

Moreover, said Douglas, the Republicans favored black equality. He hammered away at this theme ad nauseam, especially in the Butternut counties of southern Illinois. "I do not believe that the Almighty ever intended the negro to be the equal of the white man," thundered Douglas as his partisans roared approval. "He belongs to an inferior race, and must always occupy an inferior position." America was a white man's country, "made by white men, for the benefit of white men and their posterity for ever, and I am in favor of confining citizenship to white men." "Do you desire to strike out of our State Constitution that clause which keeps slaves and free negroes out of the State?" shouted Douglas rhetorically, while his supporters shouted back, "No, no."

> Do you desire to turn this beautiful State into a free negro colony, ("no, no,") in order that when Missouri abolishes slavery she can send one hundred thousand emancipated slaves into Illinois, to become citizens and voters, on an equality with yourselves? ("Never," "no.") If you desire negro citizenship, if you desire to allow

---

[14]Basler, *Works of Lincoln,* II, 461.

them to come into the State and settle with the white man, if you desire them to vote on an equality with yourselves . . . then support Mr. Lincoln and the Black Republican party, who are in favor of the citizenship of the negro.[15]

These tactics put Lincoln on the defensive. His speeches in the southern and central counties denied Douglas's accusations. Differences existed between the races, he said, that would "forever forbid [them] living together on terms of social and political equality." Lincoln assured his listeners "[that] I am not, nor ever have been, in favor of bringing about in any way the social and political equality of the white and black races [applause]—that I am not nor ever have been in favor of making voters or jurors of negroes, nor of qualifying them to hold office, nor to intermarry with white people."[16] Nor did he favor repeal of the Fugitive Slave Law, abolition of the interstate slave trade, or emancipation in the District of Columbia against the wishes of slave owners there, as Douglas had charged.

Lincoln took a more conservative position on these issues than did most Republicans in the upper North. But he could scarcely speak otherwise and hope to win in Illinois, one of the most race-conscious of the free states. And at other times in the debates he soared to a higher level of eloquence. "Let us discard all this quibbling about this man and the other man, this race and . . . the other race being inferior . . . and unite as one people throughout this land, until we shall once more stand up declaring that all men are created equal." Whether or not the black man was equal to the white man in mental endowment, said Lincoln, "in the right to eat the bread, without leave of anybody else, which his own hand earns, he is *my equal and the equal of Judge Douglas, and the equal of every living man.* [Great applause]." While the Republicans did not intend to interfere with slavery in the states where it existed, they did intend to prevent its expansion. Unlike the Democrats, they "hold that this government was instituted to secure the blessings of freedom, and that slavery is an unqualified evil to the negro, to the white man, to the soil, and to the State." The real question was the morality of bondage. If it was right, it should exist everywhere; if wrong, everything possible should be done to restrict and ultimately to end it. "It is the eternal struggle between these two principles—right and wrong—throughout the world." Douglas "*looks to no end of the institution of slavery.*" The Republicans, on the other hand, "will, if possible, place it where the public mind shall rest in the belief that it is in the course of ultimate extinction, in God's good time."[17]

Although these debates illustrated the deep differences between Republican and Democratic attitudes toward slavery, they also reflected Republican ambivalence toward racial equality and the contradictions inherent in Lincoln's commitment to both "ultimate" emancipation and the indefinite continuation of slavery where it already existed. Douglas's insistence that the Republicans could not have it both ways hit uncomfortably close to the mark. But in 1858 this was the only way for Republicans to mediate the tension between the competing values of antislavery and union.

In any case, the voters of Illinois divided almost evenly in the election. Pro-Douglas candidates for the legislature polled heavy majorities in the southern half of the state, while Lincoln supporters did similarly well in the north. Republican candidates tallied a total of 125,000 votes, the Douglas Democrats 121,000, and a handful of anti-Douglas Democrats 5,000. But Douglas carried a larger number of counties, which preserved the Democratic majority on the joint ballot in the legisla-

[15]Ibid., III, 9–10.
[16]Ibid., III, 145–146.
[17]Ibid., II, 501, III, 16, 92–93, 315.

ture and enabled the party to reelect him. Elsewhere in the free states, however, the Democrats suffered another calamity. Their fifty-three Northern congressmen were reduced to a paltry thirty-one. And Republicans won pluralities in Pennsylvania and Indiana as well as in Illinois—states that would give them the presidency in 1860 if they could retain their hold.

★ Portents of Armageddon, 1858–1859

Wedges of Sectional Division

Historians once thought that Lincoln had cleverly ruined Douglas's chances for the presidency by the question he put to him in their debate at Freeport. Could the people of a territory, Lincoln asked, lawfully exclude slavery before achieving statehood? In other words, could popular sovereignty be reconciled with the Dred Scott decision? If Douglas answered no, he would alienate many Northern Democratic voters and probably lose the current Senate contest. But if he answered yes, he would alienate the South and lose his party's presidential nomination in 1860.

The trouble with this theory is that Douglas had already alienated the South by his opposition to Lecompton, and he had already answered this question many times, beginning with his speech in June 1857 endorsing the Dred Scott decision (see page 109). At Freeport he again answered yes: the people of a territory could in effect exclude slavery despite its legal right to be there, by refusing to pass the kind of police regulations necessary to protect it. Lincoln knew that Douglas would give this answer, and he placed less importance on the question than it assumed in retrospect—indeed, the question ran somewhat counter to Lincoln's purpose, which was to identify Douglas with proslavery elements, not to alienate him from them.

Many Southern newspapers did denounce Douglas's "Freeport Doctrine," it is true, but they had already been berating Douglas for nearly a year on the Lecompton issue. Nevertheless, the Freeport Doctrine became the focus of a bitter and growing dispute that in 1860 formally split the Democratic party into Northern and Southern halves. This dispute concerned the question of a federal code of laws to protect slavery in the territories. If a territorial legislature refused to pass police regulations for this purpose, said Southerners, then Congress must do so. In February 1859, Senator Albert G. Brown of Mississippi told the Senate that unless such a federal slave code was passed, he would urge his state to secede. This set off a rancorous sectional debate in which Brown's colleague Jefferson Davis, among others, clashed ferociously with Douglas.

The Buchanan administration's renewed attempt to acquire Cuba also exacerbated sectional tensions. The President's purpose was twofold. He was an ardent expansionist and hoped to make the annexation of Cuba the centerpiece of his foreign policy. At the same time, the Cuban question might heal Democratic sectional wounds. Most Northern Democrats believed in Manifest Destiny. Whatever their attitudes toward slavery in Kansas, most were willing to welcome Cuba as a slave state. Here was an issue to bring Northern and Southern Democrats together again. Douglas endorsed annexation. The American minister in Madrid made clumsy efforts to bribe various factions in Spain to secure their support for the sale of Cuba. In Washington, Southern senators sponsored a bill for $30 million as a down payment. Republicans denounced the bid for Cuba as an outrageous maneuver to expand slavery. They managed to block the appropriation by postponements until the expiration of Congress on March 4, 1859.

In the meantime, Southern senators killed a bill for the granting of 160-acre homesteads to settlers. This measure had passed the House in February 1859 with the support of nearly all Republicans and two-thirds of the Northern Democrats. But Southerners opposed it. They saw it as a device to fill up the West with Yankee farmers. Minnesota and Oregon had just come in as states; Kansas would soon be admitted as a free state; the South was acutely conscious of the growing Northern majority in Congress and in the electoral college. Therefore Southern senators and a handful of their Northern colleagues blocked the homestead bill in the short 1858-1859 session. The simultaneous defeat of the Cuban bill by Northern votes and the homestead bill by Southern votes gave each section another issue for 1860.

The Slave-Trade Controversy

A drive to reopen the African slave trade also joined the growing list of divisive sectional issues. This movement began in the early 1850s and grew to significant proportions by 1859. Most Southerners opposed the revival of the trade. But a substantial number of prominent men endorsed repeal of the 1807 law banning the importation of slaves. Jefferson Davis condemned that law as unconstitutional and as insulting to the South. The governor of South Carolina demanded the reopening of the trade. Two-thirds of the Southern congressmen voted against a House resolution condemning the agitation to reopen the trade. In 1859, the Southern Commercial Convention passed a resolution favoring repeal of the anti-importation laws. J. B. D. DeBow, editor of the South's leading commercial periodical, became president of the African Labor Supply Association, organized in 1859 to work for repeal.

Three reasons underlay this movement. The first was the rapid escalation of slave prices in the 1850s. Between 1849 and 1859, the average price of a prime male field hand rose from $1,000 to $1,700. This not only stretched the resources of wealthy planters but also priced ordinary farmers out of the market. At a time of growing concern about the loyalty of nonslaveholders to the plantation regime, the idea of lowering prices by importation in order to widen ownership was attractive. "Our true purpose," wrote the governor of South Carolina, "is to diffuse the slave population as much as possible, and thus secure in the whole community the motives of self-interest for its support."[18]

A second reason was psychological. Many Southerners considered the African slave trade immoral. Proslavery extremists feared that such a feeling might be only the first step toward a conviction that the internal slave trade and even slavery itself were wrong. "If it is right to buy slaves in Virginia and carry them to New Orleans," asked William L. Yancey, "why is it not right to buy them in Africa and carry them there?" A Texas editor bluntly told his readers: "If you agree to slavery, you must agree to the trade, for they are one. Those who are not for us must be against us. Those who deny slavery and the slave-trade are enemies of the South."[19]

Thirdly, the drive to reopen the trade became a weapon of Southern nationalism. Instead of always standing on the defensive, said one fire-eater, the South should carry on "active aggression." The slave-trade agitation was the best means for this, because it would give "a sort of spite to the North and defiance of their opinions." Two of the foremost fire-eaters and slave-trade advocates, Yancey and Edmund Ruffin of Virginia,

---

[18]David M. Potter, *The Impending Crisis 1848-1861* (New York, 1976), p. 399.

[19]Ibid., p. 398; Ronald T. Takaki, *A Pro-Slavery Crusade: The Agitation to Reopen the African Slave Trade* (New York, 1971), p. 79.

founded the League of United Southerners in 1858 to "fire the Southern heart, instruct the Southern mind . . . and at the proper moment, by one organized, concerted action, we can precipitate the Cotton States into a revolution."[20]

Whatever its success in firing the Southern heart, the campaign to revive the African trade did not achieve its concrete goals. The lower house of the Louisiana legislature did authorize in 1858 the importation of African "apprentices" (a legal subterfuge for slavery), but the state senate did not concur. No other legislative body took action on this question.

But there appears to have been an increase in the illegal smuggling of slaves into the United States during the late 1850s. The most notorious case was that of the schooner *Wanderer,* owned by the scion of a prominent Southern family, Charles A. L. Lamar. In 1858 the *Wanderer* took on five hundred slaves in Africa, evaded British patrols, and eventually landed the four hundred surviving Africans in Georgia. Arrested by federal officials, the crew was acquitted by a Savannah jury despite firm evidence of their guilt. Lamar was even allowed to repurchase his ship at government auction for $4,000! At about the same time, a Charleston jury also acquitted the crew of another illegal trader. In the North these actions provoked outrage, which in turn called forth denunciations of Yankee hypocrisy. "What is the difference," asked a Mississippi newspaper, "between a Yankee violating the fugitive slave law in the North, and a Southern man violating . . . the law against the African slave trade in the South?"[21]

Whatever the difference, the slave-trade controversy seemed to confirm William H. Seward's description, in an 1858 speech, of an "irrepressible conflict" between slavery and freedom. Two books published within weeks of each other in 1857 punctuated this conflict: George Fitzhugh's *Cannibals All, or Slaves Without Masters;* and Hinton Rowan Helper's *The Impending Crisis of the South.*

The Rhetoric of Sectional Conflict

A member of Virginia's tidewater gentry, Fitzhugh had written numerous articles about "the failure of free society." In 1854 he collected several of these essays in a book entitled *Sociology for the South,* and he followed it with *Cannibals All* in 1857. Capitalism was a war of each against all, a form of social cannibalism, said Fitzhugh. Slavery, on the other hand, was an ancient institution that guaranteed the employer's paternal interest in his workers. "What a glorious thing to man is slavery, when want, misfortune, old age, debility and sickness overtake him." All the problems of the North stemmed from its belief in the false doctrine that all men are created equal. "Men are not born entitled to equal rights," insisted Fitzhugh. "It would be far nearer the truth to say that some were born with saddles on their backs, and others booted and spurred to ride them; and the riding does them good. . . . Slavery is the natural and normal condition of the laboring man, whether white or black. . . . We slaveholders say you must recur to domestic slavery, the oldest, the best, and most common form of Socialism."[22]

---

[20]Potter, *Impending Crisis,* p. 399; Allan Nevins, *The Emergence of Lincoln,* 2 vols. (New York, 1950), I, 406.

[21]Takaki, *A Pro-Slavery Crusade,* p. 220.

[22]Harvey Wish (ed.), *Ante-Bellum: Writings of George Fitzhugh and Hinton Rowan Helper on Slavery* (New York, 1960), pp. 58, 82, 9, 85; Nevins, *Emergence of Lincoln,* I, 200n.

Other proslavery partisans echoed Fitzhugh's arguments. George McDuffie, former governor of South Carolina, asserted that "the laboring population of no nation on earth are entitled to liberty, or capable of enjoying it." A Georgia newspaper exclaimed: "Free Society! we sicken at the name. What is it but a conglomeration of greasy mechanics, filthy operatives, small-fisted farmers, and moon-struck theorists . . . hardly fit for association with a southern gentleman's body servant."[23] A few years later, some of the small-fisted farmers and greasy mechanics in General Sherman's army would remember these words as they marched through Georgia and South Carolina.

The minimal impact of the Panic of 1857 in the South underscored Southern boasts about the superiority of their system. While many Northern businesses failed, banks closed, and factories shut down during the depression, causing unemployment and suffering among Northern workers during the winter of 1857–1858, cotton prices held firm and cotton crops set new records. This led Senator James Hammond to deliver his famous "King Cotton" speech in the Senate on March 4, 1858. Southerners were "unquestionably the most prosperous people on earth." Only the continued exports of cotton during the Panic, Hammond told the North, "saved you from destruction." This was conclusive proof of slavery's virtues. For that matter, Hammond went on:

> . . . your whole hireling class of manual laborers and "operatives," as you call them, are essentially slaves. . . . In all social systems there must be a class to do the menial duties, to perform the drudgery of life. . . . It constitutes the very mudsill of society. . . . Fortunately for the South, she found a race adapted to that purpose. . . . We use them for our purpose, and call them slaves. . . . Yours are white.[24]

One can readily imagine the political capital that Republicans made of such speeches. Several prominent Republicans came from humble origins: Nathaniel Banks had started as a bobbin boy in a textile mill; Massachusetts Senator Henry Wilson's father was a manual laborer and Wilson himself had been a shoemaker; the fathers of Thaddeus Stevens and Horace Greeley scratched a poor living from the soil; Abraham Lincoln's parents were semiliterate pioneers. These men served as living examples of upward mobility in a free-labor society. If the South thought that such men constituted the mudsill of society, this only confirmed Republican opinions of the South.[25] During the Lincoln-Douglas debates, Republicans in the audience held up banners with such slogans as "SMALL-FISTED FARMERS, MUD SILLS OF SOCIETY, GREASY MECHANICS, FOR A. LINCOLN."

Hinton Rowan Helper was at the opposite pole from George Fitzhugh. Helper grew up in western North Carolina, an area of small farmers. His 1857 book, *The Impending Crisis of the South,* dealt with slavery's impact on the Southern economy. Using selected statistics from the 1850 census, Helper portrayed a South stagnating in backwardness while the North strode forward in seven-league boots. His account contrasted the near-universal literacy and comfortable living standards of Northern farmers and workers with the ignorance and poverty of Southern poor whites. What

[23]Vernon L. Parrington, *The Romantic Revolution in America, 1800–1861,* Harvest Books ed. (New York, 1954), p. 77; Arthur C. Cole, *The Irrepressible Conflict 1850–1865* (New York, 1934), p. viii.

[24]*Selections from the Letters and Speeches of the Hon. James H. Hammond, of South Carolina* (New York, 1866), pp. 317–319.

[25]Ironically, several prominent Southern leaders had also worked their way up from modest beginnings—including Senator Hammond.

was the cause for this? "Slavery lies at the root of all the shame, poverty, ignorance, tyranny and imbecility of the South." Slavery monopolized the best land, degraded all labor to the level of bond labor, denied schools to workers, and impoverished all but "the lords of the lash" who "are not only absolute masters of the blacks [but] of all non-slaveholding whites, whose freedom is merely nominal, and whose unparalleled illiteracy and degradation is purposely and fiendishly perpetuated."[26] Although he demanded the abolition of slavery, Helper wasted no sympathy on the slaves, whom he wanted shipped back to Africa. He aimed his book at the nonslaveholding whites. He urged them to rise up, organize state Republican parties, and use their votes to overthrow the planters' rule and disenthrall the South.

Few nonslaveholders read his message, however. No Southern printer would publish *The Impending Crisis*. Helper had to move north and get it published in New York. When the book appeared in the summer of 1857, it made an immediate hit with Republicans. Horace Greeley's *New York Tribune* gave it an unprecedented eight-column review. Leading Republicans raised money to print and circulate an abridged edition as a campaign document. This infuriated Southerners, especially as the Republicans added such inflammatory captions in the abridged edition as: "Revolution—Peacefully if we can, Violently if we must."[27] Slave owners denounced *The Impending Crisis* as "incendiary, insurrectionary, and hostile to the peace and tranquility of the country."[28] Several states made circulation or possession of it a crime.

Helper's book played a role in provoking one of the most serious deadlocks in the history of Congress. The Republicans had a plurality but not a majority in the House that convened in December 1859. They nominated John Sherman of Ohio for Speaker. A moderate on slavery, Sherman had nevertheless endorsed Helper's book (without having read it), along with sixty-seven other Republican congressmen. To win the speakership, Sherman needed the support of a few border-state congressmen of the American party. A resolution introduced by a Missouri representative stating that no one who had endorsed *The Impending Crisis* was "fit to be Speaker of the House" inhibited the border-state men from voting for Sherman. The House took ballot after ballot without being able to choose a Speaker. For eight weeks the contest dragged on while tempers grew short, Northern and Southern congressmen hurled insults at one another, and members came armed to the sessions. One observer claimed that "the only persons who do not have a revolver and knife are those who have two revolvers."[29] A shootout on the floor of the House seemed a real possibility. The deadlock was finally resolved on the forty-fourth ballot, when Sherman withdrew and enough border-state Americans voted with the Republicans to elect the colorless William Pennington of New Jersey as Speaker.

The tension in Washington was heightened by John Brown's raid at Harper's Ferry, which had occurred less than two months before Congress met. This violent event climaxed more than a decade of rising sectional tensions. It also launched a year of portentous political events leading up to the presidential election of 1860.

---

[26]Wish, *Ante-Bellum*, pp. 201, 179.

[27]Potter, *Impending Crisis*, p. 387.

[28]Avery O. Craven, *The Growth of Southern Nationalism 1848–1861* (Baton Rouge, 1953), p. 251.

[29]Potter, *Impending Crisis*, p. 389.

EIGHT

The Critical Year,
1859–1860

I John Brown am now quite certain *that the crimes of this* guilty land: *will never be purged* away; *but with Blood.*

—John Brown, 1859

★ *John Brown and the Harpers Ferry Raid*

Since his exploits during 1856 as a free-state guerrilla chieftain in Kansas, John Brown had been evolving an awesome plan for a strike against slavery in the South itself. Brown was a Calvinist who believed in a God of wrath and justice. His favorite biblical passage was: "Without shedding of blood there is no remission of sins." He was certain that the sin of slavery must be atoned in blood. With the single-mindedness of religious fanaticism, he was also certain that he was God's instrument to carry out the task. He planned to lead a raiding party into the Virginia mountains. There he would attract slaves from lowland plantations to his banner. He would arm them, establish a provisional freedmen's republic that could defend the mountain passes against counterattack, and move southward along the Appalachians inspiring slave insurrections until the whole accursed system of bondage collapsed.

It was a wild scheme, but Brown managed to persuade several leading abolitionists of its practicality. From 1856 to 1859 he shuttled back and forth between Kansas, the Northeast, and settlements of former slaves in Canada, recruiting volunteers, raising money, and writing the constitution for his proposed black republic. Gerrit Smith, Thomas Wentworth Higginson, Theodore Parker, and three other Massachusetts abolitionists constituted a "Secret Six" who helped Brown raise money in New England. Ostensibly intended for Kansas, these funds were used instead to buy arms and supplies for Brown's invasion of the South.

The abolitionists who supported Brown had become convinced that moral and political actions against slavery had failed. With the Kansas-Nebraska Act, the election of Buchanan, and the Dred Scott decision, slavery had gone on from one victory to another. A violent counterstroke was the only answer. The Secret Six regarded Brown as "a Cromwellian Ironside introduced in the nineteenth century for a special purpose . . . to take up the work of the English Puritans where it had ended with the death of Cromwell—the work of social regeneration."

JOHN BROWN.
Unlike most abolitionists, Brown believed that slavery could be ended only by the sword. The fierce determination of the Old Testament patriarchs and warriors on whom Brown modeled himself is expressed by the piercing eyes in this photograph taken in 1859, the year of his raid on Harpers Ferry.

LIBRARY OF CONGRESS

Brown planned to capture the federal arsenal at Harpers Ferry, Virginia, and with the weapons seized there, to arm the thousands of slaves he expected to join him. In the summer of 1859 he rented a farm in Maryland across the river from Harpers Ferry and began gathering his seventeen white and five black recruits. Brown tried to persuade the black leader Frederick Douglass to join him. "I want you for a special purpose," he told Douglass. "When I strike, the bees will begin to swarm, and I shall want you to help hive them." But Douglass refused to participate. He tried to dissuade Brown from the mad enterprise. He could see the hopeless folly of invading Virginia and attacking federal property with an "army" of two dozen men.[1]

Situated at the confluence of the Potomac and Shenandoah rivers and surrounded by commanding heights, Harpers Ferry was a military trap. Brown's tactical plans were incredibly amateurish. He failed to inform any of the relatively few slaves in the area of his intentions. He neglected to reconnoiter the terrain around Harpers Ferry to work out an escape route. And he did nothing about laying in supplies or establishing a defensive line against an inevitable counterattack. When he took eighteen men to seize the arsenal on the night of October 16, 1859, they carried no rations.

The little band captured the undefended arsenal, armory, and rifle works. But having gained his initial objectives, Brown seemed not to know what to do next. He sat down to await slave reinforcements; but the only blacks who joined him were a

---

[1]Stephen B. Oates, *To Purge This Land With Blood: A Biography of John Brown* (New York, 1970), pp. 237, 283.

handful of bewildered slaves gathered up—along with white hostages—by patrols sent out by Brown for the purpose.

Meanwhile news of the affair spread quickly. Local citizens and nearby militia companies mobilized on October 17. They captured the bridges across the Potomac and Shenandoah, cutting off Brown's escape, and drove the raiders out of the armory, the arsenal, and the rifle works. Three local men (including a free black) and several of Brown's men, including two of his sons, were killed or mortally wounded in the fighting. Seven raiders escaped (two were later captured) and the rest were driven into the stout fire-engine house, where Brown and the remaining four unwounded invaders made their last stand. During the night of October 17-18 a detachment of U.S. marines commanded by Colonel Robert E. Lee and Lieutenant J. E. B. Stuart surrounded the engine house. Next morning, Brown having refused to surrender, the marines stormed and carried the building with the loss of one man. They killed two more raiders and wounded Brown.

Thirty-six hours after it began, John Brown's war to liberate the slaves was over. Seventeen men had been killed, including ten raiders. Brown and his six captured confederates would eventually be hanged. Not a single slave had voluntarily joined the insurrection. Brown had left behind in the Maryland farmhouse a suitcase full of correspondence with the Secret Six and other Northern sympathizers. When this was captured and publicized, the Secret Six (except Higginson, who defiantly stood his ground) went into hiding or fled to Canada. Some of them later testified before a congressional committee, but none was indicted as an accessory.

In one sense the Harpers Ferry raid was a tragic, wretched failure. But in a larger sense, perhaps, if Brown's goal was to provoke a violent confrontation and liberate the slaves, he succeeded beyond his dreams. There is some evidence that Brown realized this—that he anticipated a martyrdom that would translate him from madman to saint in the eyes of many Northerners while it provoked fear and rage in the South that would hasten the final showdown. During his swift trial by the state of Virginia for murder, treason, and insurrection, Brown discouraged all schemes to cheat the hangman's rope by forcible rescue or pleas of insanity. "I am worth inconceivably more to *hang* than for any other purpose," he told family and friends.[2]

During the month between Brown's sentencing on November 2 and his execution December 2, his demeanor won the admiration of millions in the North. He faced death with dignity. Of him it could truly be said that nothing in his life became him like the leaving of it. The peroration of his speech to the court upon his sentencing became an instant classic:

> This Court acknowledges, too, as I suppose, the validity of the law of God. I see a book kissed, which I suppose to be the Bible, or at least the New Testament, which teaches me that all things whatsoever I would that men should do to me, I should do even so to them. It teaches me, further, to remember them that are in bonds as bound with them. I endeavored to act up to that instruction. I say I am yet too young to understand that God is any respecter of persons. I believe that to have interfered as I have done, as I have always freely admitted I have done, in behalf of His despised poor, is no wrong, but right. Now, if it is deemed necessary that I should forfeit my life for the furtherance of the ends of justice, and mingle my blood further with the blood of my children and with the blood of millions in this slave country whose rights are disregarded by wicked, cruel, and unjust enactments, I say, let it be done.

[2]Ibid., p. 335.

As he walked calmly to the gallows on December 2, Brown handed one of his jailers a note: "I John Brown am now quite *certain* that the crimes of this *guilty land:* will never be purged *away;* but with Blood."[3]

Brown's posttrial behavior elevated him to a sort of sainthood in Northern antislavey circles. Ralph Waldo Emerson said that Brown would "make the gallows as glorious as the cross." Henry Wadsworth Longfellow marked the day of Brown's execution as "the date of a new Revolution, — quite as much needed as the old one." Although prominent Republicans scrambled to dissociate themselves from Brown, some of them endorsed the nobility of his aims even while condemning his means. John Brown's act may have been foolish, said John Andrew, a rising star in the Massachusetts Republican party, but "John Brown himself is right." The *Springfield Republican,* a moderate paper, declared that no event "could so deepen the moral hostility to slavery as this execution. This is not because the acts of Brown are generally approved, for they are not. It is because the nature and spirit of the man are seen to be great and noble." On the day Brown was hanged, church bells tolled in many Northern towns. Cannons fired salutes. Prayer meetings adopted memorial resolutions. This outpouring of grief was an amazing phenomenon, a symbol of how deeply the antislavery purpose had penetrated the Northern consciousness.[4]

These manifestations of Northern sympathy for Brown sent a shock wave through the South more powerful than the raid itself had done. No matter that Northern Republicans disavowed Brown's act. No matter that Northern conservatives and Democrats got up their own meetings to denounce Brown and all who sympathized with him. Southerners could see only the expressions of grief for Brown's martyrdom. They identified Brown with the abolitionists, the abolitionists with Republicans, and Republicans with the whole North. Panic seized many parts of the South. Slave patrols doubled their surveillance. Volunteer military companies cleaned their weapons and stood by for action.

Secession sentiment mushroomed after Brown's raid. "The day of compromise is passed," exulted the fire-eating *Charleston Mercury.* Harpers Ferry had convinced even "the most bigoted Unionist that there is no peace for the South in the Union." And a former Whig confirmed sadly that the affair had "wrought almost a complete revolution in the sentiments, the thoughts, the hopes, of the oldest and steadiest conservatives in all the Southern states."[5]

Northern Democrats hoped to capitalize on the raid by portraying it, in Stephen Douglas's words, as the "natural, logical, inevitable result of the doctrines and teachings of the Republican party." Because William H. Seward was the leading contender for the Republican presidential nomination, Democrats focused most of their fire on him. His "bloody and brutal" Irrepressible Conflict speech (see page 114), they charged, was the inspiration for Brown's bloody and brutal act. The Democrats succeeded in putting the Republicans on the defensive. "Brown's invasion," admitted Massachusetts Senator Henry Wilson, "has thrown us, who were in a

---

[3]Oswald Garrison Villard, *John Brown, 1800-1859: A Biography Fifty Years After* (Boston, 1910), pp. 498-499, 554.

[4]For Northern reaction to Brown's raid and its aftermath, see Oates, *To Purge This Land With Blood,* pp. 308-356, and Allan Nevins, *The Emergence of Lincoln,* 2 vols. (New York, 1950), II, 98-101.

[5]For Southern reaction, see Nevins, *Emergence of Lincoln,* II, 102-112; Oates, *To Purge This Land With Bood,* pp. 320-324; David M. Potter, *The Impending Crisis 1848-1861* (New York, 1976), pp. 380-384.

splendid position, into a defensive position. . . . If we are defeated next year we shall owe it to that foolish and insane movement of Brown's."[6]

★ The Democratic Party Breaks in Two

But political events soon put the Democrats, not the Republicans, on the defensive in the North. Southern Democrats resolved to repudiate Douglas's Freeport Doctrine and to block his nomination for president by insisting that the platform include a plank calling for a federal legal code to guarantee protection of slavery in all territories. Douglas, pledged to popular sovereignty, could not run on such a platform. At the prompting of William Lowndes Yancey, the Alabama Democratic party in January 1860 instructed its delegates to walk out of the national convention if the slave code plank was defeated. Twelve years earlier only one delegate had followed Yancey out of the national convention when a similar plank was rejected (see page 65). But this time Yancey could expect plenty of company.

When the national Democratic convention met in Charleston, South Carolina, on April 23, Douglas appeared to command a majority of the delegates but to fall short of the two-thirds that since 1836 had been necessary for the Democratic nomination. Emotions were at a fever pitch in Charleston. Yankee delegates felt like aliens in a hostile land. The tension mounted as the platform committee presented majority and minority reports to the convention. Southern partisans cheered as Yancey strode to the podium to speak for the slave code plank. The South must have security for its property, he said. "We are in a position to ask you to yield. What right of yours, gentlemen of the North, have we of the South ever invaded? . . . Ours are the institutions which are at stake; ours is the peace that is to be destroyed; ours is the property that is to be destroyed; ours is the honor at stake." Douglas's delegates supported a motion to reaffirm the 1856 popular sovereignty plank with an added provision promising to obey a definitive Supreme Court ruling on the powers of a territorial legislature over slavery.[7] Further than this the Northern Democrats could not go. The slave code plank would rub their faces in the dirt. The South was asking them to pronounce the extension of slavery a positive good. "Gentlemen of the South," declaimed an Ohio delegate, "you mistake us—you mistake us! We will not do it!"[8]

When the platform finally came to a vote after several days of debate, the popular sovereignty plank prevailed by a vote of 165 to 138 (free states, 154 to 30; slave states, 11 to 108). In a prearranged move, forty-nine delegates from eight Southern states followed Yancey out of the convention. They met in another hall, adopted the Southern rights platform, and waited to see what the main convention would do. Even after the Southern walkout, Douglas could not win two-thirds of the remaining delegates, to say nothing of two-thirds of the *whole* number, which the chairman

---

[6]Oates, *To Purge This Land With Blood,* p. 310; C. Vann Woodward, "John Brown's Private War," in Woodward, *The Burden of Southern History* (Baton Rouge, 1960), p. 46.

[7]Because the question of a territorial legislature's power over slavery was not before the Court in the Dred Scott case, Taney's pronouncement on that matter had been an *obiter dictum.*

[8]*Speech of William L. Yancey of Alabama, Delivered in the National Democratic Convention,* p. 4; William B. Hesseltine (ed.), *Three Against Lincoln: Murat Halstead Reports the Caucuses of 1860* (Baton Rouge, 1960), p. 54.

ruled necessary for nomination. After fifty-seven ballots the weary delegates gave up and adjourned, to meet again six weeks later in Baltimore.

Democratic leaders hoped that the postponement would allow tempers to cool and wiser counsels to prevail. But the jubilant Southern bolters were in no mood for reconciliation, save on their own terms. Some of them considered secession from the Democratic party the first step toward secession from the Union. On the night after the Southern exodus from the convention, an excited crowd gathered in front of the courthouse at Charleston to hear Yancey speak. He did not disappoint them. He concluded his ringing oration: "Perhaps even now, the pen of the historian is nibbed to write the story of a new revolution." The huge throng gave "three cheers for the Independent Southern Republic."[9]

The Southern bolters expected to attend the second convention in Baltimore on June 18. In alliance with Northern administration Democrats, they hoped to defeat Douglas again. But Douglas Democrats organized their own delegations from several Southern states. After a bitter fight over readmission of the Southern bolters, the Baltimore convention admitted some but rejected most of those from states where competing Douglas slates had been elected. This prompted a second walkout of Southerners. This time 110 delegates, more than a third of the total, departed to hold a Southern rights convention of their own. While the bolters nominated John C. Breckinridge of Kentucky (Buchanan's Vice President) on a slave code platform, the loyalists nominated Douglas. The divided and dispirited Democrats headed into the campaign against a united and dynamic Republican party.

★ *The Republicans Nominate Lincoln*

The Republican national convention had met at Chicago May 16 in a confident mood. Much would depend on their candidate. The party was sure to carry all but five or six Northern states and not a single Southern state, no matter whom they chose. But to win a majority of the electoral votes, they would need to carry Pennsylvania plus either Illinois or Indiana—all three of which had gone Democratic in 1856. This ruled out Salmon P. Chase, who was too radical for these states. It seemed to strengthen the candidacy of Edward Bates of Missouri, a colorless ex-Whig whom the quixotic Horace Greeley supported on the grounds that only Bates could carry the lower North. But Bates had backed the American party in 1856, which would handicap his candidacy among German Americans. Bates's lukewarm commitment to free soil was also out of tune with the party's antislavery ideology. Simon Cameron of Pennsylvania commanded the loyalty of his own state but that was all. A man of somewhat dubious integrity, Cameron had at one time or another been a Democrat, a Whig, and a Know-Nothing.

The leading candidate was Seward, who was supported by most of the delegates from the upper North. But Seward suffered from two handicaps. The first was his long career in public life. As governor and senator, he had made many enemies, including Greeley, who worked against Seward within his own New York bailiwick. Second, Seward's opposition to the Compromise of 1850, his "Higher Law" speech at that time (see page 70) and his "Irrepressible Conflict" speech in 1858 had given him a

---

[9]Robert W. Johannsen, "Douglas at Charleston," in Norman A. Graebner (ed.), *Politics and the Crisis of 1860* (Urbana, Ill., 1961), p. 90.

reputation for radicalism. Republican leaders from the lower North feared that Seward could not carry their states.

All of these factors strengthened the candidacy of Abraham Lincoln. Before the convention met, Lincoln had the support of little more than the Illinois delegation. But his lieutenants worked skillfully to pick up additional votes here and there—and, more important, to get second-choice commitments from several key states. Lincoln had all the right credentials. He was a former Whig in a party containing a majority of ex-Whigs. He had condemned slavery as a moral evil but deprecated radical action against it. He was an experienced politician who had won favorable notice in his campaign against Douglas but had not been in public life long enough to make a host of enemies. He had opposed nativism but not, like Seward, so conspicuously as to alienate nativist voters. His humble origins and homespun "honest Abe" image as a railsplitter were political assets.

The 1860 Republican platform appeared to be less radical than that of 1856. The 1860 resolutions dropped the references to polygamy and slavery as "twin relics of barbarism," condemned John Brown's raid as "the gravest of crimes," softened the language on exclusion of slavery from the territories without changing its meaning, and affirmed "the right of each state to order and control its own domestic institutions." To shed the party's nativist image, the platform opposed "any change in our naturalization laws" by which the rights of immigrants would be "abridged or impaired." The 1860 platform paid more attention than its predecessor to the economic interests of regional groups: it contained a protective tariff plank for Pennsylvania; it endorsed a homestead act to attract votes in the Midwest; it sanctioned rivers and harbors appropriations and government aid to build a transcontinental railroad. The platform was a composite of Whig and Free Soil ideas, a moderate but firm expression of the free-labor ideology of modernizing capitalism. As party platforms go, it was one of the most concise and concrete in American history—and one of the most successful in appealing to a broad spectrum of Northern voters.

The candidate matched the platform. All through the hectic night of May 17–18, frantic meetings of delegates from the lower North tried to unite on a candidate to stop Seward. Lincoln's lieutenants circulated tirelessly with the message that only their man could carry the whole North. They probably promised cabinet posts to Caleb Smith of Indiana and Simon Cameron of Pennsylvania. Lincoln had instructed his campaign managers to "make no contracts that will bind me," but in the words of his chief manager, "Lincoln ain't here, and don't know what we have to meet, so we will go ahead as if we hadn't heard from him, and he must ratify it."[10]

On the first ballot, Lincoln tallied 102 votes to Seward's $173\frac{1}{2}$ (233 necessary to nominate). In the upper North, Seward had 132 to Lincoln's 19; in the crucial tier of six states from New Jersey to Iowa, Lincoln had 62 to Seward's $3\frac{1}{2}$. Pennsylvania and several New England delegates switched to Lincoln on the second ballot, bringing him to 181 while Seward climbed to only $184\frac{1}{2}$. Still more votes trickled to Lincoln on the third ballot. At the end of the roll call he had $231\frac{1}{2}$ votes, only $1\frac{1}{2}$ short of the nomination. A dramatic hush fell over the hall as an Ohio delegate leaped to his feet and announced the switch of four votes to Lincoln. Pandemonium reigned in Chicago as the state's favorite son became the nominee. The ticket was balanced by giving the vice-presidential nomination to Hannibal Hamlin, a former Democrat from Maine.

[10] Potter, *Impending Crisis*, p. 428.

A fourth party also entered the lists in 1860. A coalition of former Southern Whigs who could not bring themselves to vote Democratic and Northern Whigs who considered the Republican party too radical formed the Constitutional Union party. This was essentially a revival of the 1856 American party shorn of its nativism. The strength of the Constitutional Unionists was concentrated in the upper South. The party adopted a platitudinous platform endorsing "the Constitution of the Country, the Union of the States, and the enforcement of the laws." It nominated John Bell of Tennessee for president and Edward Everett of Massachusetts for vice president. These men had no chance to win; the best they could hope for was to prevent a Republican victory by carrying enough electoral votes to throw the election into the House. The country braced itself for a four-party election that everyone recognized as the most crucial in its history.

★ The Campaign

The contest soon resolved itself into a two-party campaign in each section: Lincoln versus Douglas in the North and Breckinridge versus Bell in the South. The Republicans did not even put up a ticket in ten Southern states. And Douglas had no hope of carrying any of the same ten states. In the North, most of the old Whig/American constituency had gone over to the Republicans. And while Breckinridge gained the support of prominent Northern Democrats identified with the Buchanan administration, the Southern rights party could expect no Northern electoral votes. It became clear that the only way to beat Lincoln was by a fusion of the three opposing parties that might enable them to carry a solid South plus three or four crucial Northern states.

But formidable barriers stood in the way of such a fusion. The bitter divisions among Democrats could scarcely be forgiven or forgotten. A good many fire-eaters had worked to break up the party precisely in order to ensure the election of a Black Republican president and thereby to fire the Southern heart for secession. Even among Southern Democrats who deplored the schism, the gulf was now too wide to be bridged. The only fusion achieved in the South was a joint Bell-Douglas ticket in Texas, which won a paltry 24 percent of the vote against Breckinridge. Herculean efforts by party leaders in New York, Pennsylvania, Rhode Island, and New Jersey patched together fusion tickets in those states. But this proved futile, for Lincoln won a majority against the combined opposition in the first three states and an electoral plurality in New Jersey.

The likelihood that Lincoln would carry nearly all of the free states created a mood of despondency and fatalism among conservatives. At the same time a wave of mass hysteria swept through the South ominously reminiscent of the "Great Fear" in rural France during the summer of 1789. John Brown's ghost stalked the Southern imagination. The prospect of a Republican president provoked fears that an abolitionized North would let loose dozens of John Browns on the South. Every stranger became an abolitionist agent; every black man with an inscrutable face became a potential Nat Turner. Southern newspapers reported hundreds of cases of arson, poisoning, and murder attributed to slaves. Several suspected insurrectionists, black and white, were lynched; scores were whipped or tarred and feathered; hundreds of Northern whites were ordered to leave on pain of death. A severe drought in the South that summer intensified the climate of hysteria.

Southern newspapers supporting Bell or Douglas insisted that the Breckinridge press was stirring up the insurrection panic to win votes for their candidate. Most of the scare stories, said one newspaper, "turned out, on examination, to be totally false, and *all of them* grossly exaggerated."[11] Modern historians agree. But false or not, the stories contributed to the almost unbearable tension that made the South ripe for revolution. At one time or another in 1860, nearly every spokesman in the lower South threatened or warned of secession if a Republican president was elected. Even the Bell and Douglas press issued such warnings. "This Government and Black Republicanism cannot live together," said Benjamin H. Hill, a leader of the Constitutional Union party in Georgia. A Douglas newspaper in Atlanta proclaimed: "Let the consequences be what they may, whether the Potomac is crimsoned in human gore, and Pennsylvania Avenue is paved ten fathoms deep with mangled bodies . . . the South, will never submit to such humiliation and degradation as the inauguration of Abraham Lincoln."[12]

Republicans refused to take these threats seriously. They suspected, with good reason, that the warnings were aimed at Northern voters to frighten them from voting Republican. Southerners had threatened disunion in 1850, during the 1856 presidential election, during the House speakership battle in 1859, and at various other times. The latest warnings, said the Republican mayor of Chicago, were part of "the old game of scaring and bullying the North into submission to Southern demands and Southern tyranny."[13] The German-American leader Carl Schurz recalled that when Pennington was elected Speaker of the House, Southern congressmen had walked out, taken a drink, and then come back. After Lincoln's election, said Schurz, they would take two drinks and come back again.

Lincoln also refused to believe that "there will be any formidable effort to break up the Union." During the campaign, he observed the customary public silence of presidential candidates. As the election approached, he rejected pleas from conservative friends that he publish a statement to calm the South. "What is it I could say which would quiet alarm?" Lincoln asked. "Is it that no interference by the government, with slaves or slavery within the states, is intended? I have said this so often, already, that a repetition of it is but mockery, bearing an appearance of weakness, and cowardice . . . [and] encouraging bold bad men to believe they are dealing with one who can be scared into anything."[14]

Subsequent events, of course, proved that Southern threats of secession were not bluffs. Yet it is hard to see what Republicans could have done about it before the election, short of repudiating everything they stood for. "We regard every man . . . an enemy to the institutions of the South who does not boldly declare that he . . . believes African slavery to be a social, moral, and political blessing," announced a Douglas newspaper in Atlanta.[15] Under such circumstances, the Republicans could

---

[11]William L. Barney, *The Road to Secession: A New Perspective on the Old South* (New York, 1972), p. 149.

[12]Emerson D. Fite, *The Presidential Campaign of 1860* (New York, 1911), p. 165; Dwight L. Dumond, *The Secession Movement, 1860–1861* (New York, 1931), p. 106.

[13]*New York Herald*, August 1, 1860.

[14]Roy P. Basler (ed.), *The Collected Works of Abraham Lincoln*, 9 vols. (New Brunswick, N.J., 1953–1955), IV, 132–133.

[15]Barney, *Road to Secession*, p. 156.

***ABRAHAM LINCOLN AT HOME DURING THE ELECTION OF 1860.
Observing the custom that presidential candidates did not campaign
for themselves, Lincoln remained at home in Springfield, greeting
delegations of friends and supporters who came to visit him. His
6-foot, 4-inch frame towers above the crowd just to the right of the
front door.***

not have obtained a Southern hearing no matter how conciliatory they had tried to be, unless they came out foursquare for slavery.

While the main issue for the South was the Republican threat to slavery, Northern Democrats exploited racism in a fashion that had become standard. Democratic cartoons and banners proclaimed that a Black Republican victory would turn the North into a bedlam of "nigger equality," racial amalgamation, and all manner of similar evils. Cartoons showed black men kissing white women while Lincoln and Horace Greeley looked on benevolently. Such propaganda flourished especially in New York, where the Republican legislature had placed on the ballot a constitutional amendment to eliminate the discriminatory $250 property qualification for black voters. Recognizing their vulnerability on this issue, most Republican speakers and newspapers ignored the amendment or endorsed it lukewarmly. While Lincoln carried New York with 54 percent of the vote, the amendment received just 37 percent. Only two-thirds of the state's Republicans voted for it, though most upstate antislavery counties gave the amendment solid majorities.

While in the upper North the Republicans concentrated on the slavery issue, in the lower North they stressed economic issues: the homestead plank in the Midwest, the tariff plank in Pennsylvania, and the rivers and harbors and Pacific railroad planks in areas that would benefit from these measures. Only two of twenty-seven banners in a Republican rally at Lincoln's hometown of Springfield referred to slavery. "The Republicans, in their speeches, say nothing of the nigger question," complained a Pennsylvania Democrat, "but all is made to turn on the Tariff."[16] In truth, the Democrats had handed the Republicans these issues on a silver platter. During the 1859–1860 session of Congress, Democratic votes had defeated a Pacific railroad bill, a rivers and harbors bill, and an increase in the low 1857 tariff. And President Buchanan had vetoed a homestead act. Here was graphic proof to Northern voters, if any more was needed, that the South and its "doughface lackeys" were blocking measures vital to the growth and prosperity of the country.

The relationship between Republicans and abolitionists in 1860 was ambivalent. Many abolitionists denounced the Republican party as being, in Garrison's words, a "timeserving, a temporizing, a cowardly party" because it was pledged to restriction rather than destruction of slavery. Republicans' descriptions of themselves as the true "White Man's Party" because they wanted to reserve the territories for free white labor also drew abolitionist fire. So did Lincoln's statements opposing interference with slavery in the states, curtailment of the interstate slave trade, and repeal of the Fugitive Slave Law. In most areas, the Republicans held abolitionists at arm's length because association with these "fanatics" would lose votes.

But in parts of the upper North, especially New England, relations between Republicans and abolitionists were cordial. Republican gubernatorial candidates John Andrew of Massachusetts and Austin Blair of Michigan were abolitionists in all but name. So were numerous Republican senators and congressmen and virtually the whole Republican party of Vermont. Several out-and-out abolitionists campaigned for Lincoln. Most Garrisonians said privately that despite Republican shortcomings, "Lincoln's election will indicate growth in the right direction." The Radical Abolitionist party, a tiny remnant of Liberty party veterans, held a convention in 1860 and nominated Gerrit Smith for president. But this "fifth-party" nomination was little more than a gesture, and Smith received a negligible number of votes. Most political abolitionists had joined the Republican party, where they constituted a radical cell that gave the party a crusading, militant tone in the upper North.[17]

Emotion pervaded the campaign in the North as well as in the South. But whereas fear prevailed in the South, the Republicans mobilized zeal in the North. Banners, parades, mass rallies, and songs characterized this campaign even more than the log cabin and hard cider election of 1840. The free-labor symbolism of Lincoln the railsplitter was irresistible. Republican Wide Awakes marched in huge parades, singing political songs and bearing torches mounted on fence rails. (A year later many of these same men would be marching with muskets and singing "John Brown's Body.")

[16]Reinhard H. Luthin, *The First Lincoln Campaign* (Cambridge, Mass., 1944), pp. 183, 208.
[17]James M. McPherson, *The Struggle for Equality: Abolitionists and the Negro in the Civil War and Reconstruction* (Princeton, 1964), chap. 1.

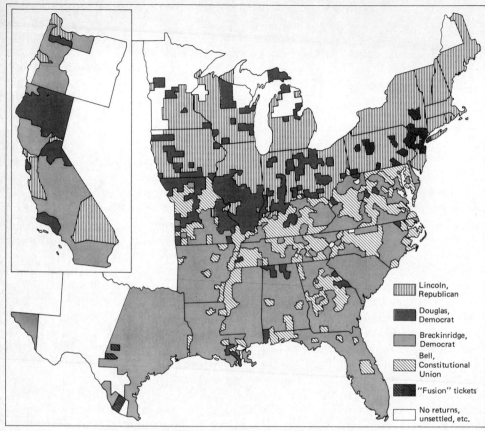

Lincoln, Republican

Douglas, Democrat

Breckinridge, Democrat

Bell, Constitutional Union

"Fusion" tickets

No returns, unsettled, etc.

COUNTIES CARRIED BY CANDIDATES IN THE 1860 PRESIDENTIAL ELECTION

Douglas broke with tradition and campaigned personally in all parts of the country. From the outset he knew that he had little chance of victory. But he took seriously the Southern threats of disunion and strove courageously to meet them head-on. His speeches contained eloquent appeals for all Americans to rally behind the Union. Although ill and exhausted, Douglas maintained a killing pace (less than a year later he died at the age of forty-eight). In many ways this was his finest hour—though reflective observers noted that part of the whirlwind the country was now reaping had been sown in Kansas six years earlier by Douglas himself.

While campaigning in Iowa, Douglas learned that the Republicans had carried the October state elections in Pennsylvania, Ohio, and Indiana. "Mr. Lincoln is the next President," said Douglas. "We must try to save the Union. I will go South." At considerable personal risk he campaigned through the lower South, denouncing disunion at every stop. He rested in Mobile on the day of the election. When Douglas observed the reaction of Alabamians to Lincoln's victory, he returned to his hotel, said his secretary, "more hopeless than I had ever before seen him."[18]

[18]Robert W. Johannsen, *Stephen A. Douglas* (New York, 1973), pp. 797–798, 803.

Table 8.1 VOTING IN THE 1860 ELECTION

	ALL STATES		FREE STATES (18)		SLAVE STATES (15)	
	Popular Votes	*Electoral Votes*	*Popular Votes*	*Electoral Votes*	*Popular Votes*	*Electoral Votes*
Lincoln	1,864,735	180	1,838,347	180	26,388	0
Opposition to Lincoln	2,821,157	123	1,572,637	3	1,248,520	120
Fusion	595,846	—	580,426	—	15,420	—
Douglas	979,425	12	815,857	3	163,568	9
Breckinridge	669,472	72	99,381	0	570,091	72
Bell	576,414	39	76,973	0	499,441	39

★ The Outcome

From the Democratic viewpoint the result was indeed discouraging. Lincoln won all the electoral votes in all of the free states except New Jersey (where he won four and Douglas three); he carried 54 percent of the popular vote in the North; and he won an absolute majority over his combined opponents in all but three Northern states (California, Oregon, New Jersey). Thus he would have garnered a majority of the electoral votes in the whole country even if his opposition had combined against him, as is shown in Table 8.1. Lincoln won no electoral votes in the slave states and scarcely any popular votes outside of a few urban counties in the border states. Douglas ran second in the North but won the electoral votes only of Missouri plus the three in New Jersey. Bell carried Virginia, Kentucky, and his native Tennessee, while Breckinridge carried the rest of the South.

In the upper North—New England and upstate New York, Michigan, Wisconsin, and Minnesota plus the Yankee counties of Ohio, Indiana, Illinois, and Iowa—Lincoln carried more than 60 percent of the vote. In the remaining portions of the free states he barely won 50 percent. Thus it was the strongly antislavery portion of the North that had carried the election and would emerge as the dominating force among congressional Republicans. This fact did not go unnoticed in the South.

Until 1856 no major party had expressed a clear opposition to slavery. Only four years later, the Northern states elected a president who hoped for the ultimate extinction of the institution. According to a New Orleans newspaper, this was "full of portentous significance. It shows, beyond all question or peradventure, the unmixed sectional animosity with which an enormous majority of the Northern people regard us of the South." The *Richmond Examiner* stated bluntly: "The idle canvass prattle about Northern conservatism may now be dismissed. A party founded on the single sentiment . . . of hatred to African slavery, is now the controlling power. . . . No clap trap about the Union . . . can alter [this] or weaken its force."[19]

---

[19]*New Orleans Daily Crescent,* November 13, 1860, and *Richmond Semi-Weekly Examiner,* November 9, 1860, in Dwight L. Dumond (ed.), *Southern Editorials on Secession* (New York, 1931), pp. 237, 223.

The reaction of antislavery men to Lincoln's election seemed to confirm Southern fears. The abolitionists Wendell Phillips and Frederick Douglass had vigorously criticized Republican defects. But the day after the election, Phillips told a celebrating crowd in Boston: "For the first time in our history the *slave* has chosen a President of the United States (Cheers). We have passed the Rubicon." No longer would the slave power rule the country, said Douglass. "Lincoln's election has vitiated their authority and broken their power. . . . It has demonstrated the possibility of electing, if not an Abolitionist, at least an *anti-slavery reputation* to the Presidency." And Charles Francis Adams, the son and grandson of presidents, a founder of the Free Soil and Republican parties in Massachusetts, declared that with Lincoln's election "the great revolution has actually taken place. . . . The country has once and for all thrown off the domination of the Slaveholders."[20]

In response to this Northern revolution, the South launched its own counterrevolution of secession.

---

[20]McPherson, *Struggle for Equality*, p. 27; Charles Francis Adams, Diary, November 7, 1860, quoted in Eric Foner, *Free Soil, Free Labor, Free Men* (New York, 1970), p. 223.

NINE

Secession and the Coming of War

Our new government is founded upon . . . the great truth that the negro is not equal to the white man; that slavery—subordination to the superior race—is his natural and normal condition.
— Alexander H. Stephens, Confederate Vice President, March 21, 1861

★ Secession of the Lower South

As the telegraph flashed news of Lincoln's election, the South Carolina legislature called a convention to take the state out of the Union. Within six weeks the six other states of the lower South had also called conventions. Their voters elected delegates after short but intensive campaigns. Each convention voted by a substantial (in most cases an overwhelming) margin to secede.[1] By February 9, 1861, three months after Lincoln's election, commissioners from these states meeting in Montgomery, Alabama, had adopted a provisional constitution for the Confederate States of America and elected Jefferson Davis provisional president. By way of comparison, the second Continental Congress took fourteen months to adopt the Declaration of Independence, and a full year elapsed between the first call for a convention in 1786 and the drafting of the U.S. Constitution; the National Assembly of France met for two years before promulgating the new constitution of 1791.

Although secession proceeded with extraordinary speed in the lower South, the appearance of solidarity masked some internal divisions. Three basic positions had

---

[1]The dates and votes on secession ordinances were as follows:

South Carolina, 20 Dec., 169-0	Georgia, 19 Jan., 208-89
Mississippi, 9 Jan., 85-15	Louisiana, 26 Jan., 113-17
Florida, 10 Jan., 62-7	Texas, 1 Feb., 166-8
Alabama, 11 Jan., 61-39	

The average vote in these seven conventions was 83 percent in favor of secession, 17 percent opposed. Five of the conventions took preliminary votes on whether to delay separate state secession in favor of some vaguely defined cooperative action by the South as a whole. These motions lost, but by a closer margin—an average of 40 percent in favor of delay, to 60 percent opposed. It is clear that a large majority of delegates in these seven states favored secession in some form.

emerged by December 1860. The first and most radical was "immediate secession." Proponents of this viewpoint believed that each state should secede on its own without waiting for collective action by the South as a whole. The immediate secessionists were strongest in the high-slaveholding counties that had gone for Breckinridge in 1860. But many nonslaveholding Democrats and slaveholding Whigs were also swept into the immediatist camp by the perceived Republican threat to white supremacy and slavery. The second position was known as "cooperation." Its supporters urged delay until the South could formulate a collective response to Lincoln's election. The cooperationists drew their greatest strength from upland counties with fewer slaves and from areas that had supported Bell or Douglas for president. The third position was one of outright opposition to secession. These "unconditional Unionists" lived mostly in the border states; they could scarcely be found in the lower South.

Except in South Carolina, where secessionist sentiment was overwhelming, cooperationist voters may have constituted 40 percent of the total in the lower South. This caused many Northerners to overestimate the strength of Southern Unionism. They failed to appreciate that cooperationism and Unionism were quite different things. The cooperationists divided into three overlapping and shifting groups, which can be labeled cooperative secessionists, ultimatumists, and conditional Unionists. All three groups believed in the right of secession, but they disagreed on method and timing. This led to much confusion. "Here in New Orleans nobody knows exactly what cooperation means," complained the New Orleans Crescent on January 5, 1861. "With some it means delay, with some conference with other states, with some it means submission." In essence, cooperative secessionists wanted the South to act as a unit, for they believed that individual state secessions would produce division and weakness. Ultimatumists wanted the Southern states to agree on an ultimatum to the Republicans demanding certain concessions. If the Republicans refused, the South would go out. Conditional Unionists urged the South to delay action to give the incoming Lincoln administration an opportunity to prove its peaceful intentions. Not until the North committed some "overt act" against Southern rights, they said, should the South take such an extreme step as secession.

Of the cooperationists, only the conditional Unionists offered much hope of preventing disunion. And they were strong only in Georgia and Louisiana. Coopera-tionists in other states insisted that their zeal for Southern rights was no less fervent than that of the immediate secessionists. "We do not associate with submissionists!" insisted Alabama cooperationists. "We scorn the Black Republican rule. . . . We intend to resist . . . but our resistance is based upon consultation, and in unity of action, with the other slave states."[2] The kinds of concessions that ultimatumists asked for would have required the Republican party to repudiate what it stood for. Ultimatumists demanded a federal slave code for all territories, a pledge not to interfere with the interstate slave trade, repeal of personal liberty laws by Northern states, compensation to slaveholders for property lost through Northern failure to enforce the Fugitive Slave Law, and other concessions of similar purport.

Republican spokesmen soon made clear the party's opposition to such conces-sions. This put the cooperationists on the defensive. By January 1861, the momentum of individual state secession became irresistible in the lower South. As each state seceded, it appointed commissioners to the other conventions about to meet. These

[2]Dwight L. Dumond, The Secession Movement, 1860-1861 (New York, 1931), pp. 201-202, 122.

commissioners gave fiery speeches urging each of the remaining states to join those that had already gone out. The barrage of mass meetings and newspaper publicity added to the pressures that caused cooperationists to cave in. Even conditional Unionists jumped aboard the secession bandwagon, for to stay off would have looked like treason to the South. The most prominent conditional Unionist, Alexander H. Stephens of Georgia, became vice president of the Confederacy.

★ Secession: Revolution or Counterrevolution?

Many Southerners proclaimed secession to be a revolution in the image of 1776. "The tea has been thrown overboard," declared the *Charleston Mercury* when Lincoln's election was announced. "The revolution of 1860 has been initiated." Pierre Soulé, former leader of the Douglas Democrats in Louisiana, said after the election that faced with a choice between "ignominy and revolution, I choose revolution." Senator Judah P. Benjamin of Louisiana described the "wild torrent of passion" that was "carrying everything before it" as "a revolution; a revolution of the most intense character" that could "no more be checked by human effort than a prairie fire by a gardener's watering pot."[3]

Benjamin was right about the intense torrent of passion sweeping the South. Mass meetings roared their approval of speakers who called for Southern independence. Secession functioned as a catharsis for the tension that had been building to a level of near hysteria since the John Brown raid a year earlier. "The minds of the people are aroused to a pitch of excitement probably unparalleled in the history of our country," wrote one Southerner. And a Virginia conservative lamented that "the desire of some for change, the greed of many for excitement . . . seems to have unthroned the reason of men, and left them at the mercy of passion."[4]

Many secessionists expected their revolution to be a peaceful one. Robert Barnwell Rhett, editor of the *Charleston Mercury,* was quoted as saying that he would eat the bodies of all men slain as a consequence of disunion, while Senator James Chesnut of South Carolina was said to have offered to drink all the blood shed in the cause. A Georgia newspaper announced: "So far as civil war is concerned, we have no fears of that in Atlanta."[5]

While hoping for peace, however, secessionists knew that most revolutions succeed only by violence. All the seceding states strengthened their militia and encouraged the formation of new volunteer military companies, which often called themselves Minute Men. As they declared themselves out of the Union, the states seized federal arsenals and forts to arm and equip these military organizations. One of the first acts of the provisional Confederate government was to authorize an army of 100,000 men.

Although many Confederates looked to 1776 as their model, secession was not

[3] *Charleston Mercury,* November 8, 1860; Soulé quoted in Willie M. Caskey, *Secession and Restoration of Louisiana* (University, La., 1938), pp. 21–22; Judah Benjamin to Samuel L. M. Barlow, December 9, 1860, S.L.M. Barlow Papers, Henry E. Huntington Library.

[4] Charles G. Sellers, "The Travail of Slavery," in Charles G. Sellers (ed.), *The Southerner as American* (Chapel Hill, 1960), pp. 69–70.

[5] E. Merton Coulter, *The Confederate States of America* (Baton Rouge, 1950), pp. 14–15; *Atlanta Daily Intelligencer,* January 28, 1861, quoted in Donald E. Reynolds, *Editors Make War: Southern Newspapers in the Secession Crisis* (Nashville, 1970), p. 174.

a revolution in the usual sense of the word. Armed revolt against an established government is by definition illegal, but most secessionists insisted that their action was legal and constitutional. Senator Louis T. Wigfall of Texas would not have favored secession "if I believed that the act of secession was one of revolution, that it was one in direct conflict with the Constitution of the United States that I am sworn to obey."[6] But he did favor it, for like most Southerners he believed in the "compact" theory of the Constitution. This theory had a long history going back to the Virginia and Kentucky Resolutions of 1798. It held that the U.S. Constitution was a compact among states that had authorized the federal government to act as their agents in the exercise of certain functions of sovereignty. But the states had never transferred the sovereignty itself. Having delegated these functions by the ratifying act of a convention, a state could withdraw from the compact and reassert its full sovereignty by the act of another convention. This was precisely what the seceding states did in 1861.

Of course, a good many Confederates believed in both the legal and the revolutionary rights of secession. "There is no incompatibility between the right of secession by a State and the right of revolution by the people," said a Southern theorist. "The one is a civil right founded upon the Constitution; the other is a natural right resting upon the law of God."[7] But as time passed, the emphasis on the right of revolution diminished while that on the legal right of secession increased, as Confederate leaders pondered the possible consequences of their action. By insisting that secession was legal rather than revolutionary, they intended to place the Confederacy on firm and safe ground in the eyes of the world. Moreover, there were those who feared that an outpouring of revolutionary rhetoric might happen to fall upon the wrong ears—after all, "liberty" and "rights" could mean something quite different to slaves than to masters. Although seceding states quoted that part of the Declaration of Independence which justified the dissolution of old governments and the formation of new ones, they did *not* quote the part which affirmed that all men are created equal and endowed with the inalienable right of liberty.

Abolitionists and Republicans were not slow to point out the incongruity—indeed the logical contradiction—of a revolution for the defense of slavery. Secession was "the oddest Revolution that History has yet seen," wrote an abolitionist editor, "a Revolution for the greater security of Injustice, and the firmer establishment of Tyranny!" The *New York Tribune* best summarized the Republican attitude: "Mr. Jefferson's Declaration of Independence was made in the interest of natural rights against Established Institutions. Mr. Jeff. Davis's caricature thereof is made in the interest of an unjust, outgrown, decaying Institution against the apprehended encroachments of Natural Human Rights." It was therefore not a revolution but a counterrevolution, a "rebellion in the interest of darkness, of despotism and oppression."[8]

Thus challenged, Confederate leaders responded that indeed they were defending established institutions. "Ours is not a revolution," said Jefferson Davis. "We are not engaged in a Quixotic fight for the rights of man; our struggle is for inherited rights." We left the Union "to save ourselves from a revolution" that threatened to make "property in slaves so insecure as to be comparatively worthless." The South's foremost journalist, J. B. D. DeBow, maintained that "we are not revolutionists; we

---

[6]*Congressional Globe,* 36th Cong., 2nd sess. (1860), 12.
[7]Jesse T. Carpenter, *The South as a Conscious Minority, 1789–1861* (New York, 1930), p. 196.
[8]*National Anti-Slavery Standard,* December 1, 1860; *New York Tribune,* May 21, 1862.

are resisting revolution. We are upholding the true doctrines of the Federal Constitution. We are conservative." On March 21, 1861, Confederate Vice President Stephens proclaimed that the "present revolution" was one to preserve "the proper status of the negro in our form of civilization." The affirmation of equality in the Declaration of Independence was wrong. "Our new government," said Stephens, "is founded upon exactly the opposite idea; its foundations are laid, its cornerstone rests, upon the great truth that the negro is not equal to the white man; that slavery—subordination to the superior race—is his natural and normal condition. This, our new government, is the first in the history of the world based upon this great physical, philosophical, and moral truth."[9]

During the secession crisis, Southerners quoted from hundreds of Republican speeches and editorials to prove that it was the Republicans who were the revolutionists, not they. Their favorites for this purpose were Seward and Lincoln. These men were the leaders of their party, said Southerners. If anyone truly represented Republican intentions, they did. In his "Irrepressible Conflict" speech, Seward had predicted the ultimate victory of the free-labor ideology. "I know, and you know, that a revolu- tion has begun," he had said in 1858. "I know, and all the world knows, that revolutions never go backward." And in his "House Divided" address, Lincoln had announced that the Republicans intended to place slavery "where the public mind shall rest in the belief that it is in the course of ultimate extinction."[10]

Whether ultimate or imminent, the extinction of slavery was precisely what the South feared. No matter how moderate the Republicans professed to be, no matter how many assurances they gave that slavery in the states would be safe under their rule, nothing could gainsay their ultimate purpose to destroy the institution. No one should "be deluded . . . into the belief that the Black Republican party is a moderate and conservative, rather than a radical and progressive party," warned the *New Orleans Delta*. "It is, in fact, essentially a revolutionary party."[11]

Secessionists conjured up a frightening scenario of future Republican actions: exclusion of slavery from the territories would bring in so many new free states that the South would be overwhelmed in Congress and encircled by free territory; Lincoln would appoint Republican justices to the Supreme Court and thus turn this bastion of Southern protection into an engine of destruction; Congress would repeal the Fugitive Slave Law and slaves would flee northward by the thousands; Congress would abolish slavery in the District of Columbia and on all federal property such as forts and arsenals, navy yards and customs houses; the government would stand by and do nothing while new John Browns led armies of insurrection into the South. "Now that the black radical Republicans have the power I suppose they will [John] Brown us all," exclaimed a South Carolinian when he learned of Lincoln's election. "We shall be in a State of Revolution forthwith," echoed another.[12]

The greatest concern of some secessionists was the possibility that the Republi-

<hr />

[9]Dunbar Rowland (ed.), *Jefferson Davis, Constitutionalist: His Letters, Papers and Speeches,* 10 vols. (Jackson, Miss., 1923), VI, 357, V, 50, 72; *DeBow's Review,* 33 (1862), 44; *Augusta Daily Constitutionalist,* March 30, 1861.

[10]George E. Baker (ed.), *The Works of William H. Seward,* 5 vols. (Boston, 1853–1884), IV, 302; Roy P. Basler (ed.), *The Collected Works of Abraham Lincoln,* 9 vols. (New Brunswick, N.J., 1953–1955), II, 461.

[11]*New Orleans Delta,* November 3, 1860.

[12]Mary Boykin Chesnut, *A Diary from Dixie,* ed. Isabel D. Martin and Myrta Lockett Avary (New York, 1905), p. 1; James L. Roark, *Masters Without Slaves: Southern Planters in the Civil War and Reconstruction* (New York, 1977), p. 6.

can party might have some attraction for nonslaveholders, especially in the border South and the upcountry. What if Hinton Rowan Helper was right about the yeomen farmers' alienation from the planter elite? "The great lever by which the abolitionists hope to extirpate slavery in the States is the aid of non-slaveholding citizens in the South," worried one editor. If the Republicans used the patronage cleverly by appointing nonslaveholders to federal offices in the South, they might build up "a party with supporters for the incoming administration here in our midst." This might prove to be the entering wedge to "Helperize" the South.[13]

To prevent such a calamity, secessionists invoked Herrenvolk democracy to remind yeomen of their racial stake in defending slavery. Lincoln's election, declared an Alabama newspaper, "shows that the North [intends] to free the negroes and force amalgamation between them and the children of the poor men of the South." Thus nonslaveholders "will never consent to submit to abolition rule," said Georgia's secessionist governor Joseph E. Brown, for they "know that in the event of the abolition of slavery, they would be greater sufferers than the rich, who would be able to protect themselves. . . . When it becomes necessary to defend our rights against so foul a domination, I would call upon the mountain boys as well as the people of the lowlands, and they would come down like an avalanche and swarm around the flag of Georgia."[14] Most nonslaveholding whites in 1861—at least in the seven states that seceded by February—seemed to respond favorably to this argument that "democratic liberty exists solely because we have black slaves" whose presence "promotes equality among the free." They therefore supported the "political revolution" of secession whose purpose was to avert the "social revolution" that would come with Republican rule.[15]

Southern political skills and Southern domination of the Democratic party had given the slave states disproportionate power in the national government. From 1789 to 1861, twenty-three of the thirty-six Speakers of the House and twenty-four of the thirty-six presidents pro tem of the Senate had been Southerners. Twenty of the thirty-five Supreme Court justices had come from slave states, and at all times since 1789 the South had had a majority on the Court. During forty-nine of these seventy-two years the president of the United States had been a Southerner—and a slaveholder. During twelve additional years, including most of the crucial 1850s, the presidents were Northern Democratic "doughfaces." Lincoln's election foreshadowed an end to all this. It was a signal that the country had turned a decisive political corner toward a future dominated by the ideology and institutions of the North. For the Old South this seemed to spell disaster, so its leaders launched a counterrevolution of independence to escape the dreaded consequences. "These are desperate means," admitted a secessionist, "but then we must recollect that we live in desperate times. Not only our property but our honor, our lives and our all are involved."[16]

---

[13]Dumond, *The Secession Movement*, p. 117n.; Daniel W. Crofts, *Reluctant Confederates: Upper South Unionists in the Secession Crisis* (Chapel Hill, 1989), p. 154.

[14]Reynolds, *Editors Make War*, pp. 125–126; Michael P. Johnson, *Toward a Patriarchal Republic: The Secession of Georgia* (Baton Rouge, 1977), p. 48; Steven Hahn, *The Roots of Southern Populism: Yeoman Farmers and the Transformation of the Georgia Upcountry, 1850–1890* (New York, 1983), pp. 86–87.

[15]J. Mills Thornton III, *Politics and Power in a Slave Society: Alabama, 1800–1860* (Baton Rouge, 1978), pp. 320, 206–207; Johnson, *Toward a Patriarchal Republic*, p. 47.

[16]Reynolds, *Editors Make War*, p. 150.

★ The Northern Response to Secession

While the lower South acted rapidly and decisively, the North floundered in uncertainty and confusion. The "lame-duck" syndrome crippled the government's will to act: President Buchanan and the current Congress held power but lacked a recent mandate; the President and Congress elected in November would not take office until March 4, by which time the Confederacy would be a fait accompli. But even if the Republicans had controlled the government during the winter, they would have been helpless to stem the tide of secession, for they had no clear conception of what to do about it.

For several weeks after the election, most Republicans urged a "Fabian policy" of "masterly inactivity." They would sit tight and do nothing to encourage secessionists or to undercut Southern Unionists. Lincoln and Seward were the chief exponents of this approach. They expected the secession fever to run its course without taking more than one or two states out of the Union. Then the good sense and basic loyalty of the South would reassert itself, and the "erring sisters" would return. This of course was a misreading of the situation in the lower South, as events soon revealed.

President Buchanan and the Crisis

Meanwhile, Buchanan took more seriously the gravity of the situation. He was in a difficult position. He believed that the crisis, having been precipitated by Lincoln's election, was Lincoln's responsibility. But Buchanan's term had nearly four months to go, and during that time the constitutional responsibility was his. He hoped that somehow he could keep the government afloat and preserve peace until relieved of his duties on March 4. Yet he was buffeted by conflicting pressures from the Southern and Northern wings of his party. Most of his advisers were Southerners. Secretary of the Treasury Howell Cobb of Georgia and Secretary of the Interior Jacob Thompson of Mississippi were secessionists marking time in Washington until their states went out. Secretary of War John Floyd of Virginia, under fire for malfeasance in office and under suspicion of treason for having transferred arms to Southern arsenals, would soon declare openly his support for secession.

Despite the Southern orientation of his administration, Buchanan could not accept disunion. His much-publicized annual message on December 3 declared secession illegal. The Union was more than a "mere voluntary association of states," said the President. It was a sovereign nation "not to be annulled at the pleasure of any one of the contracting parties." The founders of the republic were not "guilty of the absurdity of providing for its own dissolution." Thus "secession is neither more nor less than revolution." All peoples have a right of revolution against intolerable oppression, but the election of a president by constitutional procedures could not "justify a revolution to destroy this very Constitution." The Union "has been consecrated by the blood of our fathers, by the glories of the past, and by the hopes of the future." If it could be broken by the mere will of a state, the great experiment in republican self-government launched in 1776 became a failure. "Our example for more than eighty years would not only be lost, but it would be quoted as conclusive proof that man is unfit for self-government."[17]

---

[17]James D. Richardson (comp.), *Compilation of the Messages and Papers of the Presidents, 1789-1897,* 20 vols. (Washington, D.C., 1897-1913), V, 628, 630, 632-634, 637.

Most Republicans and Northern Democrats applauded this part of the President's message. It expressed the themes of nationalism for which the North was to fight during the ensuing four years. But Buchanan's next point seemed to contradict his ringing Unionist phrases. While the government must continue to "enforce the laws" in all states, said the President, it could not "coerce" a seceding state back into the Union. Republicans ridiculed this distinction between enforcement and coercion. The President had proved, jeered Seward, that "no state has the right to secede unless it wishes to" and "that it is the President's duty to enforce the laws, unless somebody opposes him."[18]

The question of what constituted "coercion" was a matter of interpretation. A few Republicans urged invasion and war if necessary to crush treason. This would unquestionably be coercion. Most Republicans in December 1860 were not ready to go this far. But they did believe that the government should defend its forts and other property in the South, collect customs duties, and carry on other functions as usual. If Southern states resisted, they would be responsible for the consequences. To secessionists, of course, such a policy was coercion. "If the President of the United States were to send a fleet to Liverpool," said Senator Wigfall of Texas, "and attempt there to enforce the laws of the United States, and to collect revenues, and that flag were fired at, would anybody say that the British Government was responsible for the blood that might follow?"[19]

Buchanan's message blamed Republicans and abolitionists for bringing on the crisis. "The incessant and violent agitation of the slavery question" had stirred "vague notions of freedom" among the slaves and created a climate of fear in the South. Unless Northerners stopped criticizing slavery and undertook in good faith to obey the Fugitive Slave Law, "disunion will become inevitable" and the South will "be justified in revolutionary resistance to the Government." To meet the South's just grievances, Buchanan recommended a constitutional amendment to protect slavery in the territories and to annul personal liberty laws in Northern states. For good measure, the President reaffirmed his recommendation for the purchase of Cuba, which would help alleviate Southern discontent by adding a new slave state to the Union.[20]

Proposals for Compromise

Buchanan's recommendations were similar to dozens of compromise measures introduced in Congress during December. To sort all of these out, the House created a special Committee of Thirty-three (one member from each state) and the Senate a Committee of Thirteen. Nearly all of the proposed compromises had two things in common: the North would make all the concessions; and Republicans would be required to give up their intention to prohibit slavery in the territories—the issue on which the party had been founded. To most Republicans this was intolerable. The party "cannot be made to surrender the fruits of its recent victory," said a Republican

---

[18]Ibid., pp. 635-636; Kenneth M. Stampp, *And the War Came: The North and the Secession Crisis, 1860-61* (Baton Rouge, 1950), p. 56.

[19]Stampp, *And the War Came*, p. 44.

[20]Richardson, *Messages and Papers of the Presidents*, V, 626-627, 630, 638, 642.

newspaper in a typical editorial. "If the will of the majority is no longer the governing power in this country, free government is at an end."[21]

A good many abolitionists preferred disunion rather than a shameful bribe in the form of a "compromise" to purchase the South's loyalty. The Garrisonian abolitionists, of course, had long denounced the Constitution as a "covenant with death" and the Union as an "agreement with hell." They had urged the free states to break loose from the sinful slaveholding Union. Now that slave states had done the breaking loose, Garrisonians were happy to see them go. They believed that secession would isolate the South and bring its peculiar institution under the ban of world opinion, end the North's obligation to return fugitive slaves, relieve the U.S. army from the duty to suppress slave insurrections, and hasten the final collapse of bondage. Some non-Garrisonians also preferred disunion to compromise. "If the Union can only be maintained by new concessions to the slaveholders," said Frederick Douglass, "if it can only be stuck together and held together by a new drain on the negro's blood, then . . . let the Union perish."[22] During the winter of 1860–1861, abolitionists who preached such doctrines encountered mob violence in many parts of the North, for Democrats and conservative Republicans blamed them for having provoked the South into secession.

But some Republicans agreed with the abolitionists in wishing to let the South go if surrender to Southern demands was the price of union. Horace Greeley's powerful *New York Tribune* expressed a willingness to "let the erring sisters depart in peace." But Greeley and other radical Republicans hedged their apparent acquiescence in disunion with so many qualifications as to render it practically meaningless. By January 1861, after congressional Republicans had stood firm against compromise on the issue of slavery in the territories, Greeley and most other "go in peace" Republicans began to denounce secessionists as traitors.

Before January, however, some conservative Republicans had hinted at a willingness to compromise on the territorial question. They endorsed the idea of extending the old Missouri Compromise line westward to the California border. This proposal became the centerpiece of a complex compromise plan introduced in the Senate Committee of Thirteen by John J. Crittenden of Kentucky. The Crittenden Compromise consisted of a series of constitutional amendments: to recognize and protect slavery in all territories south of latitude 36°30′ "now held, *or hereafter acquired*" (italics added) while prohibiting it north of that latitude; to prevent Congress from abolishing slavery in the District of Columbia or in any national jurisdiction within a slave state (e.g., forts, naval bases, arsenals); to forbid federal interference with the interstate slave trade; and to indemnify owners who were prevented by local opposition from recovering escaped slaves. These amendments were to be perpetually binding, unrepealable and unamendable for all time. Additional congressional resolutions that became part of the Crittenden Compromise undertook to modify the Fugitive Slave Law and to request states to repeal laws that conflicted with it.

Crittenden believed that his plan could win majority support in both North and South. He proposed that it be submitted to a national referendum. But Republicans in Congress opposed it. Not only did this "compromise" repudiate their platform, it also

---

[21]*Boston Daily Advertiser*, December 7, 1860, and *Des Moines Iowa State Register*, December 12, 1860, in Howard C. Perkins (ed.), *Northern Editorials on Secession* (New York, 1942), pp. 147, 157.

[22]*Douglass' Monthly*, January 1861.

promised to set off a new wave of imperialism in the Caribbean and Central America to expand slavery into territories "hereafter acquired." Passage of Crittenden's proposal, said Republicans, "would amount to a perpetual covenant of war against every people, tribe, and State owning a foot of land between here and Tierra del Fuego." It would convert the United States into "a great slave-breeding and slave-extending empire."[23] Republican votes killed the Crittenden Compromise in the Senate Committee of Thirteen on December 28. When Crittenden brought the measure to the Senate floor on January 16, Republican votes again provided the margin of defeat.[24]

Lincoln's Position

Although Lincoln made no public statements during this period, he played a crucial role in preventing concessions on the territorial issue. He quietly passed the word for Republicans to "entertain no proposition for a compromise in regard to the *extension* of slavery. The instant you do, they have us under again; all our labor is lost, and sooner or later must be done over. . . . Filibustering for all South of us, and making slave states of it, would follow. . . . The tug has to come & better now than later." Two years earlier, in his "House Divided" speech, Lincoln had said that "a crisis must be reached and passed" on the slavery question. The nation must face a decision whether it was to be ultimately a free or slave society. Now the "tug" had come, and Lincoln did not intend to back down. "If we surrender," he said in January, "it is the end of us, and of the government. They will repeat the experiment on us *ad libitum*. A year will not pass, till we shall have to take Cuba as a condition upon which they will stay in the Union."[25]

Lincoln privately assured Southern friends that his administration would not interfere with slavery in the states or in the District of Columbia, would do nothing against the interstate slave trade, would enforce the Fugitive Slave Law, and would urge Northern states to repeal or modify their personal liberty laws. Two Northern states did take such action during the secession winter. And with Lincoln's support, about two-fifths of the Republicans in Congress joined in the passage of a constitutional amendment to guarantee slavery in the states against future interference by the federal government.[26] But beyond this most Republicans would not go. As Lincoln put it in a December 22 letter to his old friend, Alexander Stephens: "You think slavery is *right* and ought to be extended; while we think it is *wrong* and ought to be restricted. That I suppose is the rub."[27]

It was indeed the rub. The lower South was seceding because a party that believed slavery wrong had come to power. No compromise could undo this fact. Although many contemporary observers, as well as some historians, believed that the Crittenden Compromise commanded widespread support in the North and the upper

---

[23]Stampp, *And the War Came*, p. 169.

[24]The vote in the Senate committee was 7 to 6, with all five Republican members in the majority. The vote on the Senate floor was 25 to 23. All 25 of the majority votes were cast by Republicans. Six Southern Democratic senators, from states soon to secede, abstained from the floor vote.

[25]Basler, *Works of Lincoln*, IV, 150, 154, 172.

[26]This Thirteenth Amendment was ratified by two states, Ohio and Maryland, before the Civil War broke out; eventually a quite different Thirteenth Amendment became part of the Constitution—one that abolished slavery in all the states.

[27]Basler, *Works of Lincoln*, p. 160.

South, it is likely that no conceivable compromise could have stopped secession in the lower South.[28] Secessionists frankly said as much from the beginning of the crisis. On December 13, before any state seceded or any compromise was voted on, thirty congressmen and senators from the lower South issued an address to their constituents: "The argument is exhausted. All hope of relief in the Union, through the agency of committees, Congressional legislation, or constitutional amendments, is extinguished, and we trust the South will not be deceived by appearances or the pretense of new guarantees. . . . The honor, safety, and independence of the Southern people are to be found only in a Southern Confederacy." Jefferson Davis said on December 2 that "no human power can save the Union, all the cotton states will go." A week later Judah Benjamin declared that "a settlement [is] totally out of our power to accomplish."[29]

★ Launching the Confederacy

Thus the delegates to the Confederate constitutional convention that met February 4 in Montgomery paid no attention to what was going on in Washington. They hammered out a provisional constitution in four days. They could do this so quickly because their constitution was in most respects a copy of the U.S. Constitution. The same was true of the permanent Confederate constitution adopted a month later. But the latter did contain some significant new provisions. The preamble omitted the general welfare clause of the U.S. Constitution and added that by ratifying the new charter, each state acted "in its sovereign and independent character." The Confederate constitution explicitly guaranteed slavery in territories as well as in states. It forbade protective (as distinguished from revenue) tariffs and outlawed congressional appropriations for internal improvements. All of these features were designed to strengthen slavery and states' rights.

The Confederate constitution also departed from the U.S. model by limiting the president to one six-year term, by giving him the power to veto separate items in appropriation bills, and by authorizing Congress to grant cabinet officers the right to speak on the floor of Congress (this was never implemented). On February 9 the convention elected Davis and Stephens provisional president and vice president. Later legislation provided for the election of permanent officers in November and for their inauguration on February 22, 1862. Until then, the delegates to the constitutional convention (plus those elected by any additional seceding states) would function as a provisional Congress.

The fire-eaters who had done so much to spur the South to secession took a back seat at Montgomery. Yancey was not even a delegate. Although Davis had been a secessionist since Lincoln's election, he was considered a moderate. Stephens had been a conditional Unionist. Part of the convention's purpose in choosing these men was to present a moderate image to the upper South, which had not seceded—yet. The same reasoning lay behind the constitutional prohibition of the foreign slave

[28]For discussions of popular support for the Crittenden Compromise, see Stampp, *And the War Came*, chaps. 8–9, David M. Potter, *Lincoln and His Party in the Secession Crisis* (New Haven, 1942), chap. 8, and Crofts, *Reluctant Confederates*, pp. 197–199.

[29]Edward McPherson, *The Political History of the United States of America During the Great Rebellion*, 2d ed. (Washington, 1865), p. 37; Davis quoted in Samuel C. Buttersworth to Samuel L. M. Barlow, December 3, 1860, Benjamin to Barlow, December 9, 1860, Barlow Papers.

trade. Some of the militant secessionists wanted to reopen the trade, but this would have alienated the upper South and crippled the Confederacy's hopes for European recognition. So instead of legalizing the trade, the convention proscribed it.

★ *The Upper South*

The question of what the eight slave states of the upper South would do was crucial. Without them, the Confederacy would have scarcely 5 percent of the industrial capacity of the Union states and less than one-fifth of the population (only one-tenth of the white population). The Confederate government sent commissioners to all eight states to woo them with appeals to interest and sentiment. But the momentum of secession seemed to have spent itself by February. Voters in Virginia, Missouri, and Arkansas elected large majorities of conditional Unionists to their state conventions. The Arkansas and Missouri conventions voted in March to reject secession. The Virginia convention did the same on April 4, though it thereafter remained in session to await further developments. The legislatures of Kentucky and Delaware refused to call conventions. In North Carolina and Tennessee, the voters rejected the calling of a convention. The Unionist governor of Maryland resisted pressure to call the legislature into session to consider the issue.

These events seemed to confirm Republican faith in Southern Unionism. But upper-South Unionists made clear that their loyalty was contingent on two factors: the incoming Republican administration must offer guarantees for the safety of slavery, and it must refrain from "coercion" of Confederate states. Many Republicans were willing to go at least halfway to meet these conditions. Seward put himself at the head of this element. Lincoln had already asked the New Yorker to serve as secretary of state. Most observers expected that Seward, a man of greater prominence and experience than Lincoln, would be the "premier" of the administration. Seward expected this himself. He became the foremost Republican proponent of a policy known as "voluntary reconstruction." This approach assumed that if the Republicans refrained from provocative acts against the seceded states and made a few timely concessions, the upper South would remain in the Union, and the lower South would eventually return. "Every thought that we think ought to be conciliatory, forbearing and patient," Seward advised Lincoln on January 27, "and so open the way for the rising of a Union Party in the seceding States which will bring them back."[30]

Accordingly, Seward backed a proposal to admit New Mexico (which included what is now Arizona) as a state. This was an apparent violation of the Republican platform, for slavery was legal in the territory. Lincoln grudgingly approved the proposal, since it was clear that the institution would not take root there. Several Southern congressmen, however, considered the New Mexico scheme a trick to divide the upper and lower South by the appearance of concession, and voted against it. So did three-quarters of the Republicans. The House killed the measure in March.

More significant was an invitation from the Virginia legislature for all states to send delegates to a "peace convention" in Washington on February 4. This was the upper South's major attempt to find some basis for voluntary reconstruction. But the enterprise was doomed from the start. Seward and his allies did manage to persuade most Republican states to send delegates as a gesture of goodwill. But the Confederate

---

[30]Allan Nevins, *The Emergence of Lincoln*, 2 vols. (New York, 1950), II, 431.

states did not participate, and the anticompromise Republicans were suspicious. Although many distinguished men attended the convention (ex-President John Tyler was chairman), they failed to develop any fresh proposals to resolve the crisis. After three weeks of labor, the convention could come up with nothing more than a modified version of the Crittenden Compromise. Congress rejected this as it had previously rejected similar proposals. Nevertheless, the peace convention did help to channel the energies of the upper South into Unionist rather than secession activities during the month before Lincoln's inauguration.

★ *Lincoln Takes the Helm*

Seward's activities alarmed anticompromise Republicans. They feared that Lincoln would defer too much to the New Yorker. Like Seward, Lincoln hoped for voluntary reconstruction through the reassertion of Southern Unionism. But he was afraid that too much forbearance would legitimize secession. Lincoln conceived his task to be one of maintaining the symbols of national authority in the South as a beacon to Unionists while at the same time reassuring Southerners that the government threatened none of their vital interests. During his trip from Springfield to Washington in February, Lincoln made many brief speeches along the way to crowds eager to see the relatively unknown prairie lawyer. Because he wished to say nothing that could be distorted, most of the speeches contained platitudes that seemed to make light of the crisis. To many observers, these speeches revealed Lincoln as a lightweight unequal to the grave occasion.

Nothing could have been further from the truth. Lincoln intended to take a reassuring but firm line in his inaugural address. The initial draft stated that "all the power at my disposal will be used to reclaim the public property and places which have fallen; to hold, occupy and possess these, and all other property belonging to the government." Seward and other advisers persuaded Lincoln to delete the reference to reclaiming federal property already seized. Seward also suggested a number of other modifications to soften the general tone of the address. The final version of Lincoln's inaugural address—the most important such speech in American history—was a careful balancing of the sword and the olive branch. It began by assuring the South— for the hundredth time—that the administration had no intention of interfering with slavery where it existed. Where hostility to the federal government was so great "in any interior locality" as to prevent the normal functioning of federal activities, the government would suspend these activities "for the time." This was the olive branch. But the Union was "perpetual," said Lincoln; secession was the "essence of anarchy," for its success would mean that a disaffected minority could break up the government at will. Lincoln intended to "take care, as the Constitution itself expressly enjoins upon me, that the laws of the Union be faithfully executed in all the States." The government would "hold, occupy, and possess" its property and "collect the [customs] duties and imposts." There would be no "invasion—no using of force . . . beyond what may be necessary for these objects." The new President closed with an eloquent peroration, part of which had been suggested by Seward:

> In *your* hands, my dissatisfied fellow countrymen, and not in *mine,* is the momentous issue of civil war. The government will not assail *you.* You can have no conflict, without being yourselves the aggressors. *You* have no oath registered in

Heaven to destroy the government, while *I* shall have the most solemn one to "preserve, protect and defend" it.

. . . We must not be enemies. Though passion may have strained, it must not break our bonds of affection. The mystic chords of memory, stretching from every battle-field, and patriot grave, to every living heart and hearthstone, all over this broad land, will yet swell the chorus of the Union, when again touched, as surely they will be, by the better angels of our nature.[31]

Ever since March 4, 1861, contemporaries and historians have debated the meaning of this address. Did the promise to enforce the laws, to collect customs duties, and to "hold, occupy and possess" federal property mean coercion? Did it mean that arsenals and forts already seized by the Confederate states would be repossessed, or only that the four forts still in federal possession—Sumter in Charleston harbor, Pickens in Pensacola Bay, and two remote posts in the Florida keys— would be held? How would the duties be collected—by ships stationed offshore? How could the laws be executed at "interior localities" if the government left vacant the offices—federal courts, land offices, post offices, and the like—necessary to execute them? Lincoln intentionally left these matters ambiguous, to avoid alienating the upper South and to give himself maximum flexibility.

Reactions to the message varied by section and party. Secessionists denounced it as a "Declaration of War." Most Republicans praised its firmness. Many Northern Democrats criticized it as either too obscure or too warlike, but Stephen A. Douglas considered it a "peace offering." The address had been aimed above all at the conditional Unionists of the upper South, and reactions of many of them, while hardly ebullient, were gratifying. "What more does any reasonable Southern man expect or desire?" asked a North Carolinian. "Are not . . . these . . . cheering assurances enough to induce the whole South to wait for the sober second thought of the North?"[32]

★ Fort Sumter and the End of Peace

The main purpose of Lincoln's inaugural message was to buy time—time for the disunion fever to subside, time for the presumed legions of Southern Unionists to regain the upper hand, time for the process of voluntary reconstruction to get under way. But on the day after his inauguration, Lincoln received some bad news that seemed likely to deny him the necessary time. From Major Robert Anderson came word that the garrison at Fort Sumter would be forced to evacuate unless resupplied within a few weeks. For more than two months Sumter had been a symbol of the Union presence in the South, a symbol out of all proportion to its intrinsic military importance. Now the Union government would be forced to act—decisively and soon—or to abandon its last effective symbol of authority in the lower South.

Sumter was a nearly completed fort on an island at the entrance to Charleston harbor. When South Carolina seceded on December 20, the fort was still unoccupied. Most of the eighty-odd U.S. soldiers in the area were stationed at Fort Moultrie, an obsolete fortification on a spit of land a mile across the harbor from Sumter. The

[31]Basler, *Works of Lincoln,* IV, 249–271, reproduces the first and final drafts of the address, with annotations of all revisions and corrections.

[32]Crofts, *Reluctant Confederates,* pp. 261–262; James G. Randall, *Lincoln the President,* 4 vols. (New York, 1945–1955), I, 308–309.

commander of the garrison, Robert Anderson, had been sent to Charleston because as a Kentuckian he would be viewed as being less provocative than his Massachusetts-born predecessor. In response to Anderson's report that Moultrie was indefensible against an attack by land, the War Department on December 11 had given him discretionary orders to move his command to Sumter if he thought an attack imminent. Anderson had every reason to expect an attack. South Carolina was going out of the Union; its officials were demanding surrender of the Charleston forts; militia companies were arming and drilling. After dusk on December 26, Anderson secretly spiked Moultrie's guns and transferred the garrison to Sumter.

Anderson believed that this move would preserve peace, for Moultrie's weakness invited attack while Sumter's strength would deter it. But the transfer outraged South Carolinians and set off reverberations that reached the White House. Commissioners from the independent republic of South Carolina had just arrived in Washington to negotiate a surrender of the forts and of other U.S. property—which they now claimed as South Carolina's property. They regarded the occupation of Sumter as a violation of an earlier pledge by Buchanan not to change the status quo in Charleston.

But the administration felt that the South had pushed it around long enough. The Northern press was hailing Anderson as a hero. "Never have I known the *entire people* more unanimous on any question," wrote an influential Buchanan Democrat. "We are ruined if Anderson is recalled or if Sumter is given up. . . . There will be hardly a man found who will not on this question be ready to attack the South."[33] Buchanan's cabinet was undergoing a shakeup owing to the departure of secessionists and their replacement by Northerners of staunch Unionist fiber. Secretary of State Jeremiah Black of Pennsylvania, Attorney General Edwin M. Stanton of Ohio, and Secretary of War Joseph Holt, a Kentucky Unionist, emerged as the strong men of the reconstructed cabinet. They stiffened the administration's backbone against Southerners who demanded that Buchanan withdraw the troops from Sumter. Buchanan astonished the South Carolinians by saying no.

The President went further and ordered reinforcements sent to Anderson. The army decided to use an unarmed merchant vessel rather than a warship for this purpose, to minimize the publicity and provocation. The ship *Star of the West* was chartered, loaded with two hundred troops and supplies, and dispatched on January 5. Despite secrecy, word leaked out, and the South Carolina militia was ready for her with shotted guns. They were more ready than Fort Sumter was, for the official notification to Anderson of the expedition had gone astray. When the *Star of the West* entered the harbor on January 9, the shore batteries opened on her, scoring one direct hit before the captain turned her around and headed back North. Lacking instructions and loath to start a war, Anderson had withheld Sumter's fire during the incident.

The North erupted in anger at this affair, while South Carolina bristled with accusations of federal aggression and with new demands for Sumter's surrender. But despite war cries on both sides, war did not come. The Buchanan administration worked out an informal truce with South Carolina that preserved the status quo for the time being. Secessionists in other states persuaded the South Carolinians to lie low until the Confederacy could complete its organization and begin to build an army. On March 1, Jefferson Davis ordered Confederate General Pierre Gustave T. Beauregard to take command at Charleston. This removed the Sumter question from the hands of the hotheaded Carolinians. Meanwhile, the Confederacy also respected a truce

---

[33]Samuel L. M. Barlow to Judah P. Benjamin, December 29, 1861, Barlow Papers.

worked out earlier between the U.S. navy and the Florida militia whereby Southern troops agreed not to attack Fork Pickens at Pensacola if the navy did not try to land reinforcements. The Confederacy sent commissioners to Washington to negotiate the surrender of both forts.

Lincoln and Fort Sumter

This was the situation confronting Lincoln when he learned on March 5, his second day as President, that Anderson's supplies would soon be exhausted. The status quo could not last much longer. The crucial question was what to do about it. The hawkish wing of the Republican party insisted that Sumter should be reinforced even at the cost of war. From all over the North came letters and telegrams with the same message. "Give up Sumpter [sic], Sir, & you are as dead politically as John Brown is physically," a correspondent told Lincoln. "You have got to fight." The editor of an influential Connecticut newspaper told the secretary of the navy: "I will gladly be one of the volunteers to sail into that harbor past all the guns of hell rather than see the flag dishonored and the government demoralized."[34] But the doves, led by Seward, urged that the fort be evacuated in the interest of avoiding war and keeping the door open for voluntary reconstruction. Seward did more than merely recommend this policy. Without authorization from Lincoln, he virtually assured Confederate commissioners in Washington that Sumter would be surrendered. He leaked similar reports to the press.

Lincoln had made no such decision, although he did lean this way for a time. General in Chief Winfield Scott advised him that it would be impossible to reinforce the fort. A poll of the cabinet on March 15 disclosed that only Postmaster General Montgomery Blair unequivocally favored reinforcement. Faced with advice from his advisers to pull out, the President wavered in his determination to "hold, occupy, and possess" the fort. But during the last two weeks of March the hawks gained the upper hand with Northern opinion. Republicans began to insist that the government *do* something to assert its sovereignty. Republican newspapers printed editorials with such titles as: "HAVE WE A GOVERNMENT?" "WANTED—A POLICY." "COME TO THE POINT." The restlessness and tension of the Northern people were approaching the breaking point. "Better almost anything than additional suspense," said one newspaper. The German-American leader Carl Schurz felt the pulse of public opinion for Lincoln and reported widespread dissatisfaction with the administration. But "as soon as one vigorous blow is struck," said Schurz, "as soon as, for instance, Fort Sumter is reinforced, public opinion in the free States will at once rally to your support."[35]

This stiffened Lincoln's initial resolve to hold the fort. So did the advice of Gustavus V. Fox, a former naval officer from Massachusetts, who suggested a plan whereby supplies and reinforcements could be run into Fort Sumter at night while cannoneers in the fort and on warships stood by to suppress the Confederate guns if they tried to interfere. Lincoln accepted the plan and on March 29 ordered Fox to prepare the expedition. At the same time he also authorized—for the second time—

---

[34]Richard N. Current, *Lincoln and the First Shot* (Philadelphia, 1963), p. 119; Bruce Catton, *The Coming Fury* (Garden City, N.Y., 1961), p. 278.

[35]Stampp, *And the War Came*, pp. 267–268; Current, *Lincoln and the First Shot*, p. 118.

WILLIAM H. SEWARD. Having served four years as governor of New York and twelve years as a U.S. senator, he was the odds-on favorite to win the Republican presidential nomination in 1860. When Lincoln won instead, Seward hoped to dominate the new administration as secretary of state and "premier," but soon discovered that Lincoln intended to run his own administration. Seward became an effective ally; in 1867 he crowned his career by negotiating the purchase of Alaska from Russia.

LIBRARY OF CONGRESS

an expedition to reinforce Fort Pickens.[36] In a switch from two weeks earlier, the entire cabinet except Seward and Secretary of the Interior Caleb Smith now approved the decision to hold Sumter.

This decision put Seward in a tight spot. His peace policy would collapse. His assurances to Confederate commissioners would be exposed as deceit. His aspirations to be premier would crumble. In an ill-advised attempt to repair the damage, he penned a memorandum to Lincoln on April 1. Seward again proposed to abandon Sumter (though to reinforce Pickens). But the most important feature of this docu-

[36]On March 12, Lincoln had ordered that Fort Pickens in Florida be reinforced. This was more feasible than reinforcement of Sumter, for Pickens was outside the harbor entrance and thus less vulnerable than Sumter, which was ringed by scores of Confederate cannon. It was also less provocative, for Pickens was not the powerful symbol to both sides that Sumter had become. But weeks passed and Lincoln received no word whether his order to reinforce Pickens had been carried out. On April 6, he finally learned that it had not. The naval commander there had cited the previous agreement not to reinforce so long as the Confederates refrained from attacking the fort and had refused to recognize new orders unless issued directly by his superiors in the Naval Department. Such orders were sent April 6; Pickens was reinforced and held by the Union through the Civil War.

ment was its foreign policy recommendations. Spain had sent troops to intervene in the troubled politics of Santo Domingo. France was casting covetous eyes toward Mexico. Seward would "demand explanations" from Spain and France and, if the explanations were not "satisfactory," would declare war. He would also "seek explanations" from Britain and Russia concerning violations of the Monroe Doctrine. Seward believed that a foreign war would reunite the country. To execute this policy there must be firm leadership, and Seward modestly offered to assume the responsibility. Lincoln gently but firmly rejected these extraordinary suggestions. He also reminded his secretary of state that whatever decisions were made or orders issued, "*I* must do it." The chastened Seward wrote no more such memoranda. There was no longer any doubt in his mind about who was premier of this administration.[37]

The President did agree to meet with a spokesman for Virginia Unionists before giving the final go-ahead for the Sumter expedition. Lincoln talked with the Virginia representative on April 4, but the meeting was unproductive. No record was kept of the conversation, and no reliable evidence of its nature exists. Whatever happened, it seems to have soured Lincoln's faith in Southern Unionism, at least temporarily. He made up his mind that very day (April 4) to proceed with the Sumter expedition. He sent a letter to Major Anderson advising him that relief was on the way.

The nature of this expedition had changed in a crucial way since Fox first suggested it. A full-scale attempt to reinforce Sumter was certain to provoke shooting, in which the North might appear to be the aggressor. This would drive the upper South into the Confederacy. Thus Lincoln conceived the idea of separating the question of reinforcement from that of provisions. He would send in supplies, but the troops and warships would stand by to go into action only if the Confederates stopped the supplies. And he would notify Southern officials of his intentions. If they opened fire on the unarmed tugs carrying provisions, they would stand convicted of attacking "a mission of humanity" bringing "food for hungry men."

Lincoln had some reason to believe that the Confederates would resist the landing of supplies. An emissary he had sent to Charleston reported the bellicose determination he found there. But if the Confederates stayed their hand, the status quo in Charleston harbor could be maintained, peace would be preserved for at least a while, and the policy of voluntary reconstruction would have a new lease on life. If the South did fire on the supply ships, the responsibility for starting a war would rest on Jefferson Davis's shoulders. On April 6, Lincoln sent a special messenger to Charleston with a dispatch notifying the governor of South Carolina "to expect an attempt will be made to supply Fort-Sumpter [sic] with provisions only; and that, if such attempt be not resisted, no effort to throw in men, arms, ammunition, will be made, without further notice, [except] in case of an attack on the Fort."[38]

The Confederates Fire the First Shot

The Confederacy accepted Lincoln's challenge. Given the assumptions that governed its policy, the Davis administration could scarcely do otherwise. Sumter had become to the South as potent a symbol of sovereignty as it was to the North. The Confederacy could not be considered a viable nation so long as a foreign power held a fort in one of its principal harbors. The Confederate provisional Congress had resolved on February

---

[37]Basler, *Works of Lincoln*, IV, 316–318.
[38]Ibid., p. 323.

15 that Sumter and other forts must be acquired "as early as practicable . . . either by negotiation, or force." Negotiation had failed; the only option left was force. The prolonged suspense had stretched Southern as well as Northern nerves to the breaking point. Any action was better than continued uncertainty. Confederate leaders also believed that a shooting war would bring the upper South to their side. Virginia secessionists had descended on Charleston with the message that Virginia would join her sister states instantly if South Carolina would "strike a blow!"[39]

On April 9, the Confederate cabinet made the fateful decision to strike a blow at Sumter. Davis ordered Beauregard to demand the fort's surrender before the relief expedition arrived. If surrender was refused, he was to batter it into submission with the heavy guns that now bore on Sumter from four sides. Only Secretary of State Robert Toombs opposed this decision. It "will lose us every friend at the North," Toombs reportedly told Davis. "You will wantonly strike a hornet's nest. . . . Legions now quiet will swarm out and sting us to death. It is unnecessary. It puts us in the wrong. It is fatal."[40]

Anderson rejected the demand for surrender. But he remarked that if left alone, his lack of supplies would force him soon to vacate the fort. When Beauregard asked him to fix a time for such a withdrawal, Anderson named April 15—unless he received supplies before then. This was unsatisfactory, for the Confederates knew that the supply ships were approaching the harbor. At 4:30 A.M. on April 12, the Confederate guns opened fire. The Union relief expedition was helpless to intervene because a mix-up in orders had diverted its strongest warship to Fort Pickens, and high seas prevented the other ships from coming to Sumter's aid. Outmanned and outgunned (the Confederate batteries fired four thousand rounds to Sumter's one thousand), the Union garrison surrendered after thirty-three hours of bombardment that destroyed large portions of the fort—though not a man on either side was killed in this first engagement of what became America's bloodiest war.

On April 14, the Confederate stars and bars replaced the stars and stripes at Fort Sumter. War had begun. And it had begun in such a way as to fulfill Toombs's prediction. Seldom in history has a counterrevolution so effectively ensured the success of the very revolution it sought to avert.

---

[39]Current, *Lincoln and the First Shot*, pp. 138–139.

[40] These words were quoted by Toombs's first biographer, Pleasant A. Stovall, *Robert Toombs* (New York, 1892), p. 226. Although one may be permitted to doubt that Toombs uttered such prescient sentiments in precisely these words, subsequent biographers and most historians have accepted the quotation as authentic.

Bibliography

ABBREVIATIONS

AH	*Agricultural History*
AHR	*American Historical Review*
CWH	*Civil War History*
JAH	*Journal of American History*
JEH	*Journal of Economic History*
JNH	*Journal of Negro History*
JSH	*Journal of Southern History*
MVHR	*Mississippi Valley Historical Review*
SAQ	*South Atlantic Quarterly*

★ Bibliographies on the Civil War and Reconstruction Era

The number of books and articles on the era of the Civil War and Reconstruction is so enormous that the following essay can provide only a selective listing of the most important and useful of them. Students desiring a more detailed bibliography should consult the following: Don E. Fehrenbacher (ed.), *Manifest Destiny and the Coming of the Civil War* (1970); David Donald (ed.), *The Nation in Crisis, 1861–1877* (1969); and the relevant portions of Frank Freidel (ed.), *Harvard Guide to American History,* rev. ed. (1974). The bibliography of James G. Randall and David Donald, *The Civil War and Reconstruction,* 2d ed. rev. (1969), contains a rich listing of items published before 1969. The essays by Charles Dew, Joe Gray Taylor, LaWanda Cox, and Harold Woodman in John B. Boles and Evelyn Thomas Nolen (eds.), *Interpreting Southern History* (1987), contain excellent reviews of recent literature on slavery, secession, the war, emancipation, Reconstruction, and the New South. For substantial bibliographies on slavery consult John D. Smith, *Black Slavery in the Americas: An Interdisciplinary Bibliography,* 2 vols. (1983). The December issue each year through 1977 of the quarterly journal *Civil War History* (1954–   ) classifies articles dealing with the Civil War era published in other journals during the previous year. Each issue of the *Journal of American History* and the May issue each year of the *Journal of Southern History* list articles published in other journals, including many articles on the Civil War era. The ongoing volumes of *Writings in American History* and *America: History and Life* contain classified listings of books and articles on all aspects of American history. For guides to the holdings of the U.S. Archives on the Civil War era, see Kenneth W. Munden and Henry Putney Beers, *The Union: A Guide to the Federal Archives Relating to the Civil War* (1986), and Henry Putney Beers, *The Confederacy: A Guide to the Archives of the Confederate States of America* (1986).

★ Biographical and Related Works

Biographies of important persons provide a great deal of information of value. The following is an alphabetical listing (by subject) of biographies of many of the principal figures of the antebellum period. In some cases more than one biography is cited, and where relevant, diaries, collected letters, and other writings of individuals are also cited.

ADAMS, CHARLES FRANCIS
Duberman, Martin, *Charles Francis Adams* (1961).

ATCHISON, DAVID
Parrish, William E., *David Rice Atchison of Missouri: Border Politician* (1961).

BANKS, NATHANIEL P.
Harrington, Fred H., *Fighting Politician: Major General N. P. Banks* (1948).

BATES, EDWARD
Cain, Marvin R., *Lincoln's Attorney General: Edward Bates of Missouri* (1965).

BELL, JOHN
Parks, Joseph H., *John Bell of Tennessee* (1950).

BENJAMIN, JUDAH P.
Evans, Eli N., *Judah P. Benjamin: The Jewish Confederate* (1988).

BIRNEY, JAMES G.
Fladeland, Betty, *James Gillespie Birney: Slaveholder to Abolitionist* (1955).

BLAIR, FRANCIS P.
Smith, Elbert B., *Francis Preston Blair* (1980).
Smith, William E., *The Francis Preston Blair Family in Politics,* 2 vols. (1933).

BLAIR, FRANCIS P., JR., and BLAIR, MONTGOMERY
See the book by William E. Smith cited in the previous entry.

BRECKINRIDGE, JOHN C.
Davis, William C., *Breckinridge: Statesman, Soldier, Symbol* (1974).

BROWN, ALBERT GALLATIN
Ranck, James B., *Albert Gallatin Brown: Radical Southern Nationalist* (1937).

BROWN, JOHN
Boyer, Richard O., *The Legend of John Brown: A Biography and a History* (1973).
Oates, Stephen B., *To Purge This Land with Blood: A Biography of John Brown* (1970).
Villard, Oswald Garrison, *John Brown, 1800–1859: A Biography* (1910).

BROWN, JOSEPH E.
Parks, Joseph Howard, *Joseph E. Brown of Georgia* (1977).

BUCHANAN, JAMES
Klein, Philip S., *President James Buchanan* (1962).

CALHOUN, JOHN C.
Coit, Margaret, *John C. Calhoun, American Portrait* (1950).
Niven, John, *John C. Calhoun and the Price of Union* (1988).
Wiltse, Charles M., *John C. Calhoun*, 3 vols. (1944–1951).

CAMERON, SIMON
Bradley, Erwin S., *Simon Cameron, Lincoln's Secretary of War: A Political Biography* (1966).

CASS, LEWIS
Woodford, Frank B., *Lewis Cass: The Last Jeffersonian* (1950).

CHASE, SALMON P.
Blue, Frederick, *Salmon P. Chase: A Life in Politics* (1987).

CLAY, HENRY
Eaton, Clement, *Henry Clay and the Art of American Politics* (1957).
Van Deusen, Glyndon G., *The Life of Henry Clay* (1937).

COBB, HOWELL
Simpson, John Eddings, *Howell Cobb: The Politics of Ambition* (1973).

COLT, SAMUEL
Rohan, Jack, *Yankee Arms Maker: The Story of Sam Colt and His Six-Shot Peacemaker* (1948).

CRITTENDEN, JOHN J.
Kirwan, Albert D., *John J. Crittenden: The Struggle for the Union* (1962).

DAVIS, JEFFERSON
Eaton, Clement, *Jefferson Davis* (1977).
Strode, Hudson, *Jefferson Davis*, 3 vols. (1955–1964).
Monroe, Haskell M., Jr., et al. (eds.), *The Papers of Jefferson Davis*, 6 vols. so far (to 1860) (1971–   ).
Rowland, Dunbar (ed.), *Jefferson Davis, Constitutionalist: His Letters, Papers and Speeches*, 10 vols. (1923).

DE BOW, JAMES B. D.
Skipper, Otis Clark, *J. B. D. De Bow, Magazinist of the Old South* (1958).

DIX, DOROTHEA
Wilson, Dorothy Clarke, *Stranger and Traveler: The Story of Dorothea Dix, American Reformer* (1975).

DOUGLAS, STEPHEN A.
Johannsen, Robert W., *Stephen A. Douglas* (1973).
Milton, George F., *The Eve of Conflict: Stephen A. Douglas and the Needless War* (1934).

DOUGLASS, FREDERICK
Foner, Philip S., *The Life and Writings of Frederick Douglass,* 4 vols. (1950–1955).
McFeely, William S., *Frederick Douglass* (1991).
Quarles, Benjamin, *Frederick Douglass* (1948).

EVERETT, EDWARD
Reid, Ronald F., *Edward Everett: Unionist Orator* (1990).

FILLMORE, MILLARD
Rayback, Robert J., *Millard Fillmore: Biography of a President* (1959).

FINNEY, CHARLES GRANDISON
Hardman, Keith, *Charles Grandison Finney, 1792–1875: Revivalist and Reformer* (1987).

FITZHUGH, GEORGE
Genovese, Eugene D., *The World the Slaveholders Made* (1969).
Wish, Harvey, *George Fitzhugh: Propagandist of the Old South* (1943).

FOX, GUSTAVUS V.
Thompson, Robert M., and Richard Wainwright (eds.), *Confidential Correspondence of Gustavus Vasa Fox, Assistant Secretary of the Navy, 1861–1985,* 2 vols. (1918–1919).

FRÉMONT, JOHN C.
Nevins, Allan, *Frémont: Pathmarker of the West* (1955).

GARRISON, WILLIAM LLOYD
Merrill, Walter M., *Against Wind and Tide: A Biography of William Lloyd Garrison* (1963).
Thomas, John L., *The Liberator: William Lloyd Garrison* (1963).
Merrill, Walter M., and Louis Ruchames (eds.), *The Letters of William Lloyd Garrison,* 6 vols. (1971–1981).

GEARY, JOHN W.
Tinkcom, Harry M., *John White Geary: Soldier-Statesman, 1819–1873* (1940).

GIDDINGS, JOSHUA
Stewart, James B., *Joshua Giddings and the Tactics of Radical Politics* (1970).

GREELEY, HORACE
Hale, William H., *Horace Greeley: Voice of the People* (1950).
Van Deusen, Glyndon G., *Horace Greeley: Nineteenth-Century Crusader* (1953).

GREGG, WILLIAM
Mitchell, Broadus, *William Gregg: Factory Master of the Old South* (1928).

GRIMKÉ, ANGELINA AND SARAH
Birney, Catherine H., *The Grimké Sisters: Sarah and Angelina Grimké* (1977).
Lerner, Gerda, *The Grimké Sisters from South Carolina: Rebels Against Slavery* (1967).
Lumkin, Katherine Du Pre, *The Emancipation of Angelina Grimké* (1974).

HALE, JOHN P.
Sewell, Richard H., *John P. Hale and the Politics of Abolition* (1965).

HAMLIN, HANNIBAL
Hunt, Harry Draper, *Hannibal Hamlin of Maine: Lincoln's First Vice-President* (1969).

HAMMOND, JAMES H.
Faust, Drew Gilpin, *James Henry Hammond and the Old South* (1982).
Bleser, Carol (ed.), *Secret and Sacred: The Diaries of James Henry Hammond, a Southern Slaveholder* (1988).

HELPER, HINTON ROWAN
Bailey, Hugh C., *Hinton Rowan Helper: Abolitionist-Racist* (1965).

HIGGINSON, THOMAS WENTWORTH
Edelstein, Tilden G., *Strange Enthusiasm, A Life of Thomas Wentworth Higginson* (1968).

HUNTER, ROBERT M. T.
Simms, Henry H., *Life of Robert M. T. Hunter: A Study in Sectionalism and Secession* (1935).

JACKSON, ANDREW
Remini, Robert, *The Life of Andrew Jackson* (1988).

JULIAN, GEORGE W.
Riddleberger, Patrick W., *George Washington Julian, Radical Republican* (1966).

LEE, ROBERT E.
Connelly, Thomas L., *The Marble Man: Robert E. Lee and His Image in American Society* (1977).
Dowdey, Clifford, *Lee* (1965).
Freeman, Douglas Southall, *R. E. Lee: A Biography,* 4 vols. (1934–1935).
Nolan, Alan T., *Lee Considered: General Robert E. Lee and Civil War History* (1991).
Dowdey, Clifford (ed.), *The Wartime Papers of R. E. Lee* (1961).

LINCOLN, ABRAHAM
Boritt, Gabor S. (ed.), *The Historian's Lincoln* (1988).
Current, Richard N., *The Lincoln Nobody Knows* (1958).
Donald, David, *Lincoln Reconsidered,* 2d ed. (1961).
Fehrenbacher, Don E., *Lincoln in Text and Context: Collected Essays* (1967).
Luthin, Reinhard, *The Real Abraham Lincoln* (1960).
McPherson, James M., *Abraham Lincoln and the Second American Revolution* (1991).
Neely, Mark E., Jr., *The Abraham Lincoln Encyclopedia* (1982).
Oates, Stephen B., *With Malice Toward None: The Life of Abraham Lincoln* (1977).
Randall, James G., *Lincoln the President,* 4th volume completed by Richard N. Current, 4 vols. (1945–1955).
Strozier, Charles B., *Lincoln's Quest for Union* (1982).
Thomas, Benjamin P., *Abraham Lincoln* (1952).
Basler, Roy P., et al. (eds.), *The Collected Works of Abraham Lincoln,* 9 vols. (1953–1955); *The Collected Works of Abraham Lincoln—Supplement, 1832–1865* (1974); and *Second Supplement, 1848–1865* (1990).
Cuomo, Mario, and Harold Holzer (eds.), *Lincoln on Democracy* (1990).

LINCOLN, MARY TODD
Baker, Jean, *Mary Todd Lincoln: A Biography* (1987).

MANN, HORACE
Messerli, Jonathan, *Horace Mann: A Biography* (1972).

MASON, JAMES M.
Mason, Virginia, *The Public Life . . . of James M. Mason* (1903).

McLEAN, JOHN
Weisenburger, Francis P., *The Life of John McLean: A Politician on the United States Supreme Court* (1937).

OLMSTED, FREDERICK LAW
Roper, Laura, *FLO: A Biography of Frederick Law Olmsted* (1973).

PARKER, THEODORE
Commager, Henry Steele, *Theodore Parker* (1936).

PHILLIPS, WENDELL
Stewart, James Brewer, *Wendell Phillips: Liberty's Hero* (1986).

PIERCE, FRANKLIN
Nichols, Roy F., *Franklin Pierce: Young Hickory of the Granite Hills* (1958).

POLK, JAMES K.
Bergeron, Paul H., *The Presidency of James K. Polk* (1987).
Quaife, Milo M. (ed.), *The Diary of James K. Polk During His Presidency,* 4 vols. (1910).
Weaver, Herbert, et al. (eds.), *The Correspondence of James K. Polk,* 7 vols. so far (1969–).

QUITMAN, JOHN A.
May, Robert, *John A. Quitman: Old South Crusader* (1985).

RHETT, ROBERT BARNWELL
White, Laura A., *Robert Barnwell Rhett, Father of Secession* (1931).

RUFFIN, EDMUND
Mathew, William M., *Edmund Ruffin and the Crisis of Slavery in the Old South* (1988).
Mitchell, Betty L., *Edmund Ruffin: A Biography* (1981).
Scarborough, William S. (ed.), *The Diary of Edmund Ruffin,* 3 vols. (1972–1989).

SCHURZ, CARL
Trefousse, Hans, *Carl Schurz: A Biography* (1982).

SCOTT, WINFIELD
Elliott, Charles W., *Winfield Scott: The Soldier and the Man* (1937).

SEWARD, WILLIAM H.
Van Deusen, Glyndon G., *William Henry Seward* (1967).
Baker, George E. (ed.), *The Works of William H. Seward,* 5 vols. (1853–1884).

SHERMAN, JOHN
Burton, Theodore E., *John Sherman* (1906).

SLIDELL, JOHN
Sears, Louis M., *John Slidell* (1925).

SMITH, GERRIT
Harlow, Ralph V., *Gerrit Smith: Philanthropist and Reformer* (1939).

STEPHENS, ALEXANDER H.
Schott, Thomas E., *Alexander H. Stephens of Georgia: A Biography* (1988).
Von Abele, Rudolph, *Alexander H. Stephens: A Biography* (1946).

STEVENS, THADDEUS
Brodie, Fawn M., *Thaddeus Stevens: Scourge of the South* (1959).

STOWE, HARRIET BEECHER
Foster, Charles H., *The Rungless Ladder: Harriet Beecher Stowe and New England Puritanism* (1954).
Wagenknecht, Edward, *Harriet Beecher Stowe: The Known and the Unknown* (1965).

SUMNER, CHARLES
Donald, David, *Charles Sumner and the Coming of the Civil War* (1960).
Palmer, Beverly Wilson (ed.), *The Selected Letters of Charles Sumner,* 2 vols. (1990).

TANEY, ROGER B.
Lewis, Walker, *Without Fear or Favor: A Biography of Chief Justice Roger Brooke Taney* (1965).
Swisher, Carl B., *Roger B. Taney* (1935).

TAPPAN, LEWIS
Wyatt-Brown, Bertram, *Lewis Tappan and the Evangelical War Against Slavery* (1969).

TAYLOR, ZACHARY
Bauer, K. Jack, *Zachary Taylor: Soldier, Planter, Statesman of the Old Southwest* (1985).
Hamilton, Holman, *Zachary Taylor,* 2 vols. (1941–1951).

TOOMBS, ROBERT
Thompson, William Y., *Robert Toombs of Georgia* (1966).

TYLER, JOHN
Chidsey, Donald B., *And Tyler Too* (1978).

VAN BUREN, MARTIN
Cole, Donald B., *Martin Van Buren and the American Political System* (1984).
Niven, John, *Martin Van Buren: The Romantic Age of American Politics* (1983).

WADE, BENJAMIN
Trefousse, Hans L., *Benjamin Franklin Wade: Radical Republican from Ohio* (1963).

WALKER, ROBERT J.
Shenton, James P., *Robert John Walker: A Politician from Jackson to Lincoln* (1961).

WALKER, WILLIAM
Carr, Albert H., *The World and William Walker* (1963).

WEBSTER, DANIEL
Bartlett, Irving H., *Daniel Webster* (1978).
Baxter, Maurice G., *One and Inseparable: Daniel Webster and the Union* (1984).
Current, Richard N., *Daniel Webster and the Rise of National Conservatism* (1963).

WELD, THEODORE
Abzug, Robert H., *Passionate Liberator: Theodore Dwight Weld and the Dilemma of Reform* (1980).

WELLES, GIDEON
Niven, John, *Gideon Welles: Lincoln's Secretary of the Navy* (1973).
Beale, Howard K., and Alan W. Brownsward (eds.), *The Diary of Gideon Welles* (1960).

WIGFALL, LOUIS T.
King, Alvy L., *Louis T. Wigfall, Southern Fire-eater* (1970).

WILMOT, DAVID
Going, Charles B., *David Wilmot, Free-Soiler* (1924).

WILSON, HENRY
Abbott, Richard H., *Cobbler in Congress: The Life of Henry Wilson* (1972).

WISE, HENRY A.
Simpson, Craig M., *A Good Southerner: The Life of Henry A. Wise of Virginia* (1985).

YANCEY, WILLIAM LOWNDES
DuBose, John Witherspoon, *The Life and Times of William Lowndes Yancey* (1892).

★ General Works on the Civil War and Reconstruction Era

Two eminent historians writing a half-century apart have produced magisterial multivolume narratives of America's sectional trauma: James Ford Rhodes, *History of the United States from the Compromise of 1850 to the McKinley-Bryan Campaign of 1896,* 8 vols. (1892–1919); and Allan Nevins, *Ordeal of the Union,* covering the years 1847–1857, 2 vols. (1947), *The Emergence of Lincoln,* covering 1857–1861, 2 vols. (1950), and *The War for the Union,* 4 vols. (1959–1971). In addition to James G. Randall and David Donald, *The Civil War and Reconstruction,* cited in the first section of this bibliography, other important one-volume studies covering all or part of this period include Peter J. Parish, *The American Civil War* (1975), and William R. Brock, *Conflict and Transformation: The United States 1844–1877* (1973), both by British historians who offer valuable perspectives on the American experience; David Herbert Donald, *Liberty and Union* (1978); Arthur C. Cole, *The Irrepressible Conflict 1850–1865* (1934); James M. McPherson, *Battle Cry of Freedom: The Civil War Era* (1988); Joel Silbey, *The American Political Nation, 1838–1893* (1991); Richard H. Sewell, *A House Divided: Sectionalism and Civil War, 1848–1865* (1988); Roger L. Ransom, *Conflict and Compromise: The Political Economy of Slavery, Emancipation, and the American Civil War* (1989); and Charles P. Roland, *An American Iliad: The Story of the Civil War* (1991).

Charles A. Beard and Mary A. Beard's sweeping survey of American history, *The Rise of American Civilization,* 2 vols. (1927), interprets the Civil War as a "Second American Revolution," by which an industrializing North destroyed the agrarian civilization of the Old South. Refinements and modifications of this interpretation can be found in Barrington Moore, *Social Origins of Dictatorship and Democracy* (1966), chap. 3: "The American Civil War: The Last Capitalist Revolution"; Margaret Shortreed, "The Anti-Slavery Radicals, 1840–1868," *Past and Present,* no. 16 (1959), 65–87; and Raimondo Luraghi, *The Rise and Fall of the Plantation South* (1978). Carl N. Degler, "The Two Cultures and the Civil War," in Stanley Coben and Lorman Ratner (eds.), *The Development of an American Culture* (1970), pp. 92–119, emphasizes cultural differences between North and South.

Wilbur J. Cash, *The Mind of the South* (1941), evokes the impact of the sectional conflict on the South; while Robert Penn Warren, *The Legacy of the Civil War* (1964), a book published during the centennial commemoration of the conflict, critically appraises the war's meaning. Several essays in Arthur S. Link and Rembert W. Patrick (eds.), *Writing Southern History: Essays in Historiography in Honor of Fletcher M. Green* (1965), evaluate historical writing about the South during the middle decades of the nineteenth century. Carl N. Degler, *The Other South: Southern Dissenters in the Nineteenth Century* (1974), offers a fresh and enlightening account of Southern whites who resisted the dominant institutions and developments in their region. Roger W. Shugg, *Origins of Class Struggle in Louisiana 1840–1875* (1939), focuses on nonelite whites in one state during the era. Superb insights into the mentality of the South's planter elite can be found in the massive collection of letters from the Jones family of Georgia, Robert M. Myers (ed.), *The Children of Pride* (1972).

Hans L. Trefousse, *The Radical Republicans: Lincoln's Vanguard for Racial Justice* (1969), analyzes the group in the North most committed to an overthrow of the Old South's institutions; while George M. Fredrickson, *The Black Image in the White Mind: The Debate Over Afro-American Character and Destiny, 1817–1914* (1972), traces the evolution of racial ideologies during the era.

Several individual historians have published collections of important and stimulating essays on the Civil War and related themes: C. Vann Woodward, *The Burden of Southern History,* rev. ed. (1968) and *American Counterpoint: Slavery and Racism in the North-South Dialogue* (1971); David M. Potter, *The South and the Sectional Conflict* (1968); David Donald, *Lincoln Reconsidered: Essays on the Civil War Era,* 2d ed., enl. (1961); Stephen B. Oates, *Our Fiery Trial: Abraham Lincoln, John Brown, and the Civil War Era* (1979); and Eric Foner, *Politics and Ideology in the Age of the Civil War* (1980). The literary critic Edmund Wilson has written a number of provocative essays in *Patriotic Gore: Studies in the Literature of the American Civil War* (1962).

Anthologies of essays and articles by various historians include: Charles Crowe (ed.), *The Age of Civil War and Reconstruction, 1830–1900,* rev. ed. (1975); Michael Perman (ed.), *Major Problems in the Civil War and Reconstruction* (1991); George M. Fredrickson (ed.), *A Nation Divided: Problems and Issues of the Civil War and Reconstruction* (1975); Robert P. Swierenga, (ed.), *Beyond the Civil War Synthesis: Politcial Essays on the Civil War Era* (1975); Irwin Unger (ed.), *Essays on the Civil War and Reconstruction* (1970); Harold D. Woodman (ed.), *The Legacy of the American Civil War* (1973); Walter J. Fraser, Jr., and Winfred B. Moore, Jr., *From the Old South to the New: Essays on the Transitional South* (1981); J. Morgan Kousser and James M. McPherson (eds.), *Region, Race and Reconstruction* (1982); Robert H. Abzug and Stephen E. Maizlish (eds.), *Race and Slavery in America* (1986); and Lloyd E. Ambrosius (ed.), *A Crisis of Republicanism: American Politics during the Civil War Era* (1990).

The history of political parties and presidential elections during the era is ably covered by several historians in Winifred E. A. Bernhard (ed.), *Political Parties in American History* (1973); Arthur M. Schlesinger, Jr. (ed.), *History of U. S. Political Parties,* 4 vols. (1973), vols. I and II; and Arthur M. Schlesinger, Jr. (ed.), *History of American Presidential Elections,* 4 vols. (1971), vol. II. The maps in Charles O. Paullin, *Atlas of the Historical Geography of the United States* (1932), provide a wealth of important data on the social, economic, and political history of this period. *Historical Statistics of the United States* (1975) and Donald B. Dodd and Wynette S. Dodd (eds.), *Historical Statistics of the South* (1973), are indispensable.

★ The Antebellum Years and the Coming of the Civil War

General Works

A brief introduction to the period is provided by John Niven, *The Coming of the Civil War* (1990). The fullest and most enlightening chronicle of the antebellum decade is David M. Potter, *The Impending Crisis 1848-1861* (1976). Avery Craven, *The Coming of the Civil War* (1942), blames extremists in both sections, particularly in the North, for whipping up popular passions that led to conflict. This "revisionist" interpretation can also be found in Avery Craven, *The Growth of Southern Nationalism 1848-1861* (1953). A less partisan history of the South, during an earlier period, is Charles S. Sydnor, *The Development of Southern Sectionalism, 1819-1848* (1948). Ulrich B. Phillips, *The Course of the South to Secession* (1939), sympathetically traces the emergence of a self-conscious Southern nationalism. William L. Barney, *The Road to Secession: A New Perspective on the Old South* (1972), is more critical of the South, while William W. Freehling, *The Road to Disunion: Secessionists at Bay 1776-1854* (1990), provides a hard-edged analysis of evolving Southern sectionalism. Don E. Fehrenbacher, *The South and Three Sectional Crises* (1980), analyzes the Missouri Compromise, the Compromise of 1850, and the Kansas-Nebraska controversy. Two useful though difficult studies of the antebellum mentality are Paul C. Nagel, *One Nation Indivisible: The Union in American Thought, 1776-1861* (1964); and Major Wilson, *Space, Time, and Freedom: The Quest for Nationality and the Irrepressible Conflict, 1815-1861* (1974). George B. Forgie, *Patricide in the House Divided: A Psychological Interpretation of Lincoln and His Age* (1979), offers a fascinating and provocative view of the sectional conflict. A superb collection of primary sources on the social and cultural landscape of the pre-Civil War years can be found in David Brion Davis (ed.), *Antebellum American Culture* (1979).

The "causes" of the Civil War have been set forth in a voluminous and at times contentious literature. For an interesting analysis of this literature, begin with Thomas J. Pressly, *Americans Interpret Their Civil War,* 2d ed. (1962). Three fine anthologies of interpretive writings, reflecting all the major viewpoints, are Edwin Rozwenc (ed.), *The Causes of the American Civil War,* 2d ed. (1972); Hans L. Trefousse (ed.), *The Causes of the Civil War* (1971); and Kenneth M. Stampp (ed.), *The Causes of the Civil War,* 2d ed. (1974). For a brief, insightful view by an Australian scholar, see Alan A. Conway, *The Causes of the American Civil War: An Historical Perspective* (1961). A British historian provides an equally useful overview in Bruce Collins, *The Origins of America's Civil War* (1981). Other useful essays that have appeared during the past thirty-five years include Thomas N. Bonner, "Civil War Historians and the 'Needless War' Doctrine," *Journal of the History of Ideas,* 17 (1956), 193-216; David Donald, "American Historians and the Causes of the Civil War," *SAQ,* 59 (1960), 251-255; Lee Benson and Cushing Strout, "Causation and the American Civil War: Two Appraisals," *History and Theory,* 1 (1961), 163-185; William Dray, "Some Causal Accounts of the American Civil War," *Daedalus,* 91 (1962), 578-592, with comment by Newton Garner, 592-598; and Eric Foner, "The Causes of the American Civil War: Recent Interpretations and New Directions," *CWH,* 20 (1974), 197-214. The essays by Joel H. Silbey, *The Partisan Imperative: The Dynamics of American Politics Before the Civil War* (1985), offer the viewpoint of the "new" political history, while Don E. Fehrenbacher, "The New Political History and the Coming of the Civil War," *Pacific Historical Review,* 54 (1985), 117-142, provides a critique of this approach.

For the intellectual odyssey of a prominent Southern historian from a revisionist viewpoint that portrayed the conflict as needless and "repressible" toward a view that North-South differences were so fundamental as to make conflict perhaps "irrepressible" after all, see the following three books by Avery Craven: *The Repressible Conflict* (1939), *The Civil War in the Making, 1815-1860* (1959), and *An Historian and the Civil War* (1964). For the mature reflections of a Northern historian, see Kenneth M. Stampp, *The Imperilled Union: Essays on the Background of the Civil War* (1980). And for a radical neorevisionist perspective, read John S. Rosenberg, "Toward a New Civil War Revisionism," *American Scholar,* 38 (1969), 250-272.

American Modernization, 1800–1860

For a stimulating though perhaps overstated exposition of the modernization thesis as applied to the antebellum United States, see Richard D. Brown, *Modernization: The Transformation of American Life 1600–1865* (1976). Douglas T. Miller, *The Birth of Modern America 1820–1850* (1970), is a useful brief study. Daniel Boorstin, *The Americans: The National Experience* (1965), offers fascinating insights and details about the changes experienced by Americans during the first half of the nineteenth century.

Three readable and informative studies of economic developments during this period are Stuart Bruchey, *The Roots of American Economic Growth 1607–1861* (1965); Douglass C. North, *The Economic Growth of the United States 1790–1860* (1961); and Thomas C. Cochran, *Frontiers of Change: Early Industrialism in America* (1981). The relevant portions of Lance E. Davis et al., *American Economic Growth: An Economist's History of the United States,* 4th ed. (1972), and Lance E. Davis and Douglass C. North, *Institutional Change and American Economic Growth* (1971), are valuable. Peter Temin, *Causal Factors in American Economic Growth in the Nineteenth Century* (1975), provides a trenchant summary of the historiography of this subject, while Stanley L. Engerman and Robert F. Gallman, "U.S. Economic Growth, 1783–1860," *Research in Economic History,* 8 (1983), provide a succinct synthesis of the latest data and interpretations. Two valuable anthologies publish many relevant articles: Douglass C. North and Robert P. Thomas (eds.), *Growth of the American Economy to 1860* (1968); and Robert W. Fogel and Stanley L. Engerman, (eds.), *The Reinterpretation of American Economic History* (1971). Stanley Lebergott, "Labor Force and Employment, 1800–1861," in National Bureau of Economic Research, *Output, Employment, and Productivity in the United States after 1800* (1966), pp. 117–210, provides important data.

The "transportation revolution" and its impact on the American economy are best described in George Rogers Taylor, *The Transportation Revolution 1815–1860* (1951). For the role of steamboats, see Louis C. Hunter, *Steamboats on the Western Waters: An Economic and Technological History* (1949); and Eric F. Haites, James Mak, and Gary M. Walton, *Western River Transportation: The Era of Early Internal Development 1810–1860* (1975). Canals and railroads are treated in Carter Goodrich, *Government Promotion of American Canals and Railroads 1800–1860* (1960); Carter Goodrich (ed.), *Canals and American Development* (1961); Albert Fishlow, *American Railroads and the Transformation of the Ante-Bellum Economy* (1965); and John R. Stover, *Iron Road to the West: American Railroads in the 1850's* (1979).

The best general treatment of agriculture during this period is Paul W. Gates, *The Farmers' Age: Agriculture 1815–1860* (1962). For the free states see Jeremy Atack and Fred Bateman, *To Their Own Soil: Agriculture in the Antebellum North* (1987). Specialized studies of value include Leo Rogin, *The Introduction of Farm Machinery . . . During the Nineteenth Century* (1931); Clarence H. Danhof, *Change in Agriculture: The Northern United States 1820–1870* (1969); and a collection of shorter pieces, Thomas C. Cochran and Thomas B. Brewer (eds.), *Views of American Economic Growth: The Agricultural Era* (1966).

For the development of industry during the antebellum decades, Victor S. Clark, *History of Manufactures in the United States,* 3 vols. (1929), vol. I, is still indispensable. For the American system of manufacturing, read Nathan Rosenberg (ed.), *The American System of Manufactures* (1969); John E. Sawyer, "The Social Basis of the American System of Manufacturing," *JEH,* 14 (1954), 361–379; Otto Mayr and Robert C. Post (eds.), *Yankee Enterprise: The Rise of the American System of Manufactures* (1982); Merrit Roe Smith, *Harper's Ferry Armory and the New Technology* (1977); and David A. Hounshell, *From the American System to Mass Production, 1800–1932* (1983). One important industry is analyzed in Peter Temin, *Iron and Steel in Nineteenth Century America: An Economic Inquiry* (1964). For the New England textile industry, see Caroline F. Ware, *The Early New England Cotton Manufacture* (1931); and Robert F. Dalzell, Jr., "The Rise of the Waltham-Lowell System and Some Thought on the Political Economy of Modernization in Ante-Bellum Massachusetts," *Perspectives in American History,* 9 (1975), 229–270. The impact of industrial change on the traditional economic order of farmers and craftsmen is analyzed in Thomas Dublin, *Women at Work: The Transformation of Work and Community in Lowell, Massachusetts, 1826-1860* (1979); Alan Dawley, *Class and Community: The Industrial Revolution in Lynn* (1976); Sean Wilentz, *Chants Democratic: New York City and the Rise of the American Working Class, 1788-1850* (1984); Steven J. Ross, *Workers on the Edge: Work, Leisure, and Politics in Industrializing Cincinnati, 1788-1890* (1985); Jonathan Prude, *The Coming of Industrial Order: Town and Factory Life in Rural Massachusetts 1810-1860* (1983); Christopher Clark, *The Roots of Rural Capitalism: Western Massachusetts, 1780-1860* (1990); Steven Hahn and Jonathan Prude (eds.), *The Countryside in the Age of Capitalist Transformation* (1985); and Bruce Laurie, *Artisans into Workers: Labor in Nineteenth-Century America* (1989).

Roger Burlingame, *March of the Iron Men: A Social History of Union Through Invention* (1938), is a sprightly history of technological innovation. More analytical is Brook Hindle, *Technology in Early America* (1966) while a good illustrated history is Brook Hindle and Steven Lubar, *Engines of Change: The American Industrial Revolution, 1790-1860* (1987). A stimulating attempt to explain the reasons for the openness of the United States to technological change can be found in H. J. Habakkuk, *American and British Technology in the Nineteenth Century* (1962). For qualifications of the Habakkuk thesis, see Carville Earle and Ronald Hoffman, "The Foundation of Modern Economy: Agriculture and the Costs of Labor in the United States and England, 1800-1860," *AHR,* 85 (1980), 1055-1094; Peter Temin, "Labor Scarcity and the Problem of American Industrial Efficiency in the 1850's," *JEH,* 26 (1966), 277-298; and Paul Uselding and Bruce Juba, "Biased Technical Progress in American Manufacturing, 1839-99," *Explorations in Economic History,* 11 (1973-74), 55-72. Also valuable are Nathan Rosenberg, *Technology and American Economic Growth* (1972); Siegfried Giedion, *Mechanization Takes Command* (1948); Irwin Feller, "Inventive Activity in Agriculture, 1837-1890," *JEH,* 22 (1962), 560-577; and Edwin T. Layton (ed.), *Technology and Change in America* (1973).

The identification of progress with technological change is traced in Arthur A. Ekirch, *The Idea of Progress in America 1815-1860* (1944); and Hugo A. Meier, "Technology and Democracy, 1800-1860," *MVHR,* 43 (1957), 618-640. For the distaste of some Americans for modernization, industry, and technology, see Leo Marx, *The Machine in the Garden: Technology and the Pastoral Idea in America* (1964); and John F. Kasson, *Civilizing the Machine: Technology and Republican Values in America* (1976). Carl Siracusa, *A Mechanical People: Perceptions of the Industrial Order in Massachusetts 1815-1880* (1979), analyzes the interaction of ideology and technology in one state. For the spreading of Yankee culture and influence through the northern tier of the Middle West, see Lois K. Mathews, *The Expansion of New England 1620-1865* (1909). The clash of Yankee and Southern migrants in the Midwest is traced in Richard L. Power, *Planting Corn Belt Culture: The Impress of the Upland Southerner and Yankee in the Old Northwest* (1953). Stimulating insights on antebellum values can be found in Daniel T. Rodgers, *The Work Ethic in Industrial America 1850-1920* (1978). Lee Soltow, *Men and Wealth in the United States 1850-1870* (1975), documents the distribution of wealth among people of various regional and ethnic groups.

Ronald G. Walters, *American Reformers 1815-1860* (1978), is a concise and important introduction to the subject. A fascinating case study is provided by Paul E. Johnson, *A Shopkeeper's Millennium: Society and Revivals in Rochester, New York, 1815-1857* (1978). One of the principal reform movements associated with modernization is analyzed in the following books: Norman A. Clark, *Deliver Us from Evil: An Interpretation of American Prohibition* (1976); William J. Rorabough, *The Alcoholic Republic: America 1790-1840* (1979); Ian R. Tyrrell, *Sobering Up: From Temperance to Prohibition in Antebellum America 1800-1860* (1979); Robert L. Hampel, *Temperance and Prohibition in Massachusetts, 1813-1852* (1982); and Jed Dannenbaum, *Drink and Disorder: Temperance Reform in Cincinnati from the Washingtonian Revival to the WCTU* (1984).

The expansion and improvement of public education during the antebellum period is discussed in Lawrence A. Cremin, *American Education: The National Experience, 1783-1876* (1980); Frederick M. Binder, *The Age of the Common School 1830-1865* (1974); Albert Fishlow, "The Common School Revival: Fact or Fancy?" in Henry Rosovsky (ed.), *Industrialization in Two Systems* (1966), pp. 40-67; Lee Soltow and Edward Stevens, *The Rise of*

Literacy and the Common School in the United States: A Socioeconomic Analysis (1981); and Carl F. Kaestle, *Pillars of the Republic: Common Schooling and American Society, 1780-1860* (1983). The relationship between education and modernizing capitalism is explored from different angles in the following works: Michael Katz, *The Irony of Early School Reform: Educational Innovation in Mid-Nineteenth Century Massachusetts* (1969); Michael B. Katz, "The Origins of Public Education: A Reassessment," *History of Education Quarterly*, 16 (1976), 381-407; Stanley K. Schultz, *The Culture Factory: Boston Public Schools 1789-1860* (1973); Carl F. Kaestle, *The Evolution of an Urban School System 1750-1850* (1973); and Carl F. Kaestle and Maris A. Vinovskis, *Education and Social Change in Nineteenth-Century Massachusetts* (1980).

For changes in the status of women and the rise of a women's rights movement, see Nancy F. Cott, *The Bonds of Womanhood: "Woman's Sphere" in New England, 1780-1835* (1977); Carl N. Degler, *At Odds: Women and the Family in America from the Revolution to the Present* (New York, 1980); Mary P. Ryan, *Cradle of the Middle Class: The Family in Oneida County, New York, 1790-1865* (1981); Catherine Clinton, *The Other Civil War: American Women in the Nineteenth Century* (1984); and Ellen Carol DuBois, *Feminism and Suffrage: The Emergence of an Independent Women's Movement in America 1848-1869* (1978).

A great deal of important information on the attitudes of Democrats and Whigs toward issues related to modernization can be found in Herbert Ershkowitz and William G. Shade, "Consensus or Conflict? Political Behavior in the State Legislatures During the Jacksonian Era," *JAH*, 58 (1971), 591-621; Harry L. Watson, *Liberty and Power: The Politics of Jacksonian America* (1990); John Ashworth: *"Agrarians" and "Aristocrats": Party Political Ideology in the United States, 1837-1846* (1983); Lawrence F. Kohl, *The Politics of Individualism: Parties and the American Character in the Jacksonian Era* (1989); and Ronald P. Formisano, *The Transformation of Political Culture: Massachusetts Parties, 1790's-1840's* (1982). For the ideology of Democrats, see Bruce Collins, "The Ideology of the Ante-Bellum Northern Democrats," *Journal of American Studies*, 11 (1977), 103-121; Jean E. Friedman, *The Revolt of the Conservative Democrats: An Essay on American Political Culture and Political Development 1837-1844* (1979); and Jean Baker, *Affairs of Party: The Political Culture of Northern Democrats in the Mid-Nineteenth Century* (1983). Robert L. Kelley, *The Transatlantic Persuasion: The Liberal-Democratic Mind in the Age of Gladstone* (1969), and Rush Welter, *The Mind of America, 1820-1860* (1975), also contain suggestive insights into the Democratic world view. Robert L. Kelley, *The Cultural Pattern in American Politics: The First Century* (1979), offers a sometimes oversimplified synthesis of the social and ideological matrix of politics. Whig attitudes are sensitively analyzed in Daniel Walker Howe, *The Political Culture of American Whigs* (1979); and Thomas Brown, *Politics and Statesmanship: Essays on the American Whig Party* (1985); while G. S. Boritt, *Lincoln and the Economics of the American Dream* (1977), explores Lincoln's Whig economic philosophy.

For the efforts of state and federal governments to provide social overhead capital and in other ways to foster economic development, consult Carter Goodrich (ed.), *The Government and the Economy 1783-1861* (1967); Oscar Handlin and Mary Handlin, *Commonwealth: A Study of the Role of the Government in the American Economy: Massachusetts 1774-1861* (1947); Louis Hartz, *Economic Policy and Democratic Thought: Pennsylvania 1776-1861* (1948); Harry Scheiber, *The Ohio Canal Era: A Case Study of Government and the Economy* (1969); Milton S. Heath, *Constructive Liberalism: The Role of the State in Economic Development of Georgia to 1860* (1954); and Peter Wallenstein, *From Slave South to New South: Public Policy in Nineteenth Century Georgia* (1987). The growing friendliness of the courts toward entrepreneurial innovation is brilliantly explored in Morton J. Horwitz, *The Transformation of American Law 1780-1861* (1977). For analyses of the major economic issue dividing Whigs and Democrats, the following works are important: Bray Hammond, *Banks and Politics in America from the Revolution to the Civil War* (1957); William G. Shade, *Banks or No Banks: The Money Issue in Western Politics 1832-1865* (1972); Roger James Sharp, *The Jacksonians Versus the Banks: Politics in the States After the Panic of 1837* (1970); and Larry Schweikart, *Banking in the American South: From the Age of Jackson to Reconstruction* (1987).

The Antebellum South and Slavery

An old but still useful survey of the antebellum South is William E. Dodd, *The Cotton Kingdom* (1919). The most up-to-date textbook is William J. Cooper, Jr., and Thomas E. Terrill, *The American South: A History* (1990), chaps. 1-14. Two collections of essays by the leading Southern scholar of a previous generation contain much of value: Ulrich B. Phillips, *Life and Labor in the Old South* (1929) and *The Slave Economy of the Old South: Selected Essays,* ed. Eugene Genovese (1968). For an attempt to separate the myth from the reality of the Southern plantation society, see Francis Pendleton Gaines, *The Southern Plantation: A Study in the Development and Accuracy of a Tradition* (1925). Lewis C. Gray, *History of Agriculture in the Southern United States to 1860,* 2 vols. (1933), still stands as the most exhaustive treatment of its subject, though many of the studies of the Southern economy cited below have modified or amplified its findings. Good microstudies of specific localities can be found in Elinor Miller and Eugene D. Genovese (eds.), *Plantation, Town, and County: Essays on the Local History of American Slave Society* (1974), and O. Vernon Burton and Robert C. McGrath (eds.), *Class, Conflict, and Consensus: Antebellum Southern Community Studies* (1982). A fine study of an important state is John Hebron Moore, *The Emergence of the Cotton Kingdom in the Old Southwest: Mississippi, 1770-1860* (1988). Religion was a powerful force in the South's cultural life; for a sensitive interpretation, consult Donald G. Mathews, *Religion in the Old South* (1977). The essays in John B. Boles (ed.), *Masters & Slaves in the House of the Lord: Race and Religion in the American South, 1740-1870* (1988), offer rich fare. Much of our perception of what life was like in the antebellum South comes from travelers' accounts; an excellent bibliography of these is Thomas D. Clark (ed.), *Travels in the Old South: A Bibliography,* 3 vols. (1956-1959), especially vol. III: *The Ante-Bellum South.* The best-known and most influential traveler was Frederick Law Olmsted. For a modern abridgment of his three books on the South, read Arthur Schlesinger (ed.), *The Cotton Kingdom* (1953). Olmsted's observations and preconceptions are analyzed by several of the essays in Dana F. White and Victor A. Kramer (eds.), *Olmsted South: Old South Critic/New South Planner* (1979).

    The economics of slavery and its relationship to Southern development—or lack thereof—have been the subject of a large scholarly literature, much of it anthologized in Harold D. Woodman (ed.), *Slavery and the Southern Economy* (1966); and Hugh G. J. Aitken (ed.), *Did Slavery Pay?* (1971). Gavin Wright, *The Political Economy of the Cotton South* (1978), contains important insights. For additional essays and primary sources on this issue, see William N. Parker (ed.), *The Structure of the Cotton Economy of the Antebellum South* (1970); and Stuart Bruchey (ed.), *Cotton and the Growth of the American Economy 1790-1860* (1967). Eugene D. Genovese, *The Political Economy of Slavery* (1965), argues vigorously that slavery inhibited Southern economic development. Robert W. Fogel and Stanley L. Engerman, *Time on the Cross: The Economics of American Negro Slavery* (1974), argue the opposite case even more vigorously, but parts of their argument have suffered withering attacks from all directions: see especially Kenneth M. Stampp et al., *Reckoning with Slavery* (1976), and Herbert G. Gutman, *Slavery and the Numbers Game* (1975). Most of the major points in the debate over slavery's impact on Southern economic development can be found in Alfred H. Conrad et al., "Slavery as an Obstacle to Economic Growth in the United States: A Panel Discussion," *JEH,* 27 (1967), 518-560. Other articles on various aspects of this question include Morton Rothstein, "The Antebellum South as a Dual Economy: A Tentative Hypothesis," *AH,* 41 (1967), 373-382; Stanley L. Engerman, "The Effects of Slavery Upon the Southern Economy," *Explorations in Entrepreneurial History,* 2nd Ser., 4 (1967), 71-97; Marvin Fishbaum and Julius Rubin, "Slavery and the Economic Development of the American South," *Explorations in Entrepreneurial History,* 2nd Ser., 6 (1968), 116-127; Julius Rubin, "The Limits of Agricultural Progress in the Nineteenth-Century South," *AH,* 49 (1975), 362-373; R. Keith Aufhauser, "Slavery and Technological Change," *JEH,* 34 (1974), 36-50; John E. Moes, "Absorption of Capital in Slave Labor in the Ante-Bellum South and Economic Growth," *American Journal of Economics,* 20 (1961), 535-541; Robert E. Gallman and Ralph V. Anderson, "Slaves as Fixed Capital: Slave Labor and Southern Economic Development," *JAH,* 44 (1977), 24-46; Fred Bateman, James Foust, and Thomas Weiss, "The Participation of Planters in Manufacturing in the Antebellum

South," *AH,* 48 (1974), 277-297; Norris W. Preyer, "Why Did Industrialization Lag in the Old South?" *Georgia Historical Quarterly,* 55 (1971), 378-389; Stanley Engerman, "A Reconsideration of Southern Economic Growth, 1770-1860," *Agricultural History,* 49 (1975), 343-361; Robert E. Gallman, "Slavery and Southern Economic Growth," *Southern Economic Journal,* 45 (1979), 1007-1022; and Fred Bateman and Thomas Weiss, *A Deplorable Scarcity: The Failure of Industrialization in the Slave Economy* (1981). See also Laurence Shore, *Southern Capitalists: The Ideological Leadership of an Elite, 1832-1885* (1986). Harold D. Woodman, *King Cotton and His Retainers: Financing and Marketing the Cotton Crop of the South* (1968), is an excellent study of the factoring system. For an account of the self-sufficiency of most parts of the South in food, see Sam B. Hilliard, *Hog Meat and Hoe Cake: Food Supply in the Old South 1840-1860* (1972). Three studies emphasize that despite the South's low rate of urbanization, the region did have important cities: Leonard P. Curry "Urbanization and Urbanism in the Old South: A Comparative View," *JSH,* 40 (1974), 43-60; Blaine A. Brownell and David R. Goldfield (eds.), *The City in Southern History* (1977); and David R. Goldfield, *Urban Growth in the Age of Sectionalism: Virginia, 1847-1861* (1977).

The institution of slavery has generated more historical writing than any other aspect of Southern history, unless it be the Confederacy itself. For recent surveys of slavery scholarship, consult David Brion Davis, "Slavery and the Post-World War II Historians," *Daedalus,* 103 (1974), 1-16; Michael Craton (ed.), *Slave Studies: Directions in Current Scholarship,* 6 (Summer 1979); and Peter J. Parish, *Slavery: History and Historians* (1989). John B. Boles, *Black Southerners, 1619-1869* (1983) provides a good introduction to the subject, while C. Duncan Rice, *The Rise and Fall of Black Slavery* (1975), places slavery in the United States in a world context. Robert William Fogel, *Without Consent or Contract: The Rise and Fall of American Slavery* (1989), refines and revises the theme of *Time on the Cross* fifteen years later, places slavery in a world context, and contains new insights on the antislavery movements in Britain and the United States.

The two classic and sharply opposed studies of slavery in the United States are Ulrich B. Phillips, *American Negro Slavery* (1918), which portrays the institution as nonrepressive and beneficial to blacks; and Kenneth M. Stampp, *The Peculiar Institution* (1956), which portrays it as repressive and harmful to blacks. Two state studies that reflect the Phillips viewpoint are Charles S. Sydnor, *Slavery in Mississippi* (1933); and James B. Sellers, *Slavery in Alabama* (1950); while state studies that tend to follow Stampp are Joe Gray Taylor, *Negro Slavery in Louisiana* (1963), and Randolph B. Campbell, *An Empire for Slavery: The Peculiar Institution in Texas* (1989). For the past three decades, nearly all studies of slavery have been influenced in one way or another by Stanley Elkins, *Slavery: A Problem in American Institutional and Intellectual Life,* 3d ed. (1976), which argues that slavery in the United States was more psychologically corrosive than in other slave societies and that this "closed" system reduced slaves to fawning, dependent, childlike "Samboes," a personality syndrome that black Americans have struggled for more than a century to overcome. The Elkins interpretation has provoked many challenges, most of which maintain that blacks underwent a wide variety of experiences and possessed a wide variety of personality types, by no means all of them dependent or Sambo-like. See especially Ann J. Lane (ed.), *The Debate Over Slavery: Stanley Elkins and His Critics* (1971); and many of the essays in such anthologies as Richard G. Brown and Stephen G. Rabe (eds.), *Slavery in American Society,* 2d ed. (1976), and Allen Weinstein, Frank Otto Gatell, and David Sarasohn (eds.), *American Negro Slavery: A Modern Reader,* 3d ed. (1979).

The principal book-length challenge to Elkins is John W. Blassingame, *The Slave Community: Plantation Life in the Antebellum South,* 2d ed. rev. (1979). Another account that stresses the slaves' ability to maintain a vital culture of their own despite the contrary pressures of slavery is George Rawick, *From Sundown to Sunup: The Making of the Black Community* (1972). The 1970s produced a cornucopia of studies of black culture in slavery, most of which emphasize especially the creative role of religion and the strength of family and kinship networks as instruments of survival in a hostile world: Eugene D. Genovese, *Roll, Jordan, Roll: The World the Slaves Made* (1974); Herbert G. Gutman, *The Black Family in Slavery and Freedom 1750-1925* (1976); Nathan Huggins, *Black Odyssey: The Afro-American Ordeal in Slavery* (1977); Albert J. Raboteau, *Slave Religion: The "Invisible Institution" in the Antebel-*

lum South (1978); Leslie H. Owens, *This Species of Property: Slave Life and Culture in the Old South* (1976); and Charles Joyner, *Remember Me: Slave Life in Coastal Georgia* (1989). The vital function of song and folklore is explored by Lawrence W. Levine, *Black Culture and Black Consciousness* (1977).

The experiences of those slaves who lived and worked in urban or industrial settings is traced in Richard C. Wade, *Slavery in the Cities* (1964); Robert S. Starobin, *Industrial Slavery in the Old South* (1970); and Ronald L. Lewis, *Coal, Iron, and Slaves: Industrial Slavery in Maryland and Virginia 1715-1865* (1979). The complicated relationship of women both black and white to the institution of slavery is analyzed in Deborah Gray White, *Ar'n't I a Woman? Female Slaves in the Plantation South* (1985); Catherine Clinton, *The Plantation Mistress: Woman's World in the Old South* (1982); and Elizabeth Fox-Genovese, *Within the Plantation Household: Black and White Women of the Old South* (1988). Otto H. Olsen, "Historians and the Extent of Slave Ownership in the Southern United States," *CWH*, 18 (1972), 101-116, documents the relatively widespread ownership of this expensive property; while William K. Scarborough, *The Overseer: Plantation Management in the Old South* (1966), analyzes a group of whites who did not own slaves but were involved in their management. William L. Van Deburg, *The Slave Drivers: Black Agricultural Labor Supervisors in the Antebellum South* (1979), portrays the role of the black slave foremen. One of the most tragic dimensions of slavery is treated in Frederick Bancroft, *Slave Trading in the Old South* (1931); and Michael Tadman, *Speculators and Slaves: Masters, Traders, and Slaves in the Old South* (1989). Legal aspects of slavery are examined in Mark Tushnet, *The American Law of Slavery, 1810-1860* (1981). Two books by James Oakes analyze the relationships among masters, slaves, Southern culture, and regional and national political economy: *The Ruling Race: A History of American Slaveholders* (1982); and *Slavery and Freedom: An Interpretation of the Old South* (1990). The essays in Willie Lee Rose, *Slavery and Freedom* (1982), contain many incisive insights.

Although large-scale revolts were relatively infrequent in the United States, those that did occur, as well as plans and rumors of others, are narrated in Herbert Aptheker, *American Negro Slave Revolts* (1943); Joseph C. Carroll, *Slave Insurrections in the United States 1800-1865* (1938); and Stephen B. Oates, *The Fires of Jubilee: Nat Turner's Fierce Rebellion* (1975). Eugene D. Genovese, *From Rebellion to Revolution: Afro-American Slave Revolts in the Making of the Modern World* (1979), places the United States experience in hemispheric context.

Much of the evidence on which an understanding of slavery can be based has been published. See especially Willie Lee Rose (ed.), *A Documentary History of Slavery in North America* (1976). An exhaustive digest of legal cases can be found in Helen T. Catterall (ed.), *Judicial Cases Concerning American Slavery and the Negro*, 5 vols. (1926-1937). Some of the most important evidence concerning the institution are the words of slaves themselves. For a large sample of these, consult John W. Blassingame (ed.), *Slave Testimony: Two Centuries of Letters, Speeches, Interviews, and Autobiographies* (1977). Many escaped or freed slaves wrote autobiographies or narratives about their experiences. For an analysis of these, see Charles H. Nichols, *Many Thousand Gone: The Ex-Slaves' Account of Their Bondage and Freedom* (1963). In the 1920s and 1930s, Fisk University and the WPA undertook to interview as many surviving ex-slaves as possible about their experiences in bondage. The transcripts of these interviews have been published in George P. Rawick (ed.), *The American Slave: A Composite Autobiography*, 41 vols. (1972-1979). Paul Escott, *Slavery Remembered: A Record of Twentieth Century Slave Narratives* (1979), is a quantitative analysis of these interviews; while Norman R. Yetman (ed.), *Life Under the "Peculiar Institution": Selections from the Slave Narrative Collection* (1970), publishes a sample of one hundred of them.

Some of the most fruitful insights concerning North American slavery are contained in studies comparing it to the institution in other New World societies. Frank Tannenbaum, *Slave and Citizen: The Negro in the Americas* (1947), and Herbert S. Klein, *Slavery in the Americas: A Comparative Study of Cuba and Virginia* (1967), maintain that slavery in North America was more repressive than in Latin America. Most of the other scholarship on the subject, however, has either modified or rejected important aspects of this interpretaton. For anthologies of various writings on the subject, see Laura Foner and Eugene D. Genovese (eds.),

Slavery in the New World (1969); Stanley L. Engerman and Eugene D. Genovese (eds.), *Race and Slavery in the Western Hemisphere: Quantitative Studies* (1975); and Vera Rubin and Arthur Tuden (eds.), *Comparative Perspectives on Slavery in New World Plantation Societies* (1977). The startlingly higher rate of slave survival and reproduction in the United States than elsewhere is documented in Philip D. Curtin, *The Atlantic Slave Trade: A Census* (1969). Two of the most challenging books in the field of comparative slavery are Carl N. Degler, *Neither Black Nor White: Slavery and Race Relations in Brazil and the United States* (1971); and Eugene D. Genovese, *The World the Slaveholders Made: Two Essays in Interpretation* (1969). An important study that compares slavery and race relations in the United States and South Africa is George M. Fredrickson, *White Supremacy: A Comparative Study in American and South African History* (1981), while Peter Kolchin, *Unfree Labor: American Slavery and Russian Serfdom* (1987), compares and contrasts these two institutions.

Although most writings about the slave South focus on the slaveowners and their slaves, two-thirds or more of the whites had no connection with slaveholding. The classic account of these people, which portrays them as a crucial element in the South's social and political structure, is Frank L. Owsley, *Plain Folk of the Old South* (1949). For a damaging critique of Owsley's interpretation, consult Fabian Linden, "Economic Democracy in the Slave South: An Appraisal of Some Recent Views," *JNH*, 31 (1946), 140–189. Another study emphasizing the inequality of wealth and economic power is Gavin Wright, " 'Economic Democracy' and the Concentration of Wealth in the Cotton South," *AH*, 44 (1970), 62–99. For other analyses of the image and reality of nonslaveholding whites, see Paul H. Buck, "The Poor Whites of the Ante-Bellum South," *AHR*, 31 (1925), 41–54; Shields McIlwaine, *The Southern Poor White* (1939); Forrest McDonald and Grady McWhiney, "The Antebellum Southern Herdsman: A Reinterpretation," *JSH*, 41 (1975), 147–166, and "The South from Self-Sufficiency to Peonage: An Interpretation," *AHR*, 85 (1980), 1095–1118; Eugene D. Genovese, "Yeoman Farmers in a Slaveholder's Democracy," *AH*, 49 (1975), 331–342; Edward Magdol and Jon L. Wakelyn (eds.), *The Southern Common People: Studies in Nineteenth-Century Social History* (1980); J. Wayne Flynt, *Dixie's Forgotten People: The South's Poor Whites* (1979); Edward Magdol and Jon L. Wakelyn (eds.), *The Southern Common People: Studies in Nineteenth-Century Social History* (1980); Steven Hahn, *The Roots of Southern Populism: Yeoman Farmers and the Transformation of the Georgia Upcountry, 1850–1890*; and Paul D. Escott, *Many Excellent People: Power and Privilege in North Carolina, 1850–1900* (1985). Ralph W. Wooster, *The People in Power: Courthouse and Statehouse in the Lower South* (1969) and *Politicians, Planters, and Plain Folk: Courthouse and Statehouse in the Upper South 1850–1860* (1975), maintains that while nonslaveholders exercised a considerable degree of political power and held many offices, their percentage of officeholding decreased during the 1850s. Other studies that trace the relationship between yeoman and planters include J. William Harris, *Plain Folk and Gentry in a Slave Society: White Liberty and Black Slavery in Augusta's Hinterlands* (1985), and Harry L. Watson, "Conflict and Collaboration: Yeomen, Slaveholders, and Politics in the Antebellum South," *Social History*, 10 (1985), 273–298. An intriguing study which argues for the Celtic roots of Southern culture, especially the yeomen farmers, is Grady McWhiney, *Cracker Culture: Celtic Ways in the Old South* (1988).

The anomalous and difficult position of free blacks in a slave society is sensitively explored in Ira Berlin, *Slaves Without Masters: The Free Negro in the Antebellum South* (1974), and Michael P. Johnson and James L. Roark, *Black Masters: A Free Family of Color in the Old South* (1984).

The Ideological Conflict over Slavery

For the international context and pre-nineteenth-century background of slavery and the antislavery movement, three books are superb: David Brion Davis, *The Problem of Slavery in Western Culture* (1966) and *The Problem of Slavery in the Age of Revolution 1770–1823* (1975); and Edmund S. Morgan, *American Slavery, American Freedom: The Ordeal of Colonial Virginia* (1975). Some of the most important interpretive articles on the reform milieu out of which abolitionism grew can be found in David Brion Davis (ed.), *Ante-Bellum Reform* (1967). Full-length studies of this milieu include Alice Felt Tyler, *Freedom's Ferment* (1944);

and Ronald G. Walters, *American Reformers 1815-1860* (1978). The evangelical impulse underlying and infusing reform movements is analyzed in Timothy L. Smith, *Revivalism and Social Reform in Mid-Nineteenth Century America* (1957); Whitney R. Cross, *The Burned-Over District* (1950); and Paul E. Johnson, *A Shopkeeper's Millennium: Society and Revivals in Rochester, New York 1815-1836* (1978). For a conservative movement against slavery, see P. J. Staudenraus, *The African Colonization Movement 1816-1865* (1961).

A good introduction to scholarship on the abolitionists is Merton L. Dillon, "The Abolitionists: A Decade of Historiography," *JSH,* 35 (1969), 500-522. Two more decades of historiography are summarized in James L. Huston, "The Experiential Basis of the Northern Antislavery Impulse," *JSH,* 55 (1990), 609-640, which also provides its own interpretation of the movement. Two collections of essays that depict the state of abolitionist historiography at the times of their publication are Martin Duberman (ed.), *The Antislavery Vanguard* (1965); and Lewis Perry and Michael Fellman (eds.), *Antislavery Reconsidered: New Perspectives on the Abolitionists* (1979). The best brief narratives of the antislavery movement are James B. Stewart, *Holy Warriors: The Abolitionists and American Slavery* (1976), and Merton L. Dillon, *Slavery Attacked: Southern Slaves and Their Allies, 1619-1865* (1989). Two older and larger studies also deal with the movement as a whole: Louis Filler, *The Crusade Against Slavery* (1960); and Dwight L. Dumond, *Antislavery: The Crusade for Freedom in America* (1961). More specialized studies that have done much to shape our understanding of the abolitionists include Gilbert Hobbs Barnes, *The Antislavery Impulse 1830-1844* (1933); Aileen S. Kraditor, *Means and Ends in American Abolitionism* (1969); Carleton Mabee, *Black Freedom: The Nonviolent Abolitionists from 1830 Through the Civil War* (1970); Ronald G. Walters, *The Antislavery Appeal: Abolitionism After 1830* (1976); Russel B. Nye, *Fettered Freedom: Civil Liberties and the Slavery Controversy 1830-1860* (1949); Lawrence J. Friedman, *Gregarious Saints: Self and Community in American Abolitionism, 1830-1870* (1982); Louis Gerteis, *Morality and Utility in American Antislavery Reform* (1987); Edward Magdol, *The Antislavery Rank and File: A Social Profile of the Abolitionists' Constituency* (1986); and Herbert Aptheker, *Abolitionism: A Revolutionary Movement* (1989). Two studies of blacks in the antislavery movement are Benjamin Quarles, *Black Abolitionists* (1969); and James H. Pease and William H. Pease, *They Who Would Be Free: Blacks' Search for Freedom 1830-1861* (1974). An important study of blacks in the North that includes material on abolitionism is Leon F. Litwack, *North of Slavery: The Negro in the Free States 1790-1860* (1961). Two anthologies offer samples of the abolitionists' own writings: John L. Thomas (ed.), *Slavery Attacked: The Abolitionist Crusade* (1965); and William H. Pease and Jane H. Pease (eds.), *The Antislavery Argument* (1965). Five books provide a full portrait of the antislavery political parties: Theodore Clarke Smith, *The Liberty and Free Soil Parties in the Northwest* (1897); Richard H. Sewell, *Ballots for Freedom: Antislavery Politics in the United States 1837-1860* (1976); Frederick J. Blue, *The Free Soilers: Third Party Politics, 1848-1854* (1973); John H. Hammond, *The Politics of Benevolence: Revival Religion and American Voting Behavior* (1979); and Gerald Sorin, *The New York Abolitionists: A Case Study of Political Radicalism* (1971). Also valuable are the essays in Alan M. Kraut (ed.), *Crusaders and Compromisers: Essays on the Relationship of the Antislavery Struggle to the Antebellum Party System* (1983). For the divisive impact of the slavery controversy on Protestant denominations, refer to C. C. Goen, *Broken Churches, Broken Nation: Denominational Schisms and the Coming of the American Civil War* (1985); and John R. McKivigan, *The War against Proslavery Religion: Abolitionism and the Northern Churches, 1830-1865* (1984).

The most lucid account of the free-labor ideology, which also contains a fine analysis of the Republican party in the 1850s, is Eric Foner, *Free Soil, Free Labor, Free Men: The Ideology of the Republican Party Before the Civil War* (1970). Howard Floan, *The South in the Northern Eyes 1831-1861* (1953), summarizes various Northern images of the South. David Brion Davis, *The Slave Power Conspiracy and the Paranoid Style* (1969), analyzes the symbolic power of these images. Three Northern groups that were generally hostile to the antislavery movement are discussed in Philip S. Foner, *Business and Slavery: The New York Merchants and the Irrepressible Conflict* (1941); Bernard Mandel, *Labor, Free and Slave: Workingmen and the Anti-Slavery Movement in the United States* (1955); and Madeline H. Rice, *American Catholic Opinion in the Slavery Controversy* (1943).

Antebellum Southern culture, values, and attitudes are analyzed in the following books, which disagree with each other on some points: David Bertelson, *The Lazy South* (1967); three books by Clement Eaton: *The Growth of Southern Civilization 1790-1861* (1961), *The Freedom of Thought Struggle in the Old South,* rev. ed. (1964), and *The Mind of the Old South,* rev. ed. (1967); and Rollin Osterweis, *Romanticism and Nationalism in the Old South* (1949). For a skillful weaving together of Northern and Southern perceptions of Southern reality, see William R. Taylor, *Cavalier and Yankee: The Old South and American National Character* (1961). Bertram Wyatt-Brown, *Southern Honor: Ethics and Behavior in the Old South* (1982) and the same author's *Yankee Saints and Southern Sinners* (1985) trace the sensitivity of Southern white men to criticism and aspersions on their honor, especially by Yankees. Also important on these themes is Kenneth S. Greenberg, *Masters and Statesmen: The Political Culture of American Slavery* (1985). Still the fullest account of proslavery ideology is William S. Jenkins, *Pro-Slavery Thought in the Old South* (1935). Two articles that place this ideology in a comparative context are Shearer Davis Bowman, "Antebellum Planters and Vormärz Junkers in Comparative Perspective," *AHR,* 85 (October 1980), 779-808; and Peter Kolchin, "In Defense of Servitude: American Proslavery and Russian Proserfdom Arguments, 1790-1860" *AHR,* 85 (October 1980), 809-827. David Donald, "The Proslavery Argument Reconsidered," *JSH,* 37 (1971), analyzes the motives of the most outspoken defenders of slavery. The antebellum theories of black racial inferiority are treated in William R. Stanton, *The Leopard's Spots: Scientific Attitudes Toward Race in America 1815-1859* (1960); and George M. Fredrickson, "Masters and Mudsills: The Role of Race in the Planter-Ideology of South Carolina," *South Atlantic Urban Studies,*II (1978), 33-48. A good selection of proslavery writings can be found in Eric L. McKitrick (ed.), *Slavery Defended: The Views of the Old South* (1963); and Drew Gilpin Faust (ed.), *The Ideology of Slavery: Proslavery Thought in the Antebellum South* (1981). For the ambivalence of some Southern whites toward slavery, consult Charles G. Sellers, "The Travail of Slavery," in Charles G. Sellers (ed.), *The Southerner as American* (1960), pp. 40-71; and James M. McPherson, "Slavery and Race," *Perspectives in American History,* 3 (1969), 460-473.

Two accounts of the slavery controversy by historians with a pronounced Southern viewpoint are Arthur Young Lloyd, *The Slavery Controversy 1831-1860* (1939); and Henry H. Simms, *A Decade of Sectional Controversy, 1851-1861* (1942). For the evolution of sectional feelings in the South, see, in addition to the books cited in the first paragraph under "General Works" for the antebellum years, Jesse T. Carpenter, *The South as a Conscious Minority 1789-1861* (1930); Robert R. Russel, *Economic Aspects of Southern Sectionalism 1840-1861* (1924) and *Critical Studies in Antebellum Sectionalism* (1972); John G. Van Deusen, *Ante-Bellum Southern Commercial Conventions* (1926); Herbert Wender, *Southern Commercial Conventions 1837-1859* (1930); Weymouth T. Jordan, *Rebels in the Making: Planters' Conventions and Southern Propaganda* (1958); and John McCardell, *The Idea of a Southern Nation* (1970). South Carolina was the foremost fire-eating state; for a fine account of why, see Lacy K. Ford, Jr., *Origins of Southern Radicalism: The South Carolina Upcountry, 1800-1860* (1988). For Southern disdain of Northern "wage slavery," see Wilfred Carsel, "The Slaveholders' Indictment of Northern Wage Slavery," *JSH,* 6 (1940), 504-520. The ambivalence of Southern attitudes toward industrialization in their own section is explored in Herbert Collins, "The Southern Industrial Gospel Before 1860," *JSH,* 12 (1946), 386-402; Theodore R. Marmor, "Anti-Industrialism and the Old South: The Agrarian Perspective of John C. Calhoun," *Comparative Studies in Society and History,* 9 (1967), 377-406; and Fred Bateman and Thomas Weiss, *A Deplorable Scarcity: The Failure of Industrialization in the Slave Economy* (1981). For the Southern propensity toward violence and martial values, see Guy A. Cardwell, "The Duel in the Old South: Crux of a Concept," *SAQ,* 66 (1967), 50-69; John Hope Franklin, *The Militant South 1800-1861* (1956); and Dickson D. Bruce, *Violence and Culture in the Antebellum South* (1979). Two studies that argue with limited success that the extent of Southern militarism has been exaggerated are Marcus Cunliffe, *Soldiers and Civilians: The Martial Spirit in America 1775-1865* (1968); and Robert E. May, "Recent Trends in the Historiography of Southern Militarism," *Historian,* 40 (1978), 213-234. An important article that argues—also with limited success—that the similarities between the North and the South were more important than the differences is Edward Pessen, "How Different from Each Other Were the Antebellum North and

South?" *AHR*, 85 (1980), 1119–1149; for a challenge to this argument, see James M. McPherson, "Antebellum Southern Exceptionalism: A New Look at an Old Question," *CWH*, 29 (1983), 230-244.

For the history of the slavery question in politics before 1844, see Donald L. Robinson, *Slavery and the Structure of American Politics 1765-1820* (1971); Glover Moore, *The Missouri Controversy 1819-1821* (1966); Richard H. Brown, "The Missouri Crisis, Slavery, and the Politics of Jacksonianism," *SAQ,* 65 (1966), 55-72; William W. Freehling, *Prelude to Civil War: The Nullification Crisis in South Carolina 1816-1836* (1966); and William J. Cooper, *The South and the Politics of Slavery 1828-1856* (1978).

Texas, Mexico, and the Compromise of 1850

For the general context of politics within which sectionalism heated up during the 1840s, see Frederick Jackson Turner, *The United States 1830-1850* (1935); and William R. Brock, *Parties and Political Conscience: American Dilemmas 1840-1850* (1979). The westering impulse that propelled Americans to and across the Mississippi during this period, undergirding the ideology of Manifest Destiny, is chronicled in Malcolm J. Rohrbough, *The Trans-Appalachian Frontier . . . 1775-1850* (1978), and Ray Allen Billington, *The Far Western Frontier 1830-1860* (1956). The racial philosophies and economic interests that rationalized expansion are analyzed by Thomas R. Hietala, *Manifest Design: Anxious Aggrandizement in Late Jacksonian America* (1985). For Texas, consult William C. Binkley, *The Texas Revolution* (1952) and *The Expansionist Movement in Texas* (1925). Frederick Merk, *Manifest Destiny and Mission in American History* (1963) and *The Monroe Doctrine and American Expansion 1843-1849* (1967), explore the expansionism of the 1840s; while in *Slavery and the Annexation of Texas* (1972), Merk narrows the focus to Texas specifically. Two studies analyze the relationship between American expansionism and the coming of the war with Mexico: David Pletcher, *The Diplomacy of Annexation: Texas, Oregon, and the Mexican War* (1973); and Norman E. Tutorow, *Texas Annexation and the Mexican War: A Political Study of the Old Northwest* (1978). Mexican viewpoints are described in Gene M. Brack, *Mexico Views Manifest Destiny: An Essay on the Origins of the Mexican War* (1975). Glen W. Price, *Origins of the War with Mexico: The Polk-Stockton Intrigue* (1967), charges Polk with deliberately provoking Mexico to war; while Charles G. Sellers, *James K. Polk, Continentalist 1843-1846* (1966), is more sympathetic to the American President. The most thorough and detailed study of the Mexican War is still Justin H. Smith, *The War with Mexico*, 2 vols. (1919). Modern studies include Otis A. Singletary, *The Mexican War* (1960); John Edward Weems, *To Conquer a Peace: The War Between the United States and Mexico* (1974); K. Jack Bauer, *The Mexican War* (1974); and John S. D. Eisenhower, *So Far from God: The U.S. War with Mexico 1846-1848* (1989). John H. Schroeder, *Mr. Polk's War: American Opposition and Dissent 1846-1848* (1973), documents antislavery and Whig opposition; while Ernest M. Lander, *Reluctant Imperialists: Calhoun, the South Carolinians, and the Mexican War* (1980), highlights the ambivalence of some Southerners toward the war. Robert W. Johannsen, *To the Halls of the Montezumas: The Mexican War in the American Imagination* (1985), focuses on the popularity of the war among Democrats and expansionists, while John D. P. Fuller focuses on the most extreme proponents of Manifest Destiny in *The Movement for the Acquisition of All Mexico* (1936).

For Northern Democrats and the Wilmot Proviso, see Chaplain Morrison, *Democratic Politics and Sectionalism: The Wilmot Proviso Controversy* (1967); and Eric Foner, "The Wilmot Proviso Revisited," *JAH,* 56 (1969), 262-279. The divisive impact of the slavery issue on Massachusetts Whigs is treated in Thomas H. O'Connor, *Lords of the Loom: The Cotton Whigs and the Coming of the Civil War* (1967); and Kinley J. Brauer, *Cotton Versus Conscience: Massachusetts Whig Politics and Southwestern Expansion 1843-1848* (1967). For evidence of how party rather than sectional divisions persisted until 1850 on issues unrelated to slavery, see Thomas B. Alexander, *Sectional Stress and Party Stress: A Study of Roll-Call Voting Patterns in the United States House of Representatives 1836-1860* (1967); and Joel H. Silbey, *The Shrine of Party: Congressional Voting Behavior 1841-1852* (1967). The Free Soil party and the 1848 presidential election are treated in Joseph Rayback, *Free Soil: The Election of*

1848 (1970); Frederick J. Blue, *The Free Soilers: Third Party Politics 1848-1854* (1973); and John Mayfield, *Rehearsal for Republicanism: Free Soil and the Politics of Antislavery* 1980).

Robert R. Russel, "What Was the Compromise of 1850?" *JSH,* 22 (1956), 292-309, undertakes to clear away myths and errors but in the process creates some new ones of his own. The fullest study of the compromise is Holman Hamilton, *Prologue to Conflict: The Crisis and Compromise of 1850* (1964). For the important role of Daniel Webster, see Robert F. Dalzell, *Daniel Webster and the Trial of American Nationalism 1843-1852* (1972). The careers of the three great senators who played such an important part in the Compromise debate are portrayed in Merrill Peterson, *The Great Triumvirate: Webster, Clay, and Calhoun* (1987). The efforts of fire-eaters to capitalize on resentment of the events that led up to the compromise are treated in Thelma Jennings, *The Nashville Convention: Southern Movement for Unity 1848-1850* (1980); while the destructive impact of these events on the Southern Whigs is narrated in Arthur C. Cole, *The Whig Party in the South* (1913).

Filibusterers, Fugitives, and Nativists

The best accounts of Southern expansionism and filibustering in the 1850s are Robert E. May, *The Southern Dream of a Caribbean Empire 1854-1861* (1973); and Charles H. Brown, *Agents of Manifest Destiny: The Lives and Times of the Filibusterers* (1979). For attempts to obtain Cuba, consult Basil Rauch, *American Interest in Cuba 1848-1855* (1948). C. Stanley Urban has written several articles on this question; see especially "The Ideology of Southern Imperialism," *Louisiana Historical Quarterly,* 39 (1956), 48-73; "New Orleans and the Cuban Question During the Lopez Expeditions of 1849-1851: A Local Study in Manifest Destiny," *Louisiana Historical Quarterly,* 22 (1939), 1095-1167; and "The Abortive Quitman Filibus-tering Expedition, 1853-1855," *Journal of Mississippi History,* 18 (1956), 175-196.

The basic study of the passage and enforcement of the Fugitive Slave Law is Stanley W. Campbell, *The Slave Catchers* (1970). Other treatments of legal aspects of the Fugitive Slave Law and related matters include Paul Finkelman, *An Imperfect Union: Slavery, Federalism, and Comity* (1980); Robert M. Cover, *Justice Accused: Antislavery and the Judicial Process* (1975); and William M. Wiecek, "Slavery and Abolition Before the United States Supreme Court, 1820-1860," *JAH,* 65 (1978), 34-59. For Northern personal liberty laws, see Thomas D. Morris, *Free Men All: The Personal Liberty Laws of the North 1780-1861* (1974). A scholarly study of the underground railroad is Larry Gara, *Liberty Line: The Legend of the Underground Railroad* (1961). For interesting insights, see also Larry Gara, "The Fugitive Slave Law: A Double Paradox," *CWH,* 10 (1964), 229-240. For the hostility of many Northern states toward blacks— fugitive or otherwise— see Eugene Berwanger, *The Frontier Against Slavery: Western Anti-Negro Prejudice and the Slavery Extension Controversy* (1971).

For the impact of immigration on the ethnic and regional distribution of the American population, see William I. Greenwald, "The Ante-Bellum Population, 1830-1861," *Mid-America,* 36 (1954), 176-189. Among the numerous studies of immigrant life and culture, the following are especially useful: Oscar Handlin, *Boston's Immigrants* (1941); Robert Ernst, *Immigrant Life in New York City 1825-1863* (1949); and Jay P. Dolan, *The Immigrant Church: New York's Irish and German Catholics 1815-1865* (1975). Still the basic narrative of nativism is Ray Allen Billington, *The Protestant Crusade 1800-1861* (1938). See also William G. Bean, "Puritan Versus Celt, 1850-1860," *New England Quarterly,* 7 (1934), 70-89; Ira M. Leonard and Robert D. Parmet, *American Nativism, 1830-1860* (1971); and Dale T. Knobel, *Paddy and the Republic: Ethnicity and Nationality in Antebellum America* (1985). The response of Catholics to nativism is explored in Robert F. Hueston, *The Catholic Press and Nativism 1840-1860* (1976); and Vincent P. Lannie, "Alienation in America: The Immigrant Catholic and Public Education in Pre- Civil War America," *Review of Politics,* 32 (1970), 503-521. For the anti-Catholic sentiments of British Protestant immigrants, consult Charlotte Erickson, *Invisible Immigrants: The Adaptation of English and Scottish Immigrants in Nineteenth Century America* (1972). Case studies of one series of ethnic conflicts are provided by David Montgomery, "The Shuttle and the Cross: Weavers and Artisans in the Kensington Riots of 1844," *Journal of Social History,* 5 (1972), 411-456; and Michael Feldberg, *The Philadelphia Riots of 1844: A Study of Ethnic Conflict* (1975).

Joel Silbey, "The Civil War Synthesis in American Political History," *CWH,* 10 (1964), 130-40; and Joel Silbey (ed.), *The Transformation of American Politics 1840-1860* (1967), argue for the primacy of nonsectional issues during much of the antebellum period. Michael Holt, "The Politics of Impatience: The Origins of Know-Nothingism," *JAH,* 60 (1973), 309-331, maintains that nativism was the most powerful political impulse in the first half of the 1850s and that it was principally responsible for breaking up the Whig party. For three books that advance a similar thesis and maintain in addition that after the demise of the Know-Nothings nativist sentiment found its way into the Republican party, see Mark L. Berger, *The Revolution in the New York Party Systems 1840-1860* (1973); Ronald P. Formisano, *The Birth of Mass Political Parties: Michigan 1827-1861* (1971); and Michael F. Holt, *Forging a Majority: The Formation of the Republican Party in Pittsburgh* (1969). Holt modifies this position and offers important new insights on politics during the 1850s in *The Political Crisis of the 1850s* (1978). Two other books that set the ethnocultural dimension of American politics in a wider context are Paul Kleppner, *The Third Electoral System 1853-1892* (1979); and Robert Kelley, *The Cultural Pattern in American Politics: The First Century* (1979). The fullest account of the matrix of nativism, ideology, and politics that gave birth to the Republican party is William E. Gienapp, *The Origins of the Republican Party, 1852-1856* (1987). Gienapp sides with those who see nativism as an important driving force in this process: see also his "Nativism and the Creation of a Republican Majority in the North before the Civil War," *JAH,* 72 (1985), 529-559. But the best study of the ideology of the Republican party sees antislavery sentiment as uppermost: Eric Foner, *Free Soil, Free Labor, Free Men: The Ideology of the Republican Party before the Civil War* (1970). An important state study takes a similar position: Stephen E. Maizlish, *The Triumph of Sectionalism: The Transformation of Ohio Politics, 1844-1856* (1983). Several of the essays in Stephen E. Maizlish and John J. Kushma (eds.), *Essays on American Antebellum Politics, 1840-1860* (1982), debate this theme. Dale Baum, "The Political Realignment of the 1850's: Know Nothingism and the Republican Majority in Massachusetts," *JAH,* 64 (1978), 959-986, raises important questions about some aspects of the ethnocultural interpretation, and his *The Civil War Party System: The Case of Massachusetts, 1848-1876* (1984), maintains the primacy of the slavery issue in the origin of the Republican party. John R. Mulkern, *The Know-Nothing Party in Massachusetts: The Rise and Fall of a People's Party* (1990), documents the complex roots of this phenomenon, while Tyler G. Anbinder, *Nativism and Politics: The Know Nothing Party in the Northern United States* (1992), argues persuasively that antislavery sentiments were important in both the birth and demise of the Know-Nothings. Gilbert Osofsky, "Abolitionists, Irish Immigrants, and the Dilemmas of Romantic Nationalism," *AHR,* 80 (1975), 889-912, demonstrates the ambivalence of abolitionists toward nativism; while Thomas J. Curran, "Seward and the Know Nothings," *New York Historical Society Quarterly,* 51 (1967), 141-159, highlights the antinativism of the foremost Republican leader. By 1856, the principal locale of the Know-Nothing political strength as a separate party had shifted to the South. For the movement there, see W. Darrell Overdyke, *The Know-Nothing Party in the South* (1950); James H. Broussard, "Some Determinants of Know-Nothing Electoral Strength in the South," *Louisiana History,* 7 (1966), 5-20; and Jean Baker, *Ambivalent Americans: The Know-Nothing Party in Maryland* (1977).

Politics and the Deepening Crisis, 1854-1860

Roy F. Nichols, "The Kansas-Nebraska Act: A Century of Historiography," *MVHR,* 43 (1956), 187-212, is a good introduction to the issues and the historiography of the vexed question of the Kansas-Nebraska Act. For the politics of the act, consult Roy F. Nichols, *The Democratic Machine 1850-1854* (1923); Robert R. Russel, "The Issues in the Congressional Struggle Over the Kansas-Nebraska Bill, 1854," *JSH,* 29 (1963), 187-210; and Gerald W. Wolff, *The Kansas-Nebraska Bill: Party, Section, and the Coming of the Civil War* (1977). Frank H. Hodder, "The Railroad Background of the Kansas-Nebraska Act," *MVHR,* 12 (1925), 3-22, contains valuable material. Alice Nichols, *Bleeding Kansas* (1954), provides a brief account of events in the disputed territory. A fuller study is James A. Rawley, *Race and Politics: "Bleeding Kansas" and the Coming of the Civil War* (1969). Two books by James C. Malin view the motives and actions of all parties, especially Northerners, with a jaundiced eye: *The Nebraska Question 1852-1854*

(1953) and *John Brown and the Legend of Fifty-Six* (1942). A detailed study of John Brown that culminates with his arrival in Kansas is Richard O. Boyer, *The Legend of John Brown* (1973). Samuel A. Johnson, *The Battle Cry of Freedom: The New England Emigrant Aid Company in the Kansas Crusade* (1954), is an informative study of the New England efforts to colonize Kansas. For the twin impacts of "bleeding Sumner" and "bleeding Kansas," see William E. Gienapp, "The Crime Against Sumner: The Caning of Charles Sumner and the Rise of the Republican Party," *CWH,* 25 (1979), 218–245.

The troubled and divisive presidency of James Buchanan is chronicled in Elbert B. Smith, *The Presidency of James Buchanan* (1975). The crucial year 1857 is dissected skillfully by Kenneth M. Stampp, *America in 1857: A Nation on the Brink* (1990). The Panic of 1857 and its political consequences are analyzed in James L. Huston, *The Panic of 1857 and the Coming of the Civil War* (1987). Charges of corruption bedeviled the Buchanan administration: this issue is exhaustively investigated by Mark W. Summers, *The Plundering Generation: Corruption and the Crisis of the Union, 1849–1861* (1987).

The Dred Scott case has received a great deal of attention. Among the more noteworthy studies are Vincent C. Hopkins, *Dred Scott's Case* (1967); Walter Ehrlich, *They Have No Rights: Dred Scott's Struggle for Freedom* (1979); and Stanley I. Kutler (ed.), *The Dred Scott Decision: Law or Politics?* (1967). All other studies, however, have been largely superseded by Don E. Fehrenbacher's exhaustive and magisterial study, *The Dred Scott Case: Its Significance in American Law and Politics* (1978), which was published in an abridged version with the title *Slavery, Law, and Politics: The Dred Scott Case in Historical Perspective* (1981). For Taney's partisan and sectional motives in this case, see also Don E. Fehrenbacher, "Roger B. Taney and the Sectional Crisis," *JSH,* 43 (1977).

The most detailed studies of the Lincoln-Douglas debates are Harry V. Jaffa, *Crisis of the House Divided* (1959), and David Zarefsky, *Lincoln, Douglas and Slavery in the Crucible of Public Debate* (1990). The full text of the debates can be found in Paul M. Angle (ed.), *Created Equal? The Complete Lincoln-Douglas Debates of 1858* (1958). For the divisive impact of the debates and of Douglas's earlier stance in the Lecompton debate on the Democratic party, consult Roy F. Nichols, *The Disruption of American Democracy* (1948). Don E. Fehrenbacher, *Prelude to Greatness: Lincoln in the 1850s* (1962), assesses Lincoln's strategy in the debates. Damon Wells, *Stephen Douglas: The Last Years, 1857–1861* (1971), and William E. Baringer, *Lincoln's Rise to Power* (1937), are also valuable for the crucial years of the late 1850s. Robert W. Johannsen, *The Frontier, the Union, and Stephen A. Douglas* (1989), pulls together fifteen essays on those and related subjects.

Ronald T. Takaki, *A Pro-Slavery Crusade: The Agitation to Reopen the African Slave Trade* (1971), argues for the importance of the slave trade issue in the sectional confrontation of the late 1850s. See also Barton J. Bernstein, "Southern Politics and Attempts to Reopen the African Slave Trade," *JNH,* 51 (1966), 16–35; and James P. Hendrix, "The Efforts to Reopen the African Slave Trade in Louisiana," *Louisiana History,* 10 (1960), 97–123. The question of reopening the trade, and the increase of the illegal trade in the 1850s, are placed in long-term context in the following books: Peter Duigan and Clarence Clendenen, *The United States and the African Slave Trade, 1619–1862* (1963); W. E. B. Du Bois, *The Suppression of the African Slave Trade to the United States 1638–1870* (1896); Warren S. Howard, *American Slavers and the Federal Law 1837–1862* (1963); and Tom Henderson Wells, *The Slave Ship* Wanderer (1967).

A good introduction to the literature on John Brown and the trauma of Harpers Ferry is Stephen B. Oates, "John Brown and His Judges: A Critique of the Historical Literature," *CWH,* 17 (1971), 5–24. Jeffrey S. Rossback, *Ambivalent Conspirators: John Brown, the Secret Six, and a Theory of Slave Violence* (1982), offers important insights on the Harpers Ferry raid. For the relationship of black leaders with Brown, see Benjamin Quarles, *Allies for Freedom: Blacks and John Brown* (1974).

For the background of the Southern Democratic insistence on a slave code for the territories, which split the Democratic party in 1860, see Arthur Bestor, "State Sovereignty and Slavery: A Reinterpretation of Proslavery Doctrine, 1846–1860," *Journal of the Illinois State Historical Society,* 54 (1961), 117–180. A revisionist interpretation of the Southern Constitutional Unionists in 1860 finds them more of a Southern rights than a Union party: John V.

Mering, "The Slave-State Constitutional Unionists and the Politics of Consensus," *JSH,* 43 (1977), 395–410. A useful narrative of the 1860 election in the South is Ollinger Crenshaw, *The Slave States in the Election of 1860* (1945). A fascinating eyewitness account of the four presidential nominating conventions can be found in William B. Hesseltine (ed.), *Three Against Lincoln: Murat Halstead Reports the Caucuses of 1860* (1960). For several brief essays on the 1860 election, see Norman A. Graebner (ed.), *Politics and the Crisis of 1860* (1961). The two basic studies of the election are Emerson D. Fite, *The Presidential Campaign of 1860* (1911); and Reinhard D. Luthin, *The First Lincoln Campaign* (1944). The question of the foreign-born vote, especially that of the Germans, is discussed by several historians in Frederick D. Luebke (ed.), *Ethnic Voters and the Election of Lincoln* (1971). Despite its title, Thomas B. Alexander's "The Civil War as Institutional Fulfillment," *JSH,* 47 (1981), 3–31, is really an intriguing study of several aspects of the election of 1860.

Secession and the Coming of War

Two essays that provide a good introduction to the historiography of secession are Ralph A. Wooster, "Secession of the Lower South: Changing Interpretations," *CWH,* 7 (1961), 117–127; and William J. Donnelly, "Conspiracy or Popular Movement: The Historiography of Southern Support for Secession," *North Carolina Historical Review,* 42 (1965), 70–84. Statistical analyses of the elections of delegates to secession conventions and of the votes in those conventions are provided by Seymour M. Lipset, "The Emergence of the One-Party South—the Election of 1860," in Lipset, *Political Man: The Social Basis of Politics* (1960), pp. 372–384; Peyton McCrary, Clark Miller, and Dale Baum, "Class and Party in the Secession Crisis: Voting Behavior in the Deep South," *Journal of Interdisciplinary History,* 8 (1978), 429–457; and Ralph Wooster, The *Secession Conventions of the South* (1962). An older but still valuable study of Southern secession is Dwight L. Dumond, *The Secession Movement 1860–1861* (1931). Studies of secession in individual states include: Harold Schultz, *Nationalism and Sectionalism in South Carolina 1852–1860* (1950); Steven A. Channing, *Crisis of Fear: Secession in South Carolina* (1970); Percy Lee Rainwater, *Mississippi: Storm Center of Secession 1856–1861* (1938); William L. Barney, *The Secessionist Impulse: Alabama and Mississippi in 1860* (1974); J. Mills Thornton, *Politics and Power in a Slave Society: Alabama 1800–1861* (1978); Michael P. Johnson, *Toward a Patriarchal Republic: The Secession of Georgia* (1977); Henry T. Shanks, *The Secession Movement in Virginia 1847–1861* (1934); Joseph Carlyle Sitterson, *The Secession Movement in North Carolina* (1939); Mary E. R. Campbell, *The Attitude of Tennesseans Toward the Union 1847–1861* (1961); Walter L. Buenger, *Secession and Union in Texas* (1984); and James M. Woods, *Rebellion and Realignment: Arkansas's Road to Secession* (1987). A superb study of the dilemma of Unionists in the upper South is Daniel W. Crofts, *Reluctant Confederates: Upper South Unionists in the Secession Crisis* (1989). For a state that did not secede, see William J. Evitts, *A Matter of Allegiances: Maryland from 1850 to 1861* (1974). The role of Southern newspapers is analyzed in Donald E. Reynolds, *Editors Make War: Southern Newspapers in the Secession Crisis* (1970); while good samples of editorials are reprinted in Dwight L. Dumond (ed.), *Southern Editorials on Secession* (1931).

Northern newspaper opinion is copiously presented in Howard C. Perkins (ed.), *Northern Editorials on Secession,* 2 vols. (1942). An old but still useful account of the Buchanan administration's handling of the crisis is Philip G. Auchampaugh, *James Buchanan and His Cabinet on the Eve of Secession* (1926). Robert C. Gunderson, *Old Gentleman's Convention* (1961); Jesse L. Keene, *The Peace Convention of 1861* (1961); and Mary Scrugham, *The Peaceable Americans of 1860–1861: A Study in Public Opinion* (1921), chronicle the futile efforts to find a compromise formula. Kenneth M. Stampp, *And the War Came: The North and the Secession Crisis 1860–61* (1950), is the best overall study of its subject; while David M. Potter, *Lincoln and His Party in the Secession Crisis,* 2d ed., with new preface (1962), is still the best study of Republican policies. See also William E. Barringer, *A House Dividing: Lincoln as President Elect* (1945). Stampp, Potter, and other historians debate the secession question in George H. Knoles (ed.), *The Crisis of the Union 1860–1861* (1965).

John S. Tilley, *Lincoln Takes Command* (1941), and Charles W. Ramsdell, "Lincoln and Fort Sumter," *JSH,* 3 (1937), 259–288, offer pro-Southern interpretations that fasten upon

Lincoln the responsibility for provoking the war. Also sympathetic to the Confederate position is Ludwell H. Johnson, "Fort Sumter and Confederate Diplomacy," *JSH,* 26 (1961), 441–466. More balanced are Richard N. Current, *Lincoln and the First Shot* (1963) and "The Confederates and the First Shot," *CWH,* 7 (1961), 357–369, and Grady McWhiney, "The Confederacy's First Shot," *CWH,* 14 (1968), 5-14. See also the Stampp and Potter studies cited in the preceding paragraph, for judicious interpretations of the Sumter crisis. Popular accounts emphasizing the military dimension are Roy Meredith, *Storm Over Sumter: The Opening Engagement of the Civil War* (1957); and William A. Swanberg, *First Blood: The Story of Fort Sumter* (1957).

Index

★

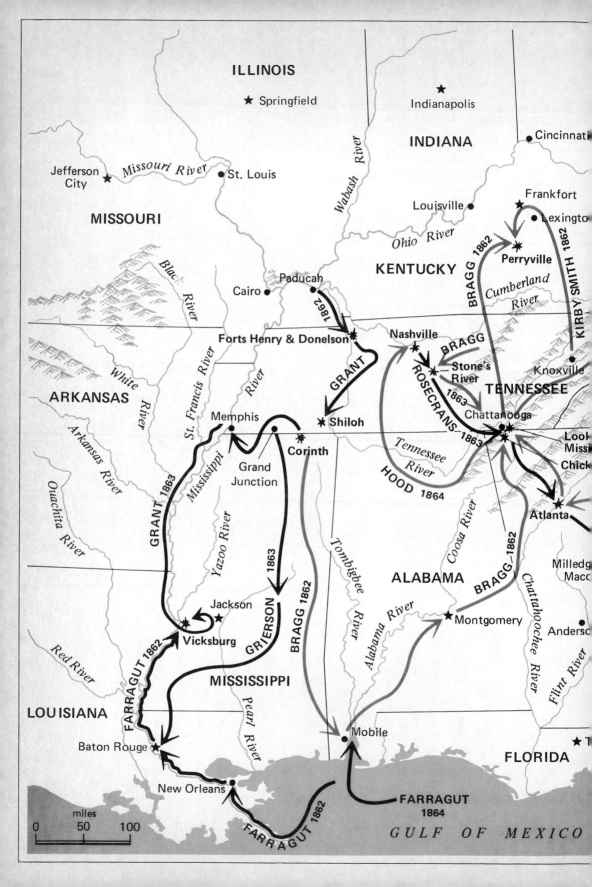

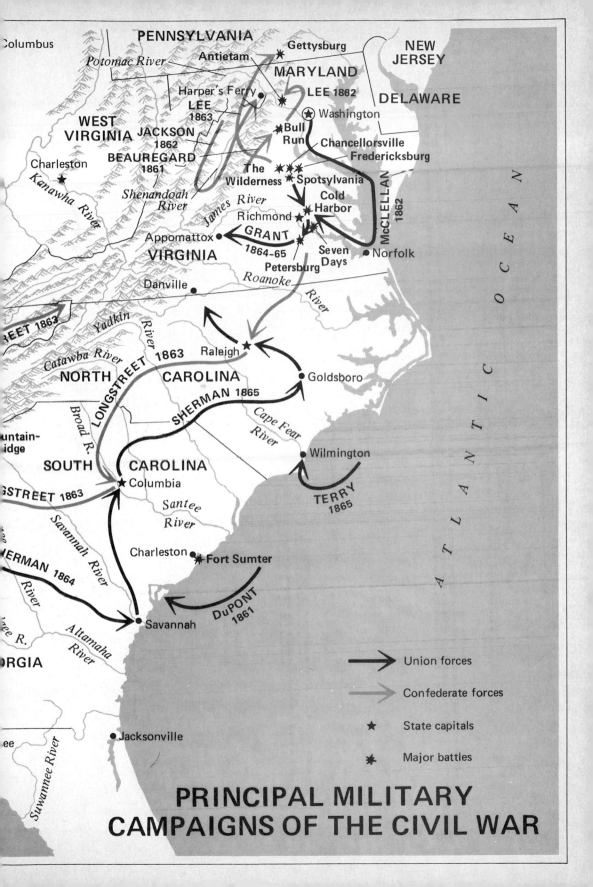

Columbus

PENNSYLVANIA

Gettysburg

NEW
JERSEY

Potomac River

Antietam

MARYLAND

DELAWARE

Harper's Ferry

LEE 1862

LEE
1863

Washington

WEST
VIRGINIA

JACKSON
1862

Bull
Run

Chancellorsville

BEAUREGARD
1861

Fredericksburg

Charleston

The
Wilderness

Spotsylvania

Kanawha River

Shenandoah
River

James River

Cold
Harbor

McCLELLAN
1862

Richmond

Appomattox

GRANT
1864-65

Seven
Days

Norfolk

VIRGINIA

Petersburg

Danville

Roanoke River

REET 1863

Yadkin River

Raleigh

NORTH

LONGSTREET 1863

CAROLINA

Goldsboro

Catawba River

Broad R.

SHERMAN 1865

Cape Fear
River

untain-
idge

SOUTH

CAROLINA

Wilmington

GSTREET 1863

Columbia

Santee
River

TERRY
1865

Savannah River

Charleston

Fort Sumter

HERMAN 1864

ee R.

Altamaha
River

Savannah

DuPONT
1861

ATLANTIC OCEAN

RGIA

Union forces

Confederate forces

State capitals

Jacksonville

Major battles

Suwannee River

PRINCIPAL MILITARY
CAMPAIGNS OF THE CIVIL WAR